Charting Literary Urban Studies

Guided by the multifaceted relations between city and text, *Charting Literary Urban Studies: Texts as Models of and for the City* attempts to chart the burgeoning field of literary urban studies by outlining how texts in varying degrees function as both representations of the city and as blueprints for its future development. The study addresses questions such as these: How do literary texts represent urban complexities – and how can they capture the uniqueness of a given city? How do literary texts simulate layers of urban memory – and how can they reinforce or help dissolve path dependencies in urban development? What role can literary studies play in interdisciplinary urban research? Are the blueprints or 'recipes' for urban development that most quickly travel around the globe – such as the 'creative city', the 'green city' or the 'smart city' – really always the ones that best solve a given problem? Or is the global spread of such travelling urban models not least a matter of their narrative packaging? In answering these key questions, this book also advances a literary studies contribution to the general theory of models, tracing a heuristic trajectory from the analysis of literary texts as representations of urban developments to an analysis of literary strategies in planning documents and other pragmatic, non-literary texts.

Jens Martin Gurr is Professor of British and Anglophone Literature and Culture at the University of Duisburg-Essen. He has 12 years of research experience in the field of Literary Urban Studies with five edited collections and some 30 essays in this field alone. As Director of the interdisciplinary Joint Centre Urban Systems at the University of Duisburg-Essen and Speaker of the Competence Field Metropolitan Research in the University Alliance Ruhr, he has directed and co-directed numerous disciplinary and interdisciplinary research projects.

Charting Literary Urban Studies

Texts as Models of and for the City

Jens Martin Gurr

Routledge
Taylor & Francis Group
NEW YORK AND LONDON

First published 2021
by Routledge
52 Vanderbilt Avenue, New York, NY 10017

and by Routledge
2 Park Square, Milton Park, Abingdon, Oxon OX14 4RN

Routledge is an imprint of the Taylor & Francis Group, an informa business

Library of Congress Cataloging-in-Publication Data
Names: Gurr, Jens Martin, 1974– author.
Title: Charting literary urban studies: texts as models of
and for the city / Jens Martin Gurr.
Description: New York, NY: Routledge, 2021. |
Includes bibliographical references and index. |
Identifiers: LCCN 2020039425 (print) | LCCN 2020039426 (ebook) |
ISBN 9780367628345 (hardback) | ISBN 9781003111009 (ebook)
Subjects: LCSH: Cities and towns–Social aspects. | Cities and towns in
literature. | Urbanization in literature. | Cities and towns–Study and teaching.
Classification: LCC HT151.G8288 2021 (print) |
LCC HT151 (ebook) | DDC 809/.93321732–dc23
LC record available at https://lccn.loc.gov/2020039425
LC ebook record available at https://lccn.loc.gov/2020039426

ISBN: 978-0-367-62834-5 (hbk)
ISBN: 978-1-003-11100-9 (ebk)

Typeset in Sabon
by Newgen Publishing UK

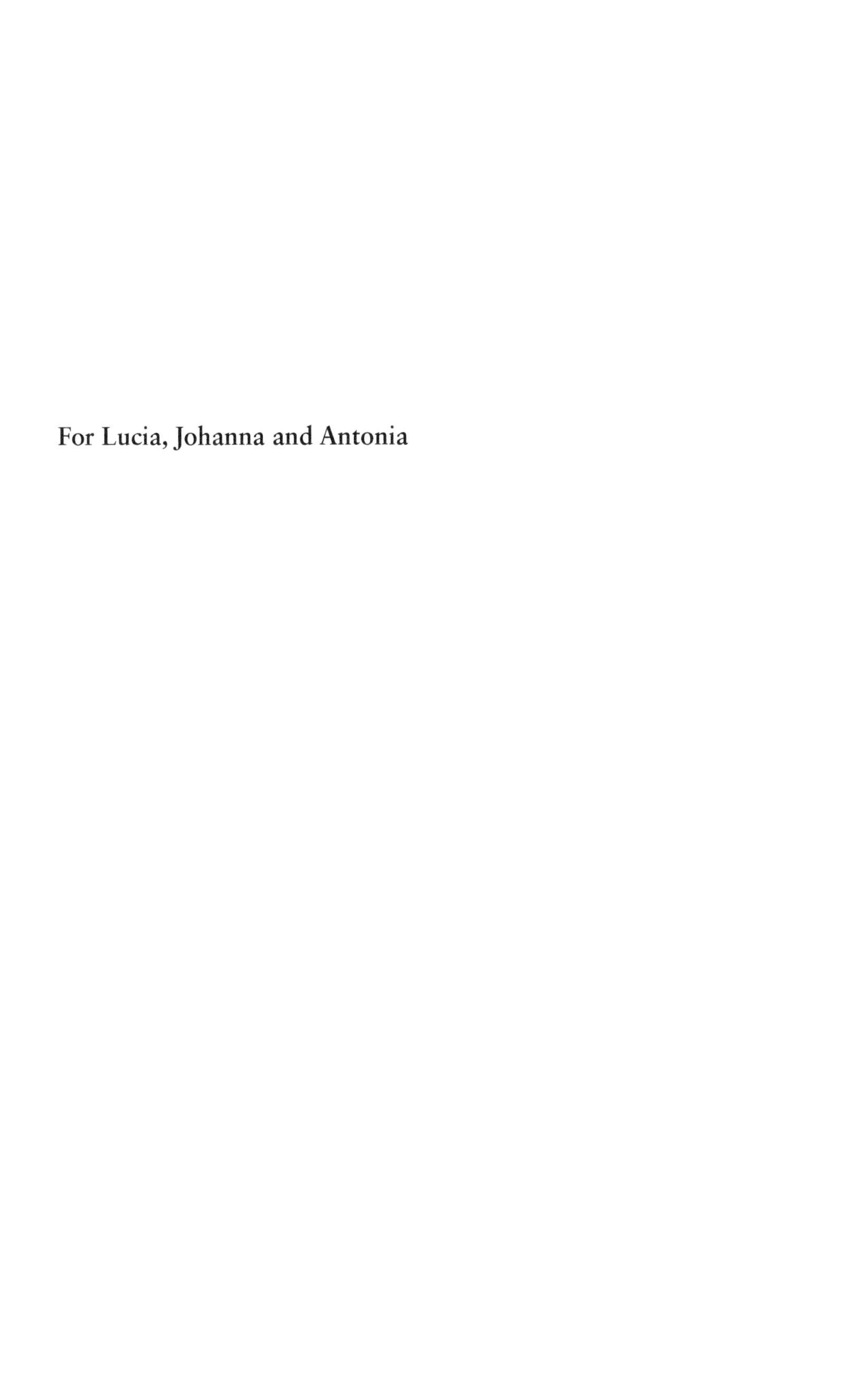

For Lucia, Johanna and Antonia

Contents

Figures

Credits List

This book builds on some long-standing research in historical as well as contemporary literary and cultural urban studies and in related fields. In addition to individual formulations and passages in several chapters, which have been used in earlier essays, I gratefully acknowledge permission from the respective publishers to re-use more extensively material from earlier essays.

Parts or earlier versions of material from the **Introduction** first appeared in:

- Jens Martin Gurr. "'Urban Complexity' from a Literary and Cultural Studies Perspective: Key Cultural Dimensions and the Challenges of 'Modeling'." *Understanding Complex Urban Systems: Multidisciplinary Approaches to Modeling*. Ed. Christian Walloth, Jens Martin Gurr, J. Alexander Schmidt. Heidelberg, New York: Springer, 2014. 133–150.
- Jens Martin Gurr. "Texte als 'Modelle von' und 'Modelle für' Stadt: Zur narrativen Modellierung von Urbanität und urbaner Komplexität." *Zeitschrift für ästhetische Bildung* 11.2 (2019) (special issue "Modell") [zaeb.net].

An earlier version of parts of **Chapter 1** first appeared in:

- Jens Martin Gurr. "'Urban Complexity' from a Literary and Cultural Studies Perspective: Key Cultural Dimensions and the Challenges of 'Modeling'." *Understanding Complex Urban Systems: Multidisciplinary Approaches to Modeling*. Ed. Christian Walloth, Jens Martin Gurr, J. Alexander Schmidt. Heidelberg, New York: Springer, 2014. 133–150.

A previous version of **Chapter 2** first appeared as:

- Jens Martin Gurr. "The Literary Representation of Urban Complexity and the Problem of Simultaneity: A Sketchy Inventory of Strategies." *Cityscapes in the Americas and Beyond: Representations of Urban Complexity in Literature and Film*. Ed. Jens Martin Gurr, Wilfried Raussert. Trier and Tempe, AZ: WVT and Bilingual Press, 2011. 11–36.

Earlier versions of parts of **Chapter 3** first appeared in:

- Jens Martin Gurr. "The Politics of Representation in Hypertext DocuFiction: Multi-Ethnic Los Angeles as an Emblem of 'America' in Norman M. Klein's *Bleeding Through: Layers of Los Angeles 1920–1986.*" *Screening the Americas: Narration of Nation in Documentary Film/Proyectando las Américas: Narración de la nación en el cine documental.* Ed. Josef Raab, Sebastian Thies, Daniela Noll-Opitz. Trier and Tempe, AZ: WVT and Bilingual Press, 2011. 153–171.
- Jens Martin Gurr, Martin Butler. "Against the 'Erasure of Memory' in Los Angeles City Planning: Strategies of Re-Ethnicizing L.A. in Digital Fiction." *Selling EthniCity: Urban Cultural Politics in the Americas.* Ed. Olaf Kaltmeier. London: Ashgate, 2011. 145–163.
- Jens Martin Gurr. "The Modernist Poetics of Urban Memory and the Structural Analogies between 'City' and 'Text': *The Waste Land* and Benjamin's *Arcades Project.*" *Recovery and Transgression: Memory in American Poetry.* Ed. Kornelia Freitag. Newcastle: Cambridge Scholars Publishing, 2015. 21–37.

An early version of **Chapter 4** was first presented as the keynote lecture at the "Schichtungen des Urbanen/Layers of the Urban" conference in Dortmund in November 2019, a double conference continued in Cincinnati in February 2020. A brief discussion of specificities of the Ruhr region in contrast to other metropolitan regions as well as a brief discussion of Jürgen Link's novel have first appeared in:

- Jens Martin Gurr. "Das Ruhrgebiet als Herausforderung für Kategorien und Ansätze der Stadtforschung." *Dérive: Zeitschrift für Stadtforschung* 58 (2015): 23–26.

An earlier version of **Chapter 5** first appeared as:

- Jens Martin Gurr. "'All those who know the term "gentrification" are part of the problem': Self-Reflexivity in Urban Activism and Cultural Production." *Resistance: Subjects, Representations, Contexts.* Ed. Martin Butler, Paul Mecheril, Lea Brenningmeyer. Bielefeld: transcript, 2017. 117–133.

Earlier versions of parts of **Chapter 6** first appeared in:

- Jens Martin Gurr. "'Without contraries is no progression': Emplotted Figures of Thought in Negotiating Oppositions, *Funktionsgeschichte* and Literature as 'Cultural Diagnosis'." *Text or Context: Reflections on Literary and Cultural Criticism.* Ed. Rüdiger Kunow, Stephan Mussil. Würzburg: Königshausen & Neumann, 2013. 59–77.

- Jens Martin Gurr. "'Urban Complexity' from a Literary and Cultural Studies Perspective: Key Cultural Dimensions and the Challenges of 'Modeling'." *Understanding Complex Urban Systems: Multidisciplinary Approaches to Modeling*. Ed. Christian Walloth, Jens Martin Gurr, J. Alexander Schmidt. Heidelberg, New York: Springer, 2014. 133–150.

Acknowledgements

I am grateful for many helpful discussions with the following colleagues over the years: Lieven Ameel, Roman Bartosch, Michael Batty, Christoph Bode, Katharina Borgmann, Barbara Buchenau, Martin Butler, Howard Davis, Helmut Demes, Georg Drennig, Michael Eisinger, Jason Finch, Florian Freitag, Kornelia Freitag, Michael Gassenmeier, Julika Griem, Walter Grünzweig, Randi Gunzenhäuser, Dieter Hassenpflug, Patsy Healey, Christoph Heyl, Uta Hohn, Julia Hoydis, Mike Hulme, Arun Jain, Rudolf Juchelka, Olaf Kaltmeier, Fabian Kessl, Alf Kimms, Ursula Kluwick, Norman M. Klein, Klaus Krumme, Rüdiger Kunow, Klaus Kunzmann, Charles Landry, Sherry Lee Linkon, Beate Löffler, Lena Mattheis, Susanne Moebus, Utku Mogultay, Hajo Neis, Rolf Parr, Frank Erik Pointner, Josef Raab, Willy Raussert, Christoph Reinfandt, Julia Sattler, J. Alexander Schmidt, Ute Schneider, Rüdiger Schultz, Christian Tagsold, Markus Taube, Sebastian Thies, Dirk Vanderbeke, Michael Wala, Christian Walloth, Hans-Werner Wehling, Renatus Widmann, Thorsten Wiechmann and Mark Williams. My sincere apologies to those I have not mentioned here.

In the last two years, the Graduate Research Group "Scripts for Postindustrial Urban Futures: American Models, Transatlantic Interventions", which is generously funded by the VolkswagenStiftung (2018–2022) and which I co-direct with our speaker Barbara Buchenau, has been a vibrant research environment. I wish to thank the principal investigators Barbara Buchenau, Kornelia Freitag, Walter Grünzweig, Randi Gunzenhäuser, Josef Raab†, Michael Wala, the group's post-doc Maria Sulimma and doctoral candidates Juliane Borosch, Florian Deckers, Elisabeth Haefs, Chris Katzenberg, Johannes Maria Krickl, Hanna Rodewald and Katharina Wood. Thanks especially to Barbara Buchenau, for many thought-provoking discussions, for excellent leadership and for being such a wonderful colleague, collaborator and friend. In fact, fruitful collaboration with colleagues from Bochum, Dortmund and Duisburg-Essen in the Ruhr Center of American Studies began in 2011 with preparations for the Graduate Research Group "Spaces – Communities – Representations: Urban Transformations in the U.S." directed by Walter Grünzweig and generously funded by MERCUR – Mercator Research Center Ruhr (2012–2015).

Since 2007, the University of Duisburg-Essen has been a truly supportive and dynamic work environment – our motto "open-minded" has often proven very fitting: I can think of few academic environments where collaboration across all faculties and academic cultures could have been more pleasant and fruitful. Moreover, the University Board (Rektorat) of the University has for many years generously supported our initiatives in the Joint Centre "Urban Systems". Thanks also to the Faculty of Humanities for generous support over the years.

Since 2008, I have had the privilege to be speaker of the University of Duisburg-Essen's Joint Centre "Urban Systems", which has been a stimulating and supportive environment for collaboration across virtually all faculties. I am grateful for the intellectual openness and generosity of many colleagues here, with whom I have collaborated in disciplinary and interdisciplinary projects in the field of urban and metropolitan research. Particular thanks go to my two co-speakers, Susanne Moebus and J. Alexander Schmidt, and to Michael Eisinger, Elke Hochmuth and Klaus Krumme. Since 2015, I have co-directed the Competence Field "Metropolitan Research" of the University Alliance Ruhr with Uta Hohn of Ruhr-University Bochum and Thorsten Wiechmann of TU Dortmund University. This, too, has been a most stimulating, collegial and supportive environment. Thanks also to Dennis Hardt, Elke Hochmuth and Felix Rudroff from the management office.

Earlier versions of several chapters have previously appeared in various essays and articles (cf. Credits List). I am grateful to the publishers for permission to re-use these materials. I have also presented many of the ideas for the book at numerous conferences and gratefully remember many helpful discussions.

Much of the research for Chapter 8 was conducted in the summer term of 2018, during which I was a Hiroshi Kitamura fellow at the University of Duisburg-Essen's Institute of East Asian Studies (IN-EAST) for six months, specifically to contribute a literary studies perspective to policy mobility research.

I gratefully acknowledge generous funding for projects and conferences from several institutions over the years, funding which has enabled research and publications that have led to this book:

- The Center for Interdisciplinary Research (ZiF) at the University of Bielefeld
- The Deutsche Forschungsgemeinschaft (DFG)
- The Emschergenossenschaft
- The German Academic Exchange Service (DAAD)
- The German Federal Ministry of Education and Research (BMBF)
- MERCUR – Mercator Research Center Ruhr
- The Ministry of Innovation, Science and Research of the State of North-Rhine Westphalia (NRW-MIWF)
- Stiftung Mercator
- VolkswagenStiftung

The publication of this book has been generously supported by the University of Duisburg-Essen's Open Access Publication Fund and by the Faculty of Humanities.

Special thanks to my wonderful team at the University of Duisburg-Essen over the years, especially to Martin Butler, Stefanie Caeners, Torsten Caeners, Christine Cangemi, Svenja Donner, Georg Drennig, Lena Heerdmann, Elke Hochmuth, Eva Marsch, Lena Mattheis, Tracey Meintrup-Cooper, Berit Michel, Beate Mrugalla, Gregor Pudzich, Adam von Wald and Mark Williams.

In the phase of preparing this book for publication, the editors at Routledge, especially Michelle Salyga and Bryony Reece, as well as my copy-editor Gail Welsh and my production manager Liz Davey, have been wonderfully competent and supportive – thanks! I also wish to thank the three anonymous reviewers for very helpful comments.

I particularly wish to thank Michael Gassenmeier for putting me on the literary urban studies trail some 20 years ago, Lena Mattheis – doctoral candidate, then collaborator – for many helpful comments on most of the chapters, designer Daniel Bläser for the beautiful cover illustration and a lot of short-notice work on some of the images, my research assistant Svenja Donner for her care and dedication in the final stages of preparing the manuscript for publication, and my secretary and office manager, Christine Cangemi, for all her support, dedication and circumspect management.

This book is for my wife Lucia, who has lived with it for more than half the time she has lived with me, and for my daughters, Johanna and Antonia, who, as children do, keep asking the right questions: "Daddy, why do people write stories about things that don't exist?" "No, why do they write stories about things that *already* exist *anyway*?" Thanks for such breakfast conversations – and for everything else.

Introduction

Talking about his magnum opus *Ulysses*, James Joyce famously told his biographer Frank Budgen: "I want [...] to give a picture of Dublin so complete that if the city one day suddenly disappeared from the earth it could be reconstructed out of my book" (Budgen 69f.). Joyce here facetiously suggests a double function of texts that is central to this book's interest in the relation between 'the city' and 'the text': Texts can be *representations of* the city – *Ulysses* as "a picture of Dublin" – and they can be *blueprints for* the city – "[Dublin] could be reconstructed out of my book".

Guided by such a dual understanding of the relations between city and text, this book attempts to chart the burgeoning field of literary urban studies by addressing questions such as these: How do literary texts represent urban complexities – and how can they capture the uniqueness of a given city? How do literary texts simulate layers of urban memory – and how can they reinforce or help dissolve path dependencies in urban development? What role can literary studies play in interdisciplinary urban research? Are the blueprints or 'recipes' for urban development that most quickly travel around the globe – take the 'creative city', the 'green city' or the 'smart city' – really always the ones that best solve a given problem, or is the global diffusion of such travelling urban models not least a matter of their narrative packaging? The book engages these key questions by advancing a literary studies contribution to the general theory of models and by tracing a heuristic trajectory from the analysis of literary texts as representations of urban developments to an analysis of literary strategies in planning documents and other pragmatic, non-literary texts. These suggestions, it is hoped, will be of interest to scholars both in literary studies and in various fields of urban research as well as to students in these areas. Given this interdisciplinary orientation, I have cut short a number of more in-depth discussions that would have been in order had the book been addressed to a literary studies readership alone.

After decades of scholarship on literary representations of the city, the emerging field of literary urban studies[1] has more recently also begun to read literary and non-literary texts side by side and to consider both the pragmatic functions of literary texts and the 'literariness' of planning documents (cf. Ameel 2016, 2017, 2019; Buchenau/Gurr 2016, 2018; Keunen/Verraest), important work that this book builds upon and seeks to continue. Here, a key influence has been the sustained interest in the role of narratives in urban planning, design and development; urban planner Leonie Sandercock has even spoken of the "story turn in planning" (2010).[2]

Planning invariably makes use of narratives, as becomes apparent in the designs for a building to be erected on a single plot of land, the construction of a new quarter or the transformation of an entire city, all of which have to plot the transition from a present into a desired future state. In all these planning cases, narratives describe the process in texts, images, maps or animations, thus seeking to attract, convince or generate support from owners, city administrators, investors and other stakeholders. In this vein, governance and planning scholar Merlijn van Hulst has described "storytelling as a model *of* and a model *for* planning". In doing so, he has especially drawn attention to the "future-directedness" of both narrative and planning: "Through telling and listening to stories, actors in the present not only make sense of the past, but also prepare for the future" (van Hulst 300). It is this "future-directedness" (van Hulst 300) and the (at least potential) openness of planning – alternative developments are always at least imaginable – which make it possible to read planning texts as "future narratives" in the sense of literary scholar Christoph Bode (cf. Bode/Dietrich): A "future narrative" is a narrative that describes more than one potential continuation in a given situation and thus does not – as the more common "past narratives" do – present a development as having already happened in the past and thus as no longer allowing for different outcomes. Rather, "future narratives" portray the future as being open and subject to intervention. In "future narratives", this is made explicit in the form of decision points – or "nodes", as Bode calls them – in the narrative, which can either simply be bifurcations or may offer three or more alternatives. Each of these potential paths into the future can then, in turn, contain further nodes. Nodal structures, I will argue, are common also in literary texts seeking to represent an urban experience of constantly having a choice between different potential courses of action (cf. Chapter 3). In the practice of planning, most plans – whether they are master plans for an entire district or smaller-scale plans for an individual building – do not explicitly present alternatives. In other words, they do not flesh out alternatives in narrative descriptions or visualisations, let alone with considerations of anticipated costs, benefits and impacts. However, any planning document, sometimes implicitly, refers to different possible futures and thus contains at least one node; in the simplest form – and this may even be the most common one – the alternatives may only be that a plan may or may not be realised. Thus, any plan for the future is essentially a "future narrative", because even where it is presented as a 'must' without alternatives, it contains – at least implicitly – the decision point of realisation or non-realisation.

While, as part of the "story turn in planning", numerous studies from the field of planning research and planning theory have engaged with the role of narratives in planning (if frequently with an inflationary and fuzzy use of the term 'narrative'), this is hardly true to the same extent for literary and cultural studies despite their specific competence in the analysis of narratives. Thus, there is as yet no substantial narratology of urban planning, although recent work by Lieven Ameel, Bart Keunen and Sofie Verraest points in the direction pursued here (cf. especially Ameel 2016, 2017, 2019, 2021; Keunen/Verraest). These studies have shown the potential of narratological and rhetorical analyses of planning documents: Specific underlying plot patterns and their generic implications – as well as central tropes and references to established patterns of narrative sense-making – have thus been shown to suggest or predetermine outcomes, path dependencies, inclusions and exclusions. Thus, a literary studies approach to planning texts can frequently show them to be profoundly 'literary' (cf. the discussion of the 'Garden City' concept in Chapter 8), but it can also help explain their – often unintended, occasionally highly problematic – political implications.

In contrast to 'traditional' literary studies approaches interested in literary representations of cities, the field of literary urban studies as it has evolved and as I understand it, is also centrally concerned with the real-world city and its challenges. This is, therefore, a more thoroughly interdisciplinary field requiring literary scholars to leave their comfort zone and to engage with, say, the theory and practice of planning or with approaches to modelling urban complexities in economics, mobility science, or the social sciences. Literary scholar Eric Prieto has described the concerns of what he calls "geocentered" criticism as follows:

> [The] geocentered study of authors or works should lead away from the individual author and work and toward a more general kind of knowledge, one that breaks through the aesthetic frame that sets works of literature off from the world and seeks to use the study of literature as a way to better think about the world around us.[3]
>
> (25)

While I sympathise with the real-world commitment, I see no reason to "brea[k] through the aesthetic frame" and I do believe it is *one* task of literary studies also to provide detailed readings of individual texts. Moreover, it may precisely be an understanding of the aesthetic functions and appeal of texts – literary as well as pragmatic – that can help explain their very real impact. Literary urban studies thus understood, more so than established approaches to studying 'literature and the city', must be concerned with conceptualising the relation between the textual and the material city, between 'the city' and 'the text'.[4]

Here, an understanding that regards texts as models can be particularly fruitful. According to a general theory of models (cf. Stachowiak 131–133), all models share the characteristics of being (1) representational, (2) reductive and (3) pragmatic. A model may therefore be defined as a simplified physical, digital or mental representation of a more complex outside entity to which it must be functionally or structurally similar in order to function as a model. Models are devised or chosen for a specific purpose and – depending on that purpose – will selectively focus on different characteristics, elements or connections of the system perceived as central to this purpose while disregarding others. Thus, a map of a city with colour-coding in green, yellow or red to represent high, medium or low average incomes per district is a model of that city in that it (1) represents the city, (2) does so in a highly selective, simplified, abstracted and aggregate form, and (3) does so for specific purposes – possibly to support decisions about where to launch social cohesion programmes – while it would be largely useless for other objectives.

Moreover, mathematician and information theorist Bernd Mahr has argued that models should additionally be understood in their dual nature of always being both "models *of*" something and "models *for*" something:

> A model is always based on something *of* which it is a model, i.e. departing from which or referring to which it has been produced or chosen, its matrix. The purpose of building or choosing a model is its use [...] One of the typical uses of models is their use as a *means of designing* [*or creating*] something. [Here] models are samples, pre-formations or specifications [...] The notion of the model can therefore only be explained convincingly if it is acknowledged that a model is always both a *model of something* and a *model for something.*[5]
>
> (2015, 331f.; italics original; my translation)

Adapting this notion, a model can be understood as being to varying degrees both the *descriptive* rendering of an entity *of* which it is a model and – at least implicitly – the *prescriptive* blueprint for the design or transformation of a future entity *for* which it is a model. With reference to the relation between the city and the text, a text can thus be understood as an urban model in that it is – again to varying degrees – *descriptive* in its representation of the city and – again at least implicitly – *prescriptive* in that it formulates directions or options for a different future city. This dual nature is also evident in the fact that texts not only represent an external urban reality but contribute to shaping perceptions of the urban and thus to highlighting that a different city is at least conceptually possible. Moreover, as the increasingly frequent collaboration between planning experts and science fiction writers shows, literary texts as models *of* and models *for* urban realities also have a crucial role to play in developing scenarios. Thus, the German Federal Institute for Building, Urban and Spatial Research (BBSR) in 2015 issued a study entitled *Learning from Science Fiction Cities: Scenarios for Urban Planning* (my translation; cf. BBSR).

The notion of texts as models lends itself to being applied to both literary and pragmatic, non-literary texts such as planning documents. However, more clearly than in Mahr's original conceptualisation, where "model of" and "model for" are two sides of the same coin or may only be gradually more or less prominent in different models,[6] "model of" and "model for" are here introduced as a heuristic distinction based on which the field of literary urban studies can be charted or mapped.[7]

There has recently been an increased interest in adapting a general theory of models (with frequent references to Stachowiak and especially to Mahr) to literary studies and in disciplinary literary and cultural studies approaches to the theory of models (cf. several contributions in Bahlke/Siegert/Vogl as well as in Dirks/Knobloch; Wendler). Pioneering work has been done, for instance, in two research training groups in Münster and Jena.[8] Expanding and refocusing such work, this book specifically conceptualises literary texts as models complementary to the currently dominant quantitative models in urban research, a notion I develop in more detail in Chapter 1.

An attempt at charting the field of literary urban studies requires a fundamental decision about structure: Does one proceed chronologically by epoch, which would suggest an interest in the succession of literary representations of cities in different periods? Or regionally, by city, in which case one would be likely to catalogue representations of different cities?[9] Or does one proceed by different genres, which would hardly do justice to the overlaps and transfers between literary and planning texts (for these, cf. for instance Ameel 2016, 2019). All of these, I believe, would in different ways strengthen a focus on questions of 'representation', would therefore lead away from what I have called the 'real-world concerns' of literary urban studies and would not necessarily be helpful to a more conceptual discussion of the relation between text and city. However, since I do believe that some concepts are best introduced in sustained readings of individual texts, this study deliberately works both with chapters that take their cue from a representational challenge and that use texts largely to provide examples, and with chapters interested in an individual text. Moreover, I do analyse in some detail texts from a range of different genres and text types – poetry and docu-fiction in multimedia hypertext (Chapter 3), novels (Chapter 4), urban activist writings (Chapter 5), planning documents (Chapter 8), as well as a range of shorter examples discussed throughout.

In conceptualising different subfields of research, approaches and guiding questions in literary urban studies, this study follows three interrelated trajectories, each involving a reversal of the research focus and direction of inquiry:

1. from texts as *descriptive* models *of* key urban structures, developments and characteristics to texts as *prescriptive* blueprints *for* the planning, design and development of cities;
2. from the question of how the city shapes writing to that of how texts shape the city;
3. from the study of literary texts on the city to the analysis of planning documents and other pragmatic, non-literary texts central to urban planning and development.

Tracing these three trajectories, the study proceeds as follows: **Chapter 1**, "Interdisciplinary Urban Complexity Research and Texts as Qualitative Models", outlines a contribution of literary urban studies to inter- and transdisciplinary urban complexity research by discussing textual models of the urban as complementary to the currently dominant quantitative models. Without denying their usefulness for a vast number of purposes, it will be argued that quantitative models are characterised by abstraction and aggregation and thus are generally not concerned with local or individual specificity. On the other hand, qualitative models are frequently designed to capture just that. More narrowly, literary texts serve as a particular type of qualitative model: By focusing precisely on the representation of specific places, of individual responses and of patterns of sense-making, they are diametrically opposed to quantitative models in their selection of which elements of complex urban reality to include or to leave out. As an alternative form of 'modelling' urban complexity, literary texts are thus shown to function as a complementary type of 'urban model'.

Chapter 2, "Literary Models of Urban Complexity and the Problem of Simultaneity: A Sketchy Inventory of Strategies", develops a typology of literary strategies in the representation of urban complexity. It takes its cue from the insight – formulated by Georg Simmel, Kevin Lynch and others – that an overwhelming simultaneity is quintessential to the urban experience. Arguing that, given the linearity of print, the representation of this simultaneity poses the main challenge to literary models of the city, *and* that the representation of urban simultaneity invariably involves or at least implies most other key facets of complexity, I here use a wide range of texts from the seventeenth to the twenty-first century to develop a typology of literary strategies of nonetheless representing, simulating or suggesting this simultaneity. It is precisely the use of such strategies, this chapter argues, which enables literary texts to function as models *of* urban complexity.

Continuing the inquiry into texts as models *of* the city, **Chapter 3**, "Palimpsests, Rhizomes, Nodes: Texts as Structural and Functional Urban Models", builds on the typology developed in Chapter 2 to provide theoretical concepts and extended case studies for the analysis of texts as structural and functional models of urban complexities. More specifically, using T.S. Eliot's "The Waste Land" as a quintessential topographical poem *and* as a central text in discussions of urban memory, and Norman Klein's 2003 multimedia database narrative *Bleeding Through: Layers of Los Angeles 1920–1986* as arguably one of the most ambitious attempts at using hypertext database structures to represent urban complexities, I here discuss textual strategies of simulating rhizomatic and palimpsestic urban structures as well as textual simulations of cities as spatialised and layered urban memory. Here, Walter Benjamin's notion of "superposition", the simultaneous perception of different layers of the past, will play a central role.

Chapter 4, "Reversing Perspectives: Urban Memory in Built and Literary Post-Industrial Cities", is the first of three chapters suggesting and performing a shift of attention: It attempts to apply the concepts outlined in the previous chapters – palimpsest, superposition, rhizome – first to physical sites in the polycentric post-industrial conurbation of the Ruhr region in Germany and only then to literary texts representing these sites in particular and the region generally. In doing so, it addresses the question of how concepts from literary urban studies can help understand the real-world city. Second, it argues that concepts of historical layering – usually applied to 'old' European cities such as Rome, Berlin, London, Paris or St. Petersburg – also fit post-industrial conurbations. The chapter proposes a distinction between the 'palimpsest' and Benjamin's notion of "superposition", which is here understood as an analytical concept rather than an involuntary perception. By doing justice to an observer's knowledge, it allows for an understanding of what might be called a 'remembered presence', which, though it may have left no physical traces, may nonetheless be crucial to understanding the history and meanings of a site.

Chapter 5, "Urban Activist Writing and the Transition from 'Models *of*' to 'Models *for*' Urban Developments" engages with a corpus of activist writing from anti-gentrification and 'right to the city' movements and identifies aesthetic strategies of subverting commodification common in such writing. It does so in order to highlight activist writing as a text type that systematically blends the descriptive and the prescriptive characteristics of models: While critically commenting on current urban developments, activist writing clearly pursues an agenda in blueprinting desirable urban developments. The central case study here is Christoph Schäfer's highly allusive and self-reflexive visual essay *Die Stadt ist unsere Fabrik/The City is our Factory* (2010).

Entitled "Narrative Path Dependencies: From Scenario Building in Literary Texts to the Narratology and Rhetoric of Pragmatic Texts", **Chapter 6** completes the reversal of perspectives: It builds on selected concepts from narratology, metaphor theory, research on cognitive models and *Funktionsgeschichte* to develop a theoretical framework for the comparative analysis of the real-world functions of literary texts, for instance in scenario building, and of the literary strategies in and functions of pragmatic texts such as planning documents. Developing further recent narratological research on planning texts in literary urban studies, the chapter proposes the notion of what I call "narrative path dependencies" in planning texts.

Co-authored with Barbara Buchenau, a long-standing fellow thinker in the realm of urban North American studies, **Chapter 7**, "'Scripts' in Urban Development: Procedural Knowledge, Self-Description, and Persuasive Blueprint for the Future" introduces the concept of 'scripts' in urban development as persuasive combinations of these three components. Developed in an inter-institutional research group we co-direct (speaker: Barbara Buchenau, co-speaker: Jens Martin Gurr), the notion of 'scripts' proposed here draws on uses and implications of the term in a wide variety of disciplines and fields, which each contribute vital components to an understanding of how scripts function as a particularly powerful type of model: They often deliberately blur the descriptive and the normative characteristics of models and thus simultaneously function as models *of* and models *for* urban developments. We then draw on an ongoing collaborative research project on the transatlantic comparison of scripts in post-industrial urban transformations to: (a) illustrate the implications of this type of research for the theory and practice of literary urban studies and (b) to point out how a surprisingly limited number of such scripts permute, intersect and reinforce each other in global urban developments.

Building on key insights developed in Chapters 1–7, **Chapter 8**, "From the 'Garden City' to the 'Smart City': Literary Urban Studies, Policy Mobility

Research and Travelling Urban Models", develops a literary studies approach to policy mobility research and more specifically to research on 'global urbanism' and the global diffusion of blueprints for urban development. The chapter initially points out the lack of attention to narrative patterns, rhetoric, visualisation and other strategies of persuasion in policy mobility research (hitherto mainly in the fields of political science, economics, human geography, planning studies and studies of the built environment). In order to highlight the extent to which such travelling models rely on – broadly speaking – literary strategies for their persuasive effect, the chapter then offers a detailed analysis of the narrative structures, plot patterns, visualisations, and of the use of literary and cultural references, collective symbols and established patterns of interpretation in planning documents, policy papers, marketing materials and other pragmatic, non-literary texts central to the diffusion of the 'Garden City' concept. Such strategies can to a significant extent explain the ease and speed with which the concept was adopted in a variety of different cultural contexts and the changes it underwent in the process. The chapter thus shows how literary studies can decisively contribute to research on global policy mobility, especially in the field of travelling models and concepts in urban development. Finally, this approach to policy mobility is briefly shown to be applicable to other key fields in recent global urban development, such as the numerous blueprints for 'smart' or 'sustainable' urban development. While such globally prevalent developments can arguably be claimed simply as instances of similar solutions to similar challenges, this diagnosis significantly underestimates the extent to which such projects rely on globally circulating narratives, imaginaries and iconic visual representations.

As a whole, this book charts literary urban studies and thus contributes to the development of this vibrant emerging research field through the application of existing as well as newly developed methods to partly new materials not generally discussed in literary studies. It does so by advancing a literary studies contribution to the general theory of models and by introducing the notion of texts across different genres and text types as – to varying degrees – descriptive models *of* the city and prescriptive models *for* the city. Taking my cue from Joyce's light-hearted remark about the double function of texts – "to give a picture of [the city]" and to serve as a blueprint from which it "could be reconstructed" (Budgen 69f.), I thus also seek to explore Yi-Fu Tuan's notion that "the personality of certain cities (nineteenth-century London, for instance) owes much to the influence of a powerful literature. A great city may be seen as the construction of words as well as stone" (686).

Notes

1 The Association for Literary Urban Studies (ALUS), founded and spearheaded by Lieven Ameel and Jason Finch, has been instrumental here; its website provides a helpful bibliography of work in literary urban studies: https://blogs.helsinki.fi/hlc-n. Two important collections have been edited by Tambling and Lindner/Meissner.

2 Cf. also Childs; Cohen; Eckstein/Throgmorton; Filep/Thompson-Fawcett/Rae; Healey; Ivory; Kaplan; Keunen/Verraest; Mandelbaum; Sandercock 2003; Tewdwr-Jones; Throgmorton 1996, 2003; van Hulst.

3 For a discussion of this passage, cf. also Mattheis 80.
4 The relation of the material and the textual city might also be conceptualised in the light of the material turn in literary studies; in this view, city texts can be seen as material artefacts that form part of the material city while also imaginatively intervening in its formation.
5 Mahr's original reads as follows: "Einem Modell liegt immer etwas zugrunde, *wovon* es ein Modell ist, d.h. von dem ausgehend oder auf das Bezug nehmend es hergestellt oder gewählt wurde, seine Matrix. Zweck der Herstellung oder der Wahl eines Modells ist sein Gebrauch [...] Zu den typischen Gebrauchsweisen von Modellen gehört ihr Gebrauch als *Mittel der Gestaltung*. Für die Gestaltung sind Modelle Vorbilder, Vorformen oder Spezifikationen [...] Der Begriff des Modells lässt sich daher nur dann überzeugend erklären, wenn man berücksichtigt, dass ein Modell immer zugleich ein *Modell von etwas* und ein *Modell für etwas* ist" (2015, 331f.). Cf. also Mahr 2004, 2008; for this dual nature of models, cf. also Geertz 93 and Yanow.
6 To be sure, Mahr clearly states that models "can be used for very different purposes: models can be descriptive for us, like Bohr's model of the atom, prescriptive, like [an ISO standard], conceptual, like the architecture of a software system [and several further purposes]" (2015, 332).
7 Van Hulst's discussion of "storytelling" as "a model *of* and a model *for* planning" is in keeping with the "story turn in planning" (Sandercock 2010), but makes no reference to the theory of models and does not develop the notion of "model of" and "model for" any further.
8 These are the Münster RTG 1886 "Literarische Form: Geschichte und Kultur ästhetischer Modellbildung" (cf. for instance Erdbeer 2015a, 2015b) as well as the Jena RTG 2041 "Modell Romantik" (cf. for instance Matuschek/Kerschbaumer).
9 This would also make it difficult to justify the inclusion or exclusion of specific cities (unless one restricted the discussion to a handful of 'global cities' from the start).

References

Ameel, Lieven. "A *Bildungsroman* for a Waterfront Development: Literary Genre and the Planning Narratives of Jätkäsaari, Helsinki." *Journal of Urban Cultural Studies* 3.2 (2016): 167–187.

Ameel, Lieven. *The Narrative Turn in Urban Planning: Plotting the Helsinki Waterfront*. New York: Routledge, 2021.

Ameel, Lieven. "The Sixth Borough: Metaphorizations of the Water in New York City's Comprehensive Waterfront Plan Vision 2020 and Foer's 'The Sixth Borough'." *Critique* 60.3 (2019): 251–262. https://doi.org/10.1080/00111619.2018.1556203.

Ameel, Lieven. "Towards a Narrative Typology of Urban Planning Narratives *for*, *in*, and *of* Planning in Jätkäsaari, Helsinki." *Urban Design International* 22 (2017): 318–330. https://doi.org/10.1057/s41289-016-0030-8.

Association for Literary Urban Studies (ALUS). https://blogs.helsinki.fi/hlc-n.

Bahlke, Friedrich, Bernhard Siegert, Joseph Vogl, eds. *Modelle und Modellierung*. Paderborn: Fink, 2014.

BBSR (Bundesinstitut für Bau-, Stadt- und Raumforschung). *Von Science-Fiction-Städten lernen: Szenarien für die Stadtplanung*. Bonn: BBSR, 2015.

Bode, Christoph, Rainer Dietrich. *Future Narratives: Theory, Poetics, and Media-Historical Moment*. Berlin, Boston: de Gruyter, 2013.

Buchenau, Barbara, Jens Martin Gurr. "City Scripts: Urban American Studies and the Conjunction of Textual Strategies and Spatial Processes." *Urban Transformations in the U.S.A.: Spaces, Communities, Representations*. Ed. Julia Sattler. Bielefeld: transcript, 2016. 395–420.

Buchenau, Barbara, Jens Martin Gurr. “On the Textuality of American Cities and their Others: A Disputation.” *Projecting American Studies: Essays on Theory, Method and Practice*. Ed. Frank Kelleter, Alexander Starre. Heidelberg: Winter, 2018. 135–152.

Budgen, Frank. *James Joyce and the Making of* Ulysses [1934]. Bloomington: Indiana University Press, 1960.

Childs, Mark C. “Storytelling and Urban Design.” *Journal of Urbanism* 1.2 (2008): 173–186.

Cohen, Philip. “Stuff Happens: Telling the Story and Doing the Business in the Making of Thames Gateway.” *London’s Turning: Thames Gateway; Prospects and Legacy*. Ed. Philip Cohen, Michael J. Rustin. Aldershot: Ashgate, 2008. 99–124.

Dirks, Ulrich, Eberhard Knobloch, eds. *Modelle*. Frankfurt/Main, Berlin, Bern, Bruxelles, New York: Peter Lang, 2008.

Eckstein, Barbara, James A. Throgmorton, eds. *Story and Sustainability: Planning, Practice, and Possibility for American Cities*. Cambridge, MA: MIT Press, 2003.

Eliot, T.S. “The Waste Land.” Eliot. *Collected Poems: 1909–1962*. London: Faber & Faber, 1974. 61–86.

Erdbeer, Robert Matthias. “Poetik der Modelle.” *Textpraxis* 11 (2015a). www.uni-muenster.de/textpraxis/robert-matthias-erdbeer-poetik-der-modelle.

Erdbeer, Robert Matthias. “Poetik der Modelle – Überlegungen zu einer literarischen Modelltheorie.” *Erwägen – Wissen – Ethik/Deliberation – Knowledge – Ethics: Forum für Erwägungskultur/Forum for Deliberative Culture* 26.3 (2015b): 359–362.

Filep, Crystal Victoria, Michelle Thompson-Fawcett, Murray Rae. “Built Narratives.” *Journal of Urban Design* 19.3 (2014): 298–316.

Geertz, Clifford. *The Interpretation of Cultures: Selected Essays*. London: Fontana Press, 1993.

Healey, Patsy. “Planning in Relational Space and Time: Responding to New Urban Realities.” *A Companion to the City*. Ed. Gary Bridge, Sophie Watson. Oxford: Blackwell, 2000. 517–530.

Ivory, Chris. “The Role of the Imagined User in Planning and Design Narratives.” *Planning Theory* 12.4 (2013): 425–441.

Kaplan, Thomas J. “Reading Policy Narratives: Beginnings, Middles, and Ends.” *The Argumentative Turn in Policy Analysis and Planning*. Ed. Frank Fischer, John Forester. London: UCL Press, 1993. 167–185.

Keunen, Bart, Sofie Verraest. “Tell-Tale Landscapes and Mythical Chronotopes in Urban Designs for Twenty-First Century Paris.” *CLCWeb: Comparative Literature and Culture* 14.3 (2012). https://doi.org/10.7771/1481–4374.2038.

Klein, Norman M., Rosemary Comella, Andreas Kratky. *Bleeding Through: Layers of Los Angeles 1920–1986* [DVD and Book]. Karlsruhe: ZKM digital arts edition, 2003.

Lindner, Christoph, Miriam Meissner, eds. *The Routledge Companion to Urban Imaginaries*. London, New York: Routledge, 2019.

Mahr, Bernd. “Ein Modell des Modellseins: Ein Beitrag zur Aufklärung des Modellbegriffs.” *Modelle*. Ed. Ulrich Dirks, Eberhard Knobloch. Frankfurt/Main, Berlin, Bern, Bruxelles, New York: Peter Lang, 2008. 187–218.

Mahr, Bernd. “Modelle und ihre Befragbarkeit: Grundlagen einer allgemeinen Modelltheorie.” *Erwägen – Wissen – Ethik/Deliberation – Knowledge – Ethics: Forum für Erwägungskultur/Forum for Deliberative Culture* 26.3 (2015): 329–342.

Mahr, Bernd. “Das Mögliche im Modell und die Vermeidung der Fiktion.” *Science & Fiction: Über Gedankenexperimente in Wissenschaft, Philosophie und Literatur*. Ed. Thomas Macho, Annette Wunschel. Frankfurt/Main: Fischer, 2004. 161–182.

Mandelbaum, Seymour J. “Telling Stories.” *Journal of Planning Education and Research* 10.3 (1991): 209–214.

Mattheis, Lena. *Translocal Narratability in Contemporary Anglophone Fiction*. Dissertation manuscript, University of Duisburg-Essen, 2019.

Matuschek, Stefan, Sandra Kerschbaumer, eds. *Romantik erkennen – Modelle finden*. Leiden: Ferdinand Schöningh, 2019.

Prieto, Eric. “Geocriticism, Geopoetics, Geophilosophy, and Beyond.” *Geocritical Explorations: Space, Place, and Mapping in Literary and Cultural Studies*. Ed. Robert T. Tally. New York: Palgrave Macmillan, 2011. 13–27.

Sandercock, Leonie. “From the Campfire to the Computer: An Epistemology of Multiplicity and the Story Turn in Planning.” *Multimedia Explorations in Urban Policy and Planning: Beyond the Flatlands*. Ed. Leonie Sandercock, Giovanni Attili. Dordrecht, Heidelberg, New York: Springer, 2010. 17–37.

Sandercock, Leonie. “Out of the Closet: The Importance of Stories and Storytelling in Planning Practice.” *Planning Theory & Practice* 4.1 (2003): 11–28.

Schäfer, Christoph. *Die Stadt ist unsere Fabrik/The City is our Factory*. Leipzig: Spector Books, 2010.

Stachowiak, Herbert. *Allgemeine Modelltheorie*. Wien, New York: Springer, 1973.

Tambling, Jeremy, ed. *The Palgrave Handbook of Literature and the City*. London: Palgrave, 2016.

Tewdwr-Jones, Mark. *Urban Reflections: Narratives of Place, Planning and Change*. Bristol: Policy Press, 2011.

Throgmorton, James A. “Planning as Persuasive Storytelling in a Global-Scale Web of Relationships.” *Planning Theory* 2.2 (2003): 125–135.

Throgmorton, James A. *Planning as Persuasive Storytelling: The Rhetorical Construction of Chicago’s Electric Future*. Chicago: University of Chicago Press, 1996.

Tuan, Yi-Fu. “Language and the Making of Place: A Narrative-Descriptive Approach.” *Annals of the Association of American Geographers* 81.4 (1991): 684–696.

van Hulst, Merlijn. “Storytelling, a Model *of* and a Model *for* Planning.” *Planning Theory* 11.3 (2012): 299–318.

Wendler, Reinhard. *Das Modell zwischen Kunst und Wissenschaft*. Munich: Fink, 2013.

Yanow, Dvora. “Cognition Meets Action: Metaphors as Models *of* and Models *for*.” *Political Language and Metaphor: Interpreting and Changing the World*. Ed. Terrell Carver, Jernej Pikalo. London: Routledge, 2008. 225–238.

1 Interdisciplinary Urban Complexity Research and Texts as Qualitative Models

This chapter attempts to sketch a literary and cultural studies approach to the modelling of urban complexity: After briefly commenting on what I perceive as a neglect of cultural phenomena in much urban modelling, I will discuss key characteristics of urban complexity from a literary and cultural studies perspective and will relate these to technical or mathematical notions of complexity. My third section engages with the need for reduction and compression in modelling and with the resulting limitations of urban models before discussing the fundamentally different status of the model in urban complexity studies on the one hand and in literary and cultural studies on the other hand. The chapter thus sets out to show how literary and cultural studies engage with urban complexity and what such an engagement can contribute to truly interdisciplinary work on urban complexity and urban systems. I will argue that literary texts specifically can bring back into the discussion those features of urban complexity that resist quantitative modelling but that are nonetheless crucial to a differentiated understanding of the functioning of urban systems.

The Neglect of 'Culture' in Urban Complexity Research

In his masterful study *Die komplexe Stadt: Orientierungen im urbanen Labyrinth* (2009), one of the most ambitious attempts to provide urban studies with an integrating research agenda, Frank Eckardt goes so far as to propose complexity as *the* key characteristic of the city and calls for a transdisciplinary research programme organised around the integrating paradigm of 'complexity'. However, Eckardt then largely pursues a sociological programme.

'Complexity' is indeed central to much work in urban modelling (cf. for instance Albeverio *et al.*; Batty 2013; Portugali 2011; Walloth/Gurr/Schmidt; for a brief and accessible account, cf. Gurr/Walloth). Inter- and transdisciplinary methodological discussions of urban modelling might highlight questions such as the following:

- How is 'urban complexity' understood, defined and 'modelled' in various disciplines and what is the relation to urban reality these models claim?

- Which subsystems or combinations of subsystems are being modelled by researchers of various disciplines – e.g. is the city considered as a social, ecological, economic, technical or cultural system?
- What are the – normative and/or descriptive – aims and interests pursued with different types of models? Are they designed fundamentally to understand interdependencies within or explain the functioning of urban systems – or do they seek to aid decision-making in concrete situations?
- How can central non-quantifiable phenomena that are especially relevant to a 'humanities' understanding of urban complexity be integrated into the dominant types of models? To what extent can they complement mathematical models?
- Which issues and strategies in dealing with urban complexity are already cross-disciplinary? What are the interfaces between disciplines and what bridges can be built here?
- Which of the issues and strategies specific to the individual disciplines dealing with urban complexity can be regarded as complementary? What are the implications of the specific sign systems in which these models are mediated? Are there parallels or analogies between quantitative and narrative models?
- According to which criteria do we make decisions concerning parameters to be included or excluded? To what extent are selection criteria for inclusion and exclusion complementary in different disciplines?
- How can the insights from various types of models be integrated?

It seems that, despite much talk of multi-, inter- or transdisciplinary research in (urban) complexity, the perspective of culture is curiously absent in discussions of urban modelling.[1] More specifically, while the consideration of actors and groups of actors and their behaviour as an important dimension of 'culture' as studied by the social sciences is clearly central to modelling endeavours, patterns of symbolic representation and patterns of perception and interpretation as less tangible elements of the city largely resist quantitative modelling and are a conspicuous absence in models of urban complexity. A few prominent examples may suffice here: The "Preface" to one of the most ambitious collections on the topic, Albeverio *et al.*'s *The Dynamics of Complex Urban Systems* (2008), in its plea for a "fruitful collaboration between natural science" and "regional science" mentions "physics, mathematics, computer science, biology …" (omission original) on the side of "natural science" and "architecture, geography, city plannings [sic], economics, sociology …" (omission original) on the side of "regional science" (v) – and the volume, comprehensive as it is, does not contain anything even remotely from the field of cultural studies. Even in the exhaustive and masterful 2009 *Encyclopedia of Complexity and Systems Science*, Michael Batty's state-of-the-art contribution on "Cities as Complex Systems: Scaling, Interaction, Networks, Dynamics and Urban Morphologies" (1041–1071) does not even mention 'culture', nor do concepts like 'individuality' play any role. Similarly, "Springer Complexity", according to the description for what is arguably the leading and most prominent book series in the field, is said to "cut across all traditional disciplines of the natural and life sciences, engineering, economics, medicine, neuroscience, social and computer science" (Portugali *et al.* front matter). Moreover, the outline for Springer's "Understanding Complex Systems" (UCS) series states the aim of the programme as follows: "UCS is explicitly transdisciplinary", its first "main goal" being "to elaborate the concepts, methods and tools of complex systems at all levels of description and in all scientific fields, especially newly emerging areas within the life, social, behavioural, economic, neuro- and cognitive sciences (and derivatives thereof)" (Portugali 2011, front matter). The mental, non-institutional dimension of culture in the form of symbolically mediated patterns of perception and interpretation of human environments, it seems, hardly features in discussions of urban complexity.

Characteristics of (Urban) Complexity: Urban Systems Research and the Perspective of Literary and Cultural Studies

Many of the characteristics of urban complexity frequently discussed in research on complex urban systems[2] are those that are also of interest to literary and cultural studies. Portugali (2006) conveniently defines the complexity of the city thus: "a very large number of interacting parts, linked by a complex network of feedback and feedforward loops, within a system that is open to and, thus part of, its environment" (657; cf. also Portugali 2011, 232). Further characteristics of complexity frequently discussed include self-organisation, emergence, non-linearity, phase transitions, density, mobility (as one cause of change over time and as the occasion for increased interaction and mixing), ethnic and cultural multiplicity, heterogeneity and hybridity, violence, conflicts over the use of space, intersections of technology and virtual spaces with physical spaces, overlapping and intersecting spatial scales – from the local to the global – and their interdependencies, as well as complex interferences, interdependencies or intersections in the interaction between multiple players, intentions or force fields. Together, these make urban systems prime examples of translocal networks of complex relationships, connections and interdependencies subject to rapid change over time. Moreover, as already indicated in Portugali's working definition, the city is of course an open or dissipative rather than a closed system (in the technical sense): It exchanges goods, energy, information, people, money, etc. with its environment. All these characteristics, it seems, are more or less part and parcel also of urban simulation models in the more technically oriented disciplines concerned with urban modelling from a complex systems perspective.

However, the 'softer', less easily quantified and modelled characteristics of urban complexity are no less central to the 'urban experience'. In this vein, in addition to the 'usual suspects' such as "hierarchy and emergence, non-linearity, asymmetry, number of relationships, number of parts", Mainzer (374) also lists the following features: "values and beliefs, people, interests, notions and perceptions" (they appear in a visualisation, hence in no particular order – the order is mine). Additionally, while the notion of a system's 'history' – in the sense that previous developments have an impact on the present and future course of the system – is central to urban modelling (if only in the sense that past developments can be extrapolated for predictive purposes), one specific aspect of a city's history is of particular importance to an understanding of urban systems from the perspective of literary and cultural studies: This is the notion of the city as a palimpsest, a form of layered spatialised memory (this is discussed in detail in Chapters 3 and 4).[3] Individual and collective memory and the way it is physically manifested in and evoked by the built environment is a prime concern in many literary texts (for a detailed discussion of a specific key text, cf. Chapter 3).

Arguably the central challenge to literary 'modelling', however, lies in the multiplicity of sense impressions and the resulting sensual overload and semiotic 'overkill' as a result of a multiplicity of sign systems and ceaseless semiosis. In this vein, Georg Simmel in his influential 1903 essay "The Metropolis and Mental Life", one of the crucial texts in the early phase of urban studies, defines "the psychological conditions which the metropolis creates" as marked by the "*intensification of nervous stimulation* which results from the swift and uninterrupted change of outer and inner stimuli [...] the rapid crowding of changing images, the sharp discontinuity in the grasp of a single glance, and the unexpectedness of onrushing impressions" (13; italics original).

In his 2011 study *Complexity, Cognition and the City*, in a remarkably similar way, Portugali speaks of

> the really complex situation that concerns individuals under a bombardment of information, that is, under a multiplicity of messages from a multiplicity of sources and of all kinds. This is typical of the dynamics of cities: every agent operating in the city is continually subject to a multiplicity of messages in the form of views, noises, smells etc. In order to behave and survive, the agent [...] must make sense of all those signals and messages. (232f.)

As I will argue in Chapter 2, it is precisely the representation of simultaneity that poses the greatest challenge in the narrative representation of urban complexity.

Urban Complexity in Technical and Literary Models: Information, Compression, the Limits of Modelling – and the Status of the Model

In two chapters jointly authored with Herman Haken that largely go back to an earlier joint essay (Haken/Portugali), Portugali (2011) elaborates on the amount of information contained in the physical structure of the city.[4] In the subchapter tellingly entitled "How Many Bits to the Face of the City" (179–186), the authors argue: "From the point of view of information theory, the face of the city is a message. As a message it conveys and transmits different quantities of Shannonian information" (Portugali 2011, 201). Conceived in terms of informational complexity, it is obvious that the city contains a virtually endless amount of information – even if we just take its physical shape and ignore, for the moment, the interaction of millions of humans each with their own thoughts, hopes, anxieties, etc.

As far as the 'measurement' of complexity from a literary and cultural studies perspective is concerned, it is evident that most mathematical or technical measures are hardly helpful: Neither algorithmic or Kolmogorov complexity (a measurement of the length of the minimal programme that reproduces a given sequence; for a discussion, cf. Li/Vitányi), nor Bennett's notion of logical depth (essentially a measure of the time required for a given bit string to be computed and reproduced), nor effective complexity in the sense of Gell-Mann (for a discussion, cf. for instance Gell-Mann 1995a and 1995b), nor the measure of informational entropy, nor the question of calculability as in P- or NP-problems, nor dynamic complexity are really helpful here. It seems that, when descriptions of urban systems and the specific forms of complexity they exhibit are concerned, it does not really matter whether we are looking at Kolmogorov complexity, effective complexity or logical depth – the multiple interdependencies, overlapping scales, forms of self-organisation, etc., yield an astonishing degree of complexity by any definition. However, this complexity is not beyond comprehension or calculability: "The significant achievement of complexity theories is to show that even [under such complex conditions] a scientific approach is possible" (Portugali 2011, 232). The solution, Portugali argues, lies in what he refers to as "information compression" (2011, 231–233).

Compression and strategic 'reduction' of complexity are of course part and parcel of any modelling process, as Stachowiak's notion of "reduction" ["Verkürzung"] as central to any model already makes clear (132). The crucial task, of course, is to decide what can safely be left out or abstracted so as not to distort the overall picture. This will naturally depend on what the model is supposed to achieve – whether, for instance, to help understand all interdependencies within a system or whether to capture only those features of a system perceived as relevant to a specific investment decision. In both cases, the heuristic nature of the model is not to be ignored. In this context, Cohen and Stewart aptly remark:

> Mathematical descriptions of nature are not fundamental truths about the world, but models. There are good models and bad models and indifferent models, and what models you use depends on the purposes for which you use it and the range of phenomena which you want to understand [...] Reductionist rhetoric [...] claims a degree of correspondence between deep underlying rules and reality that is never justified by any actual calculation or experiment.
>
> (410)

Lefebvre similarly comments on the need for reduction in dealing with 'complexity' but also on the inherent dangers:

> Reduction is a scientific procedure designed to deal with complexity and chaos of brute observations. This kind of simplification is necessary at first, but it must be quickly followed by the gradual restoration of what has thus been temporarily set aside for the sake of analysis. Otherwise a methodological necessity may become a servitude, and the legitimate operation of reduction may be transformed into the abuse of *reductionism*.
>
> (105f.; italics original)

In a related vein, David Byrne in an excellent overview on *Complexity Theory and the Social Sciences* aptly remarks that complexity science is "clearly quantitative" (54) in its aims and methods, and appropriately points out three more fundamental caveats and limits to quantitative analysis and modelling:

1. the limits to formalisation of any mathematical system established by Gödel;
2. the limits to capacity of measurement central to deterministic chaos; and
3. the working limits for expression of mathematical formalism derived from the non-linearity of the real systems with which chaos/complexity is concerned

(for an excellent discussion of these caveats, cf. 54–71)

More specifically and with a view to practical limitations in the modelling of urban systems, Portugali (2012a) in an enlightening state-of-the-art article on "Complexity Theories of Cities: Achievements, Criticism and Potentials", comments on a key problem in many contemporary applications of complexity theory in urban modelling:

> There is nothing wrong [...] in sophisticated simulation models crunching huge quantities of data by means of fast computers. What's wrong is [...] that simulation models originally designed as media by which to study phenomena of complexity and self-organization become the message itself.
>
> (52)

As a result, "practitioners of urban simulation models tend to overlook the non-quantifiable urban phenomena" (52).[5]

In his "Introduction" to the same volume, Portugali (2012b, 4) attempts to account for this loss by commenting on the research motivation of scholars in CTC (complexity theories of cities): "Some are physicists for whom cities is [sic] just another source for quantitative data with which to test their models, while others are urbanists who see CTC as the new and more sophisticated generation of the 'old' quantitative approach to cities. By so doing they overlook the qualitative message of CTC" (4).[6] He then incisively asks: "But what about the uniqueness of cities – of the properties that differentiate them from material and organic entities, how do these [relate] to their complexity and dynamics?" (4). Thus, what is missing, according to Portugali, is only the analysis of what distinguishes cities generally from other complex systems; he does not appear to be interested in the arguably more important question what makes an individual city unique – as in studies on the "intrinsic logic ['Eigenlogik'] of cities" (cf. Berking/Löw) – let alone in the uniqueness of individuals and their response to the city.

What is the consequence of this type of reduction? While Rolf Lindner (92) has argued that "[t]he city of sociologists [...] is frequently a non-sensual place, a city one does not hear, smell, taste, more precisely, a Non-Place",[7] I would argue that this is even more true of the city of quantitative modellers and complexity theorists.

Purely quantitative approaches are similarly problematic when it comes to defining the elusive notion of 'urbanity' or when it comes to defining the 'metropolis': 'Metropolis' and, to a lesser extent, 'city', it seems, are not merely descriptive terms, but more or less strongly imply normative elements, even a utopian promise – and this, I would argue, is largely a cultural promise that is difficult to categorise. However, the concept of the metropolis of course is not only normative. It does make sense to classify cities according to various criteria, and many historical as well as recent attempts to define the metropolitan character of cities are very enlightening.[8] Thus, the concept of 'metropolis' – just like 'urbanity' – curiously oscillates between descriptively designating a quantifiable status of centrality as a financial centre, a traffic node, a centre of research and education or of the media industry on the one hand, and a normative requirement of a far less tangible 'je ne sais quoi', a metropolitan 'feel' of cultural promise (for a more detailed discussion, cf. Gurr 2010, 2015): Frankfurt/Main may be a financial metropolis, because, second to London, it is the seat of the most important European stock exchange and of several important banks, but is it a cultural metropolis? Berlin, although certainly not a financial centre, is a metropolis, because it is a capital with over three million residents, but it also appears to have the intangible cultural 'flair' a metropolis in the wider sense also seems to need. Even in scholarly discourse, the descriptive and the normative components of the concept of 'metropolis' are not always neatly distinguished. Despite their undisputed achievements in dealing with a range of aspects of urban complexity – demographic developments, material and energy flows, mobility planning and innumerable others – it is here, in understanding the qualitative phenomena such as urbanity, individuality, place-specificity, individual patterns of interpretation and sense-making – that quantitative models show their limitations.

This, I argue, is where literary and cultural studies come in: For although it is, of course, possible to include certain 'subjective' features into a model (for instance by including group-specific cultural preferences, as is common in agent-based modelling and other types of urban simulation models), what is individual, unique, historically and personally specific and not reducible to an underlying pattern, is what disappears in abstracting from the individual and in the aggregation of preferences, needs, desires, hopes, fears into an equation. It is precisely this individuality and specificity both of different urban environments in their "intrinsic logic" (*sensu* Berking/Löw) and of human behaviour, of perceptions and patterns of sense-making that literary texts model in uniquely differentiated ways. It is in literary texts that the "non-sensual" city of sociologists (*sensu* Lindner) and quantitative modellers becomes perceptibly individualised.[9]

From the perspective of literary and cultural studies, the question is how the complexity of the urban text is 'modelled' in literature (and other media, though I do not discuss them here). Despite the universally diagnosed importance of complexity as a key characteristic of the urban and despite the widely perceived affinity between the city and the novel (and film) – and a look at innumerable 'urban' poems and narrative fictions confirms that the issue is indeed central to 'urban literature' – the specific issue of how literary texts represent urban complexity has received very limited explicit scholarly attention. In most of the innumerable studies on urban imaginaries in literature and film, though occasionally implied, complexity – let alone simultaneity – almost universally does not feature as a theme in itself.[10]

A further key issue that needs to be addressed in comparative discussions of 'urban modelling' in technical complexity research and in literary studies is the fundamentally different status of the 'model' in both fields: While in technical urban complexity research, the model is the *result* of scientific endeavour, in literary and cultural studies, the literary text functions as the 'model' and is thus the *object of study* rather than the *result* of the scholar's own work. Thus, Mahr's rather casually enumerative formulation of the two alternative ways in which models come into being – "no object is a model per se. Models are *built* or *chosen*" (331; italics original) – here constitutes a fundamental distinction between different research cultures and their dominant forms of engaging with models.

Bridging the Gap: Parallels between Quantitative and Textual Models

Despite the fundamentally different status of the 'model' in urban complexity modelling on the one hand and in literary and cultural studies on the other hand, there are a number of important parallels and points of intersection between the two types of 'model' and in the understanding of complexity: What most technical notions of complexity share is that they measure the complexity of a system in terms of the length or the complexity of the description or representation of that system. A number of complexity theorists have even argued that "complexity is not primarily a characteristic of the object that is being described, but of the description" (Richter/Rost 112; my translation).[11] This notion might lend itself as a bridge between technical or mathematical and cultural conceptualisations of complexity. Ultimately, what is relevant to literary studies, one might argue, is not so much the complexity of the city itself, but the representation of this complexity, i.e. its description in the 'model' of the literary text. Literary studies are thus concerned with the challenge of 'modelling' it, or, in the terminology of literary studies, of 'representing' it. Thus, where technical and mathematical complexity research is concerned with the mathematical description of complexity, literary and cultural studies of urban complexity are concerned with the challenges of verbal representation.

Gell-Mann's notion of "effective complexity" provides a further important connection between a technical and a literary understanding of complexity:

> A measure that corresponds much better to what is usually meant by complexity in ordinary conversation, as well as in scientific discourse, refers not to the length of the most concise description of an entity (which is roughly what AIC [algorithmic information content] is), but to the length of a concise description of a set of the entity's regularities. Thus something almost entirely random, with practically no regularities, would have effective complexity near zero. So would something completely regular, such as a bit string consisting entirely of zeroes. Effective complexity can be high only in a region intermediate between total order and complete disorder.
>
> (1995b, 16)

This seems precisely to be the case with cities: In the sense of "effective complexity", they are systems in which there are multiple regularities as well as contingencies, and hence systems in which "a concise description of a set of the entity's regularities" would be extremely long. Thus characterised by an intricate combination of both order and disorder, cities have long been understood as systems of extremely high "effective complexity" (take Jane Jacobs's classic formulation that cities are "problems in organized complexity", 449). Somewhat speculatively, we might argue that literary texts as models of reality are *per se* combinations of order and disorder: In frequently highly structured and ordered ways, they represent complexity and multiplicity, even disorder, and overlay disorder with order – established plot structures, schemata or typological patterns of interpretation (cf. Koschorke 29ff.) – and thus structurally replicate key patterns of urban complexity (for a detailed discussion of texts as structural and functional urban models, cf. Chapter 3; for the structural analogies between city and text, cf. also Sharpe/Wallock).

Moreover, if we regard 'scenario building' and the testing of alternative parameter settings in their impact on a given system as a crucial function of urban systems modelling – a notion I discuss in some detail in Chapter 6 – then a further parallel emerges: One of the central functions of literature, according to one understanding, is that it serves as a form of symbolic action, as a social experiment free from the constraints of everyday life – literature as 'de-pragmatised behaviour in rehearsal' ['entpragmatisiertes Probehandeln'][12] which makes it possible symbolically to try out in fiction different scenarios or potential solutions for key societal issues. Here, too, given the descriptive, representational as well as the – at least implicitly – prescriptive, speculative, exploratory function of texts, this conceptualisation – developed in the wake of Mahr's understanding of the model – of texts as both descriptive "models *of*" and prescriptive "models *for*" urban structures, developments and functions, seems highly appropriate.

The different procedures used in different fields and disciplines to represent, reduce (or: constitute in the first place) and seek to 'manage' complexity do justice to different facets of urban complexity in varying degrees: Mobility systems or energy flows lend themselves to being modelled in the sense of complex systems research far more than do processes of sense-making or conflicting patterns in the perception and use of space, which find privileged expression in verbal models of literary texts. Even the selection criteria for facets to be included in (and, conversely, excluded from) the model are virtually diametrically opposed: that which is individual, specific or characteristic in literary texts as opposed to that which can be generalised, aggregated and quantified in quantitative models.

Moreover, the boundaries between numerical, visual and narrative models do not necessarily coincide with disciplinary boundaries, as the example of modelling urban complexity in social cartography shows (for a detailed discussion cf. Gurr/Schneider; for questions of statistics and cartography, cf. Schneider 2006, 2011a, 2011b, 2014; for mapping in literary studies, cf. Mattheis; Moretti; Rossetto): Here, visualisations are regularly preceded by quantitative models, which in turn may be informed by underlying – often unquestioned – narratives. Similar forms of overlay and transfer between quantitative and visual models are to be found in different methods of mathematical optimisation such as graph theory or in the geometrical 'tesselation' of areas as they occur in the optimisation of infrastructures, logistics networks, scheduling problems or evacuation scenarios. What is more, qualitative and quantitative representations of complexity by no means have to correspond: some forms of complexity may be easy to describe qualitatively but may be extremely difficult to quantify (and vice versa).

Nonetheless, a number of strategies in dealing with complexity are rather similar, and there are a large number of overlaps, interactions and transfers between different basic types of models. There are, for instance, a number of remarkable parallels and analogies between algorithmic and aesthetic/literary strategies of representing and reducing complexity (sometimes only reduction may make representation possible in the first place). Thus, a number of literary strategies of reducing complexity – for instance, the metonymic strategy of telling one story and suggesting that innumerable others would also have been worth telling, or the breaking of linearity by means of partition and distribution (for a typology of such strategies, cf. Chapter 2) – are paralleled in mathematics and information technology in the handling of complex calculations and large quantities of data by means of distributed computing, randomisation or decomposition (for an accessible discussion, cf. Schultz).[13]

Despite such parallels, analogies and processes of exchange, the different methods of modelling complexity cannot be seamlessly integrated or converted into one another: My point is not that key qualitative elements of the urban should somehow nonetheless be quantified in order to be integrated into numerical models after all. Such different models might rather complement each other, for instance by mutually setting off shortcomings and by filling in each other's blind spots. This kind of integration of various approaches to modelling, I argue, is crucial to a more refined understanding of complex urban systems.

What, then, can the study of cities and urban complexity learn from literary and cultural studies? It may be the insight that the irreducible element of individual psychological responses to a given urban environment, that is, human desires, hopes and fears, are very often crucial to understanding that environment. What literary and cultural studies as I conceive them can contribute is an understanding of precisely those elements of urban complexity that cannot be measured, modelled, classified or studied in terms of information theory. Literary texts as an alternative form of 'modelling' urban complexity enable *different* views and may draw attention to blind spots in other models, thus not only functioning as a type of 'sanity check' but as a further, different and complementary type of 'urban model'.

Further inter- and transdisciplinary research across the disciplines should enlarge on the implications of differences and complementarities between different types of models. What seems clear, however, is that insights into the limitations of quantitative models and the complementary achievements of qualitative models productively tie in with recent insights into the limits of planning and plannability, with discussions of planning under and for conditions of uncertainty, or of the role of emergent processes for the practice of planning – what can be planned is very often not what will make a place distinctive (cf. for instance Walloth 2014, 2016). These discussions therefore also tie in with notions of a 'new modesty' in planning. It is precisely the need to integrate these different perspectives to come to a meaningful understanding of the complex dynamic of 'urban systems' that makes this kind of interdisciplinary dialogue so necessary, so challenging and so rewarding.

Notes

1 The same is true of the roles and functions of urban culture in urban systems. For discussions of the functions of urban culture and the contribution of urban cultural studies to transdisciplinary urban research, cf. for instance Butler/Gurr; Gurr/Butler 2011, 2013.
2 For enlightening explicit or implicit definitions of urban complexity and its defining features, cf. for instance Batty 2009, *passim*; Eckardt *passim*; Mainzer 374 *et passim*; Portugali 2000; Portugali 2006, 652–657 *et passim*; Portugali 2011, 232ff. *et passim*; Portugali 2012b, 4f.
3 For various aspects of the notion of the city as a palimpsest, cf. Assmann; Harvey 66; Hassenpflug 2006, 2011; Huyssen; Martindale; Sharpe/Wallock 9; Suttles. For the palimpsest in literary studies, cf. especially Dillon.
4 Cf. Portugali 2011, ch. 8: "Shannonian Information and the City" (167–187) and ch. 9: "Semantic Information and the City" (187–210); cf. also Haken/Portugali.
5 Similarly, Portugali (2012a, 54) argues that "[q]ualitative urban phenomena do not lend themselves to quantitative-statistical analysis and thus are of little interest to mainstream CTC".
6 Portugali (2011, 227) somewhat schematically accounts for this by commenting on the different methodologies of the natural as opposed to the social sciences: "The methodological tools of the 'hard' sciences are reductionism, mathematical formalism, statistical analysis and explanation, while those of the 'soft' humanities and social theory are the exact opposite: anti-reductionism, understanding in place of

explanation, and hermeneutics in place of analysis." Like Portugali, Mainzer calls for a recognition of the qualitative features of a system and argues that complexity science can function as a connection: "Contrary to any reductionistic kind of naturalism and physicalism we recognize the characteristic intentional features of human societies. Thus the complex system approach may be a method of bridging the gap between the natural sciences and the humanities that was criticized in Snow's famous 'two cultures'" (12). For an enlightening if frequently schematic problematisation of "the two cultures" in the context of complexity theories and cities, cf. Portugali 2011, 9–52; cf. also Stephen Read and several other contributions in Portugali *et al.*

7 The German original reads: "Die Stadt der Soziologen hingegen ist für gewöhnlich ein unsinnlicher Ort, eine Stadt, die man nicht hört, nicht riecht, nicht schmeckt, genau genommen ein Nicht-Ort" (Lindner 92). Marc Augé's notion of the "non-place" is not quoted here, but clearly implied, it seems.

8 Cf. especially Danielzyk/Blotevogel, who distinguish between the (1) innovation and competition function, (2) decision and control function, (3) gateway function, and (4) symbolic function. For an early influential study, cf. Hall; for a widely debated recent contribution, cf. Sassen; for a survey, cf. Bronger.

9 Here, the inquiry into the "knowledge *of* literature" (cf. Hörisch; my italics) or into the strategies of producing knowledge *in* literature may be especially relevant: What are the specific achievements of literature and of literary texts as a unique form of generating, storing, transmitting and mediating knowledge (cf., for instance, Felski; Fluck; Gurr 2013; Gymnich/Nünning)? It has been argued that literary texts represent knowledge – or create it in the first place – in ways fundamentally different from discursive, expository texts (cf., for instance, Glomb/Horlacher; Hörisch). Specific literary strategies thus become "devices for articulating truth" (Felski 84). This centrally concerns questions of genre and questions of literary modelling generally: In which ways do literary (and maybe especially poetic) texts function differently from discursive texts (for an example, cf. Gurr 2017) or what are the specific cognitive achievements of narrative as opposed to, say, quantitative models of complex matters?

10 Cf. for instance Alter; Balshaw/Kennedy; Barta; Brooker 1996, 2002; Caws; Harding; Keunen/Eeckhout; Lehan; Lenz/Riese; McNamara; Scherpe; Smuda; Teske; Wirth-Nesher; Wolfreys 1998, 2004, 2007. A few observations on urban complexity are to be found, for instance, in Keunen or Brandt.

11 The German original reads: "Komplexität ist nicht in erster Linie eine Eigenschaft des beschriebenen Objekts, sondern der Beschreibung selbst" (Richter/Rost 112).

12 This is the view formulated, among others, by Kenneth Burke, Dieter Wellershoff, Wolfgang Iser or Glomb/Horlacher.

13 I am grateful to Alf Kimms, professor of Logistics and Operations Research at the University of Duisburg-Essen's Mercator School of Management, and an expert on quantitative strategies of optimisation, for helpful discussions on these parallels.

References

Albeverio, Sergio, Denise Andrey, Paolo Giordano, Alberto Vancheri, eds. *The Dynamics of Complex Urban Systems: An Interdisciplinary Approach.* Heidelberg: Physica, 2008.

Alter, Robert. *Imagined Cities: Urban Experience and the Language of the Novel.* New Haven: Yale University Press, 2005.

Assmann, Aleida. "Geschichte findet Stadt." *Kommunikation – Gedächtnis – Raum: Kulturwissenschaften nach dem 'Spatial Turn.'* Ed. Moritz Csàky, Christoph Leitgeb. Bielefeld: transcript, 2009. 13–27.
Augé, Marc. *Non-Places: Introduction to an Anthropology of Supermodernity*. London: Verso, 1995.
Balshaw, Maria, Liam Kennedy. "Introduction." *Urban Space and Representation*. Ed. Balshaw, Kennedy. London: Pluto, 2000. 1–21.
Barta, Peter I. *Bely, Joyce, and Döblin: Peripatetics in the City Novel*. Gainesville: University Press of Florida, 1997.
Batty, Michael. "Cities as Complex Systems: Scaling, Interaction, Networks, Dynamics and Urban Morphologies." *Encyclopedia of Complexity and Systems Science*. Ed. Robert A. Meyers. Berlin: Springer, 2009. Vol. 1, 1041–1071.
Batty, Michael. *The New Science of Cities*. Cambridge, MA: MIT Press, 2013.
Berking, Helmuth, Martina Löw, eds. *Die Eigenlogik der Städte: Neue Wege für die Stadtforschung*. Frankfurt/Main: Campus, 2008.
Brandt, Stefan L. "The City as Liminal Space: Urban Visuality and Aesthetic Experience in Postmodern U.S. Literature and Cinema." *Amerikastudien/American Studies* 54.4 (2009): 553–581.
Bronger, Dirk. *Metropolen – Megastädte – Global Cities: Die Metropolisierung der Erde*. Darmstadt: Wissenschaftliche Buchgesellschaft, 2004.
Brooker, Peter. *Modernity and Metropolis: Writing, Film and Urban Formations*. Houndmills: Palgrave, 2002.
Brooker, Peter. *New York Fictions: Modernity, Postmodernism, the New Modern*. London: Longman, 1996.
Burke, Kenneth. *The Philosophy of Literary Form: Studies in Symbolic Action*. Berkeley: University of California Press, 1974 [reprint; orig. ed.: Baton Rouge: Louisiana State University Press, 1941].
Butler, Martin, Jens Martin Gurr. "Urbane Populärkultur als Bewertungspraxis und -ressource: Zum normativen Potential populärkultureller Inszenierung und diskursiver Aneignung urbaner Räume." *Place-Making in urbanen Diskursen*. Ed. Ingo H. Warnke, Beatrix Busse. Berlin, Munich, Boston: de Gruyter, 2014. 369–384.
Byrne, David. *Complexity Theory and the Social Sciences: An Introduction*. London, New York: Routledge, 1998.
Caws, Mary Ann, ed. *City Images: Perspectives from Literature, Philosophy, and Film*. New York: Gordon and Breach, 1991.
Cohen, Jack, Ian Stewart. *The Collapse of Chaos: Discovering Simplicity in a Complex World*. Harmondsworth: Penguin, 1995.
Danielzyk, Rainer, Hans Heinrich Blotevogel. "Leistungen und Funktionen von Metropolregionen." *Metropolregionen und Raumentwicklung, Part 3: Metropolregionen. Innovation, Wettbewerb, Handlungsfähigkeit*. Ed. Jörg Knieling. Hannover: Verlag der ARL, 2009. 22–29.
Dillon, Sarah. *The Palimpsest: Literature, Criticism, Theory*. New York: Continuum, 2007.
Eckardt, Frank. *Die komplexe Stadt: Orientierungen im urbanen Labyrinth*. Wiesbaden: Verlag für Sozialwissenschaften, 2009.
Felski, Rita. *Uses of Literature*. Oxford: Blackwell, 2008.
Fluck, Winfried. *Das kulturelle Imaginäre: Eine Funktionsgeschichte des amerikanischen Romans, 1790–1900*. Frankfurt/Main: Suhrkamp, 1997.
Gell-Mann, Murray. *The Quark and the Jaguar: Adventures in the Simple and the Complex*. London: Abacus, 1995a.

Gell-Mann, Murray. "What is Complexity?" *Complexity* 1.1 (1995b): 16–19.

Glomb, Stefan, Stefan Horlacher, eds. *Beyond Extremes: Repräsentation und Reflexion von Modernisierungsprozessen im zeitgenössischen britischen Roman*. Tübingen: Narr, 2004.

Gurr, Jens Martin. "Das Ruhrgebiet als Herausforderung für Kategorien und Ansätze der Stadtforschung." *Dérive: Zeitschrift für Stadtforschung* 58 (2015): 23–26.

Gurr, Jens Martin. "Urbanity, Urban Culture and the European Metropolis." *Britannien und Europa: Studien zur Literatur-, Geistes- und Kulturgeschichte; Festschrift für Jürgen Klein*. Ed. Michael Szczekalla. Frankfurt/Main: Peter Lang, 2010. 241–255.

Gurr, Jens Martin. "Views on Violence in Shelley's Post-Peterloo Prose and Poetry: Contradiction, Ambivalence, Ambiguity?" *Romantic Ambiguities: Abodes of the Modern*. Ed. Sebastian Domsch, Christoph Reinfandt, Katharina Rennhak. [Studies in English Romanticism 20]. Trier: WVT, 2017. 83–93.

Gurr, Jens Martin. "'Without contraries is no progression': Emplotted Figures of Thought in Negotiating Oppositions, *Funktionsgeschichte* and Literature as 'Cultural Diagnosis'." *Text or Context: Reflections on Literary and Cultural Criticism*. Ed. Rüdiger Kunow, Stephan Mussil. Würzburg: Königshausen & Neumann, 2013. 59–77.

Gurr, Jens Martin, Martin Butler. "Against the 'Erasure of Memory' in Los Angeles City Planning: Strategies of Re-Ethnicizing L.A. in Digital Fiction." *Selling EthniCity*. Ed. Olaf Kaltmeier. London: Ashgate, 2011. 145–163.

Gurr, Jens Martin, Martin Butler. "On the 'Cultural Dimension of Sustainability' in Urban Systems: Urban Cultures as Ecological 'Force-Fields' in Processes of Sustainable Development." *Healthy and Liveable Cities/Gesunde und lebenswerte Städte*. Ed. Stefanie Caeners, Michael Eisinger, Jens Martin Gurr, J. Alexander Schmidt. Stuttgart: avedition, 2013. 138–151.

Gurr, Jens Martin, Ute Schneider. "Strategien zur Bewältigung urbaner Komplexität: Zum Zusammenwirken visueller, verbaler und quantitativer Modelle." *Komplexität und Einfachheit: DFG-Symposion 2015*. Ed. Albrecht Koschorke. Stuttgart: Metzler, 2017. 256–275.

Gurr, Jens Martin, Christian Walloth. "Introduction: Towards a Transdisciplinary Understanding of Complex Urban Systems." *Understanding Complex Urban Systems: Multidisciplinary Approaches to Modeling*. Ed. Christian Walloth, Jens Martin Gurr, J. Alexander Schmidt. Heidelberg, New York: Springer, 2014. 1–12.

Gymnich, Marion, Ansgar Nünning, eds. *Funktionen von Literatur: Theoretische Grundlagen und Modellinterpretationen*. Trier: WVT, 2005.

Haken, Herman, Juval Portugali. "The Face of the City is its Information." *Journal of Environmental Psychology* 23.4 (2003): 385–408.

Hall, Peter. *The World Cities*. London: Weidenfeld & Nicolson, 1966.

Harding, Desmond. "*Ulysses* and *Manhattan Transfer*: A Poetics of Transatlantic Literary Modernism." Harding. *Writing the City: Urban Visions & Literary Modernism*. New York: Routledge, 2003. 97–136.

Harvey, David. *The Condition of Postmodernity: An Inquiry into the Origins of Cultural Change*. Oxford, London: Blackwell, 1989.

Hassenpflug, Dieter. "Once Again: Can Urban Space be Read?" *Reading the City: Developing Urban Hermeneutics/Stadt lesen: Beiträge zu einer urbanen Hermeneutik*. Ed. Dieter Hassenpflug, Nico Giersig, Bernhard Stratmann. Weimar: Verlag der Bauhaus-Universität, 2011. 49–58.

Hassenpflug, Dieter. "Walter Benjamin und die Traumseite der Stadt." Hassenpflug. *Reflexive Urbanistik: Reden und Aufsätze zur europäischen Stadt.* Weimar: Verlag der Bauhaus-Universität, 2006. 7–22.

Hörisch, Jochen. *Das Wissen der Literatur*. Munich: Fink, 2007.

Huyssen, Andreas. *Present Pasts: Urban Palimpsests and the Politics of Memory*. Palo Alto: Stanford University Press, 2003.

Iser, Wolfgang. *Das Fiktive und das Imaginäre: Perspektiven literarischer Anthropologie*. Frankfurt/Main: Suhrkamp, 1993.

Jacobs, Jane. *The Death and Life of Great American Cities*. New York: Random House, 1961.

Keunen, Bart. "Living with Fragments: World Making in Modernist City Literature." *Modernism*. Ed. Astradur Eysteinsson, Vivian Liska. Amsterdam: Benjamins, 2007. 271–290.

Keunen, Bart, Bart Eeckhout. "Whatever Happened to the Urban Novel?" *Postmodern New York City: Transfiguring Spaces – Raum-Transformationen*. Ed. Günter Lenz, Utz Riese. Heidelberg: Winter, 2003. 53–69.

Koschorke, Albrecht. *Wahrheit und Erfindung: Grundzüge einer Allgemeinen Erzähltheorie*. Frankfurt/Main: Fischer, [3]2013.

Lefebvre, Henri. *The Production of Space* [1974]. Trans. Donald Nicholson-Smith. Oxford: Blackwell, 1991.

Lehan, Richard. *The City in Literature: An Intellectual and Cultural History*. Berkeley: University of California Press, 1998.

Lenz, Günter, Utz Riese, eds. *Postmodern New York City: Transfiguring Spaces – Raum-Transformationen*. Heidelberg: Winter, 2003.

Li, Ming, Paul Vitányi. *An Introduction to Kolmogorov Complexity and its Applications*. New York, Berlin: Springer, 1993.

Lindner, Rolf. "Textur, '*imaginaire*', Habitus. Schlüsselbegriffe der kulturanalytischen Stadtforschung." *Die Eigenlogik der Städte: Neue Wege für die Stadtforschung*. Ed. Helmuth Berking, Martina Löw. Frankfurt/Main: Campus, 2008. 83–94.

Mahr, Bernd. "Modelle und ihre Befragbarkeit: Grundlagen einer allgemeinen Modelltheorie." *Erwägen – Wissen – Ethik/Deliberation – Knowledge – Ethics: Forum für Erwägungskultur/Forum for Deliberative Culture* 26.3 (2015): 329–342.

Mainzer, Klaus. *Thinking in Complexity: The Computational Dynamics of Matter, Mind and Mankind*. Berlin: Springer, [5]2007.

Martindale, Charles. "Ruins of Rome: T.S. Eliot and the Presence of the Past." *Arion* 3.2–3 (1995): 102–140.

Mattheis, Lena. *Translocal Narratability in Contemporary Anglophone Fiction*. Dissertation manuscript, University of Duisburg-Essen, 2019.

McNamara, Kevin R., ed. *The Cambridge Companion to the Literature of Los Angeles*. Cambridge: Cambridge University Press, 2010.

Moretti, Franco. *Atlas of the European Novel, 1800–1900*. London, New York: Verso. 1998.

Portugali, Juval. *Complexity, Cognition and the City*. Understanding Complex Systems (UCS). Berlin, Heidelberg: Springer, 2011.

Portugali, Juval. "Complexity Theories of Cities: Achievements, Criticism and Potentials." *Complexity Theories of Cities Have Come of Age: An Overview with Implications to Urban Planning and Design*. Ed. Juval Portugali, Han Meyer, Egbert Stolk, Ekim Tan. Berlin, Heidelberg: Springer, 2012a. 47–62.

Portugali, Juval. "Complexity Theory as a Link Between Space and Place." *Environment and Planning A* 38 (2006): 647–664.

Portugali, Juval. "Introduction." *Complexity Theories of Cities Have Come of Age: An Overview with Implications to Urban Planning and Design*. Ed. Juval Portugali, Han Meyer, Egbert Stolk, Ekim Tan. Berlin, Heidelberg: Springer, 2012b. 1–5.
Portugali, Juval. *Self-Organization and the City*. Berlin, Heidelberg: Springer, 2000.
Portugali, Juval, Han Meyer, Egbert Stolk, Ekim Tan, eds. *Complexity Theories of Cities Have Come of Age: An Overview with Implications to Urban Planning and Design*. Berlin, Heidelberg: Springer, 2012.
Read, Stephen. "Meaning and Material: Phenomenology, Complexity, Science and 'Adjacent Possibilities'." *Complexity Theories of Cities Have Come of Age: An Overview with Implications to Urban Planning and Design*. Ed. Juval Portugali, Han Meyer, Egbert Stolk, Ekim Tan. Berlin, Heidelberg: Springer, 2012. 105–127.
Richter, Klaus, Jan-Michael Rost. *Komplexe Systeme*. Frankfurt/Main: Fischer, 2002.
Rossetto, Tania. "Theorizing Maps with Literature." *Progress in Human Geography* 38.4 (2014): 513–530.
Sassen, Saskia. *The Global City: New York, London, Tokyo*. Princeton: Princeton University Press, [2]2001.
Scherpe, Klaus R., ed. *Die Unwirklichkeit der Städte: Großstadtdarstellungen zwischen Moderne und Postmoderne*. Reinbek: Rowohlt, 1988.
Schneider, Ute. "Die Farbe der Religion: Topographie und Topik der 'Deux France'." *Journal of Modern European History* 9 (2011a): 117–139.
Schneider, Ute. "Inquiries or Statistics? Agricultural Surveys and Methodological Considerations in the Nineteenth Century." *The Golden Age of State Enquiries*. Ed. Nadine Vivier. Turnhout: Brepols, 2014. 43–57.
Schneider, Ute. *Die Macht der Karten: Eine Geschichte der Kartographie vom Mittelalter bis heute*. 3rd enl. and updated ed. Darmstadt: Primus, 2011b.
Schneider, Ute. "'Den Staat auf einem Kartenblatt übersehen!' Die Visualisierung der Staatskräfte und des Nationalcharakters." *Kartenwelten: Der Raum und seine Repräsentation in der Neuzeit*. Ed. Christof Dipper, Ute Schneider. Darmstadt: Primus, 2006. 11–25.
Schultz, Rüdiger. "Uncertainty in Urban Systems: How to Optimize Decision Making Using Stochastic Programming." *Understanding Complex Urban Systems: Multidisciplinary Approaches to Modeling*. Ed. Christian Walloth, Jens Martin Gurr, J. Alexander Schmidt. Berlin, Heidelberg: Springer, 2014.
Sharpe, William, Leonard Wallock. "From 'Great Town' to 'Nonplace Urban Realm': Reading the Modern City." *Visions of the Modern City: Essays in History, Art, and Literature*. Ed. Sharpe, Wallock. Baltimore: Johns Hopkins University Press, 1987. 1–50.
Simmel, Georg. "The Metropolis and Mental Life" [1903]. *The City Cultures Reader*. Ed. Malcolm Miles, Tim Hall, Iain Borden. London: Routledge, [2]2004. 12–19.
Smuda, Manfred, ed. *Die Großstadt als "Text."* Munich: Fink, 1992.
Stachowiak, Herbert. *Allgemeine Modelltheorie*. Vienna, New York: Springer, 1973.
Suttles, Gerald D. "The Cumulative Texture of Local Urban Culture." *American Journal of Sociology* 90.2 (1984): 283–304.
Teske, Doris. *Die Vertextung der Megalopolis: London im Spiel postmoderner Texte*. Trier: WVT, 1999.
Walloth, Christian. "Emergence in Complex Urban Systems: Blessing or Curse of Planning Efforts?" *Understanding Complex Urban Systems: Multidisciplinary Approaches to Modeling*. Berlin, Heidelberg: Springer, 2014. 121–132.

Walloth, Christian. *Emergent Nested Systems: A Theory of Understanding and Influencing Complex Systems as well as Case Studies in Urban Systems*. Berlin, Heidelberg: Springer, 2016.

Walloth, Christian, Jens Martin Gurr, J. Alexander Schmidt, eds. *Understanding Complex Urban Systems: Multidisciplinary Approaches to Modeling*. Berlin, Heidelberg: Springer, 2014.

Wellershoff, Dieter. *Literatur und Lustprinzip*. Cologne: Kiepenheuer & Witsch, 1973.

Wirth-Nesher, Hana. *City Codes: Reading the Modern Urban Novel*. Cambridge: Cambridge University Press, 1996.

Wolfreys, Julian. *Writing London: The Trace of the Urban Text from Blake to Dickens*. London: Palgrave, 1998.

Wolfreys, Julian. *Writing London 2: Materiality, Memory, Spectrality*. London: Palgrave, 2004.

Wolfreys, Julian. *Writing London 3: Inventions of the City*. London: Palgrave, 2007.

2 Literary Models of Urban Complexity and the Problem of Simultaneity

A Sketchy Inventory of Strategies

Complexity as Simultaneity

An appropriate entry into a discussion of literary strategies of representing urban complexity is afforded by juxtaposing a passage each from Kevin Lynch's influential 1960 *The Image of the City* and from Lessing's 1766 "Laocoon", his classic discussion of the "limits of painting and poetry", as the subtitle puts it. In his discussion, Lynch highlights both the role of complexity as a key characteristic of urban environments *and* the centrality of simultaneity as a key component of this complexity. He speaks of urban environments as surroundings in which

> [a]t every instant, there is more than the eye can see, more than the ear can hear, a setting or a view waiting to be explored. Nothing is experienced by itself, but always in relation to its surroundings, the sequences of events leading up to it, the memory of past experiences [...] Nearly every sense is in operation and the image [we form of the city] is the composite of them all.
>
> (1f.)

In chapter XIII of "Laocoon", Lessing discusses a literary attempt at representing just such a moment of retinal indulgence in the contemplation of a painting:

> What architecture, what masses of light and shadow, what contrasts, what multiplicity of expression! Where do I begin, where do I cease to feast my eyes? If the painter so delights me, how much more will the poet do so? I open the book and I find myself – cheated. I find four good, plain lines, which might serve as the caption to a painting, in which we might find the material for a painting, but which are not themselves a painting.[1]
>
> (73; my translation)

In the course of "Laocoon", Lessing famously goes on to argue that literature is deficient in representing simultaneity, a point I discuss in some detail in the course of this chapter.

On the one hand, the representation of co-existing impressions is arguably the crux of any attempt to narrate urban complexity, for simultaneity, the notion of innumerable things – momentous or trivial – happening at the same time, is surely a central characteristic of urban complexity. On the other hand, it is simultaneity which in literary texts poses particular representational challenges. Other key aspects of complexity – multiple causal dependencies, conflicts of interest over the use of space, or social and cultural heterogeneity, for instance – pose no principal narrative challenge. From a narratological perspective, representations of simultaneity are therefore of particular interest when discussing attempts to represent complexity. Somewhat provocatively, we might argue that representations of urban complexity must therefore centrally be attempts to prove wrong Lessing's assumption that literature is deficient in the compelling representation of simultaneity. They must, as Nabokov's narrator in *Lolita* has it, "put the impact of an instantaneous vision into a sequence of words; their physical accumulation in the page impairs the actual flash, the sharp unity of the impression" (99).

It is interesting to note that even Frank Eckardt in what is one of the most sustained and ambitious engagements with urban complexity – here from a sociological angle – begins his reflections on urban complexity with a quotation from Döblin's *Berlin Alexanderplatz* (cf. Eckardt 7). However, although it is central to Döblin's endeavour, the notion of simultaneity as a key component of complexity hardly plays a role at all in Eckardt's study.

The same is true of most of the innumerable studies on urban imaginaries in literature and film, in which, though occasionally implied, complexity – let alone simultaneity – almost universally does not feature as a theme in itself.[2] However, as a look at innumerable 'urban' poems and narrative fictions and at numerous anthologies (cf. for instance Baron; Lopate; Meller/Slogsnat) reveals, the issue is indeed central to 'urban literature'.

As far as the centrality of simultaneity to representations of urban complexity is concerned, it is interesting to consider the multiple characteristics of 'complexity' which Eckardt explicitly and implicitly discusses: multiplicity, density, mobility, intersections of the global and the local, cultural hybridity, violence, conflicts over the use of space, intersections of technology and virtual spaces with physical and experienced space, complex interferences, interdependencies, disparities, or intersections in the interaction between multiple players, layers, intentions, or force fields. This chapter argues that many of these aspects of urban complexity pose challenges in the representation of simultaneity, in other words: Strategies of narrating urban complexity are to a considerable extent strategies of narrating simultaneity. Conversely, the representation of urban simultaneity as a key component of urban complexity invariably involves or at least implies *other* forms of complexity – complexities of cause and effect, of intersecting spatial scales, or ethical complexities. As a case in point, I begin with a few observations on the connection between the complexity of urban environments and ethical complexities in a number of texts from various epochs since the seventeenth century and in de Certeau's discussion of urban complexity in his influential chapter "Walking in the City" in *The Practice of Everyday Life*.

Making no attempt at anything like completeness, the final and longest part of this chapter then attempts a sketchy inventory of strategies in the representation of simultaneity as arguably the central component of narrative representations of urban complexity. In my examples, I deliberately draw on British, American and continental texts, because the literary traffic of ideas does not stop at borders and these strategies are remarkably ubiquitous in literary cultures whose authors engaged in literary dialogue and read each others' works for centuries.

Simultaneity as a Key to other Forms of Complexity

In the following, I explore the connection between the complexity of simultaneity and the ethical complexities of urban life[3] as merely one out of many fields – the connection could equally be pointed out between simultaneity and other forms of complexity. That the representation of complexity as simultaneity frequently involves the representation of other complexities – causal, spatial or ethical – may be illustrated by means of Sir John Denham's 1642 topographical long poem "Coopers Hill". This text also lends itself to discussing one of the central strategies of attempting to cope with urban complexity – the attempt to escape the throng and get a view of the to-and-fro from above. Cooper's Hill, located in Egham, Surrey, a few miles from Windsor Castle and about 20 miles south-west of central London, is a vantage point some 220 feet above its surroundings (but, given the distance, is hardly 'above' London). Though one would hardly have been able to see anything in detail (cf. O Hehir xxiii–xxvii), it does serve as the point from which conceptually to survey London:

> Exalted to this height, I first looke downe
> On *Pauls*, as men from thence upon the towne. [...]
> So rais'd above the tumult and the crowd
> I see the City in a thicker cloud
> Of businesse, then of smoake, where men like Ants
> Toyle to prevent imaginarie wants. [...]
> Some study plots, and some those plots t'undoe,
> Others to make'em, and undoe'em too [...]
> Blinded with light, and sicke of being well,
> In tumults seeke their peace, their heaven in hell.
> (Denham 110–113, ll. 13–46; italics original)

Oxymoronic and paradoxical phrases here suggest the complexities of London, then a city of some 350,000 people, with the incessant bustle of the crowd in mindless pursuit of "businesse" rendered in the image of ants.[4] It is important to note that "businesse" here is also to be read as 'busy-ness' in the sense of a pointless state of being busy. What is readily apparent here is the suggestion of a close association between urban density and complexity on the one hand and morally questionable human behaviour on the other hand. Moreover, the depiction of the city from a vantage point "rais'd above the tumult and the crowd" in a striking way invites comparison with Michel de Certeau's widely cited distinction between the "walker's" and the "voyeur's" perspective on the city (92f.): The "walker" finds himself in the midst of the city's complexity and without the sense of control and order which a view from above would yield (cf. 92). In de Certeau's sense, walkers "follow the thicks and thins of an urban 'text' they write without being able to read it" (93). In contrast to this, the "voyeur's" perspective on the city is characterised by the view from an elevated location, which to some extent makes the beholder feel in control and makes the city appear as a legible text. De Certeau here speaks of the "pleasure of 'seeing the whole,' of looking down on, totalizing the most immoderate of human texts" (92). As de Certeau notes, with the view from above on the city, "[t]he gigantic mass is immobilized before the eyes" (91). This view from above "makes the complexity of the city readable, and immobilizes its opaque mobility in a transparent text" (92). De Certeau's observation that "[t]he desire to see the city preceded the means of satisfying it. Medieval or Renaissance painters represented the city as seen in a perspective that no eye had yet enjoyed" (92) strikes one as highly pertinent in the context of Denham's depiction of the city from a "height [...] above the tumult and the crowd", which surely also owes something to panoptic illustrations such as Claes Van Visscher's famous 1616 panorama of London (cf. Meller/Slogsnat 8f.). Indeed, it seems that the mere 220 feet of Cooper's Hill – if hardly physically, then at least imaginatively[5] – provide for exactly the kind of perspective which, according to de Certeau, "makes the complexity of the city readable" (92) – but it also allows the "voyeur" to "be lifted out of the city's grasp" and out of the moral complexities of urban life with its "extremes of ambition and degradation" (de Certeau 91f.).

Eighteenth-century representations of London – whether in the poetry of Swift, Pope, Gay or Johnson, in the novels of Fielding, or in the *Spectator* essays of Addison and Steele – similarly make clear that the representation of complexities of the city in terms of size, architecture, growth, mobility, density, etc. are inseparable from ethical judgements of the city and its complexities. Samuel Johnson's 1738 tirade in "London" is representative here. The asyndetic enumeration of criminal doings and chaotic events simultaneously suggests urban complexity in the sense of a chaotic simultaneity of multiple events *and* of ethical entanglements and moral degradation:[6]

> Here Malice, Rapine, Accident, conspire,
> And now a Rabble rages, now a Fire;
> Their Ambush here relentless Ruffians lay,
> And here the fell Attorney prowls for Prey;
> Here falling Houses thunder on your Head,
> And here a female Atheist talks you dead.[7]
>
> (S. Johnson ll. 13–18)

In a related vein, in a passage Raymond Williams has drawn attention to, Fielding writes in his 1751 *Enquiry into the Causes of the Late Increase of Robbers*:

> Whoever considers the Cities of London and Westminster, with the late vast increase of their suburbs, the great irregularity of their buildings, the immense numbers of lanes, alleys, courts and bye-places, must think that had they been intended for the very purpose of concealment they could not have been better contrived.
>
> (qtd. in Williams 61)

Fielding here points to the link between crime and the physical complexity of the built environment of the city. In this context of how the city's complexity fosters and shields criminal activity, Williams perceptively points out the connection between the "teeming, mazelike [...] impenetrable city" and the "urban 'private eye' " (61).[8]

The notion of the city's conduciveness to crime and to the decline of political culture has even repeatedly been argued to form a cornerstone of American political thought. One of the classic early American instances of associating urban density and complexity with moral and political degradation is Jefferson's 1787 letter to James Madison, significantly written from Paris:

> I think our governments will remain virtuous for many centuries; as long as they are chiefly agricultural; and this will be as long as there shall be vacant lands in any part of America. When they get piled upon one another in large cities, as in Europe, they will become corrupt as in Europe.
>
> (Jefferson 422)

In 2003, in his novella "Bleeding Through", in which he imaginatively explores the perversions of twentieth-century city planning in Los Angeles (cf. also Chapter 3), Norman M. Klein ties representations of violence and murder in the city to the "longstanding American distrust of urban democracy" (25) and explicitly evokes the Jeffersonian tradition: "Many Americans believe, as they did in Jefferson's day, that equality can survive only in a small town. By contrast, fascism flourishes in crowds" (25). From petty blue-collar delinquency via back-street violence and murder to the grand schemes of organised crime or corporate fraud, crime in all its variations is indeed overwhelmingly associated with the city, as witnessed by the innumerable *films noirs*, thrillers and other genres of urban crime film.[9]

Strategies of Representing Urban Simultaneity: Towards an Inventory

Although Lessing's claims have long been disputed, his 1766 "Laocoon" as a discussion of the "limits of painting and poetry" is demonstrably still central to discussions of literary representations of simultaneity.[10] In what is essentially a semiotic argument based on the differing sign systems used in painting and literature (for this is what is meant by the seemingly more narrow term of "*Poesie*" ['poetry']), Lessing here argues:

> If it is true that painting in its imitation uses means entirely different from those of literature – the former using figures and colours in space, the latter articulated sounds in time – and if the signs unquestionably need to be comfortably related to that which they signify, then signs arranged in contiguity can only designate objects which are contiguous, signs arranged in sequence can only designate objects which appear in sequence or whose parts appear in sequence.[11]
>
> (XVI, 77f.; my translation)

Language, according to this argument, cannot persuasively represent simultaneity "because the coexistence of bodies here collides with the consecutive nature of speech" (Lessing XVII, 87; my translation).[12]

In what is probably the most widely cited passage from the treatise, Lessing summarises his views on the shortcomings of literature:

> This remains true: The sequence of time is the domain of the poet, just as space is the domain of the painter [...] If several things which in reality have to be surveyed at once if they are to create a whole were to be narrated to the reader one after the other in order to create a picture of the whole for him, this is an intrusion of the poet into the domain of the painter – and one in which the poet wastes a lot of imagination without any use.[13]
>
> (XVIII, 90; my translation)

As Lessing famously argues with reference to Homer's description of the shield of Achilles in the *Iliad*, a solution to the problem of representing multiple elements (which in a visual depiction could be surveyed at once) is to temporalise static descriptions into a sequence:

> For Homer does not paint the shield as a finished and complete one but as a shield in the making. Here, too, he has availed himself of the celebrated device of transforming the coexistence prevalent in his subject matter into consecutiveness [...] We do not see the shield but the divine master as he makes the shield.[14]
>
> (XVIII, 93; my translation)

As we will see, this is also one of the strategies employed in the representation of simultaneity as a key component of urban complexity. However, there is a range of other strategies of describing, suggesting or simulating simultaneity. The following is an attempt at a sketchy and idealised inventory with no claim to completeness.[15]

Declarative Complexity

Arguably the simplest form of representing urban complexity and simultaneity are declarative representations, i.e. passages which state that something is complex without 'showing' or performing complexity. These frequently take the form of 'suggesting' complexity by means of metaphors or similes such as the often clichéd urban 'maze' or 'labyrinth'[16] to express an individual's sense of being lost.[17] Though surely a way of representing the city as 'complex', this alone is more a thematic notion than a strategy of representation. If the city is merely declared to resemble a maze without representing it *as* a maze, for our purposes this is not of great interest and as such has little or nothing to do with simultaneity. In the more interesting cases, however, the text will also assume labyrinthine qualities itself or will have the experiential potential of allowing readers to experience the disorientation suggested by the notion of the labyrinth.

Synecdochic Representations

The second strategy is what I term the 'synecdochic representation of simultaneity', which consists in narrating one strand of action and suggesting that there would have been innumerable others that would also deserve to be told. This is apparent for instance in Djuna Barnes's "The Hem of Manhattan", her account of a boat-trip around the island of Manhattan in 1917:

> Somewhere, everywhere over there in that world that we had been around [...] actresses were getting their beauty sleep or were at school learning arduously a new dance. Somewhere a man was killing a gnat and somewhere else a man building a bomb. Someone was kissing, and someone was killing, someone was being born, and someone was dying. Some were eating and drinking, and others were starving. Some were thinking and others were not. Waiters moved about in the great hotels.
>
> (74)

The suggestion is that many of these simultaneous events and actions would yield stories worth telling. Moreover, the text appears to employ a further strategy reminiscent of the one Lessing found in Homer's temporalisation in describing the shield of Achilles: Barnes's text artificially slows down the process of perception, of having to take in all the sights of the city. The observer here withdraws, as it were, from the midst of the bustle to the "hem" and, by taking the comparatively slow boat around the island – as opposed to a drive or walk through the city – significantly slows down the "rapid crowding of changing images, the [...] onrushing impressions" as Simmel described "the psychological conditions which the metropolis creates" (13). Suggestively drawing attention to the more sedate taking in of the city this allows for, Barnes states: "Manhattan Island has passed before me in review" (72). In some ways, observing Manhattan from the "hem" leads to a form of being "lifted out of the city's grasp" and its complexities similar to that de Certeau (92) ascribes to visions from above.

Even more directly, the technique of highlighting the need to 'select' from countless simultaneous stories equally worth telling is apparent in the much-quoted voice-over conclusion to Jules Dassin's 1948 New York film *The Naked*

City: "There are eight million stories in the Naked City. This has been one of them."

A related technique is to be found in Paul Auster's "City of Glass", the opening text of his *New York Trilogy*, which is centrally concerned with the representation of urban complexities and, as a storehouse of various strategies, will feature in several parts of my discussion. Quinn, attempting to follow Stillman, is suddenly confronted with the dilemma of two Stillmans alighting from the train:

> There was nothing he could do now that would not be a mistake. Whatever choice he made – and he had to make a choice – would be arbitrary, a submission to chance. Uncertainty would haunt him to the end. At that moment, the two Stillmans started on their way again. The first turned right, the second turned left. Quinn craved an amoeba's body, wanting to cut himself in half and run off in two directions at once [...] For no reason, he went to his left, in pursuit of the second Stillman. After nine or ten paces, he stopped [...] There was no way to know [...] He went after the first Stillman.
>
> (Auster 68)

In a novel so self-consciously concerned with the complexities of linguistic representation, there is at least the suggestion that the text, too, has to make a choice and that the untold story of the 'other' Stillman would also be worthwhile. In other words, the narrative problem of having to choose between simultaneous events, i.e., a problem of discourse (*how* to narrate simultaneity), is here represented on the story level by turning the need to choose into a problem for one of the characters.

Experiential Strategies

In this vein, what might be called the 'performative or experiential representation of simultaneity' is a central strategy that recurs with remarkable consistency throughout the centuries from eighteenth-century representations of the city all the way to contemporary urban fiction.[18] Complexity and simultaneity are here frequently enacted by means of a suggestive asyndetic sequence of impressions simulating the chaotic and "rapid crowding of changing images" (Simmel 13), which allows readers to 'experience' the sense of being overpowered by the simultaneity of multiple impressions. I would here like to discuss three central examples of texts which both descriptively employ the *topos* of the maze or labyrinth *and* in various ways perform labyrinthine complexity. Here, the sense of disorientation induced by the maze is rendered as an important component of complexity.

In book VII of *The Prelude*, "Residence in London",[19] in a passage on "private courts/Gloomy as coffins, and unsightly lanes", which "may [...] entangle our impatient steps", Wordsworth refers to these physical complexities as "those labyrinths" (VII, ll. 180–185). But *The Prelude*, arguably the central Romantic city text, also allows readers to '*experience*' complexity by confronting them with "the unexpectedness of onrushing impressions" (Simmel 13):

> Rise up, thou monstrous ant-hill on the plain
> Of a too busy world! Before me flow,
> Thou endless stream of men and moving things!
> [...] the quick dance
> Of colours, lights, and forms; the deafening din;
> The comers and the goers face to face,
> Face after face [...]
> Meanwhile the roar continues, till at length,
> Escaped as from an enemy we turn
> Abruptly into some sequestered nook.
> (Wordsworth 1850, VII, ll. 149–170)

Note the "meanwhile" (l. 168) as an indication of the simultaneity of these impressions. The culmination of what in the course of book VII are literally hundreds of lines of such frenzied, breathlessly asyndetic description of this

> [...] anarchy and din,
> Barbarian and infernal, – a phantasma,
> Monstrous in colour, motion, shape, sight, sound!
> (Wordsworth VII, ll. 686–688)

is the rendering of Bartholomew Fair. In a further passage of some 50 lines of largely asyndetic enumeration, Wordsworth summarises his impressions as follows:

> All out-o'-the-way, far-fetched, perverted things,
> All freaks of Nature, all Promethean thoughts
> Of man, his dullness, madness, and their feats
> All jumbled up together to compose
> A Parliament of Monsters, Tents and Booths
> Meanwhile, as if the whole were one vast mill,
> Are vomiting, receiving on all sides,
> Men, Women, three-years Children, Babes in arms.
> O, blank confusion! True epitome
> Of what the mighty City is itself.
> (VII, ll. 714–723)

It may bear pointing out that, here too, "meanwhile" indicates the simultaneity of sense impressions which, like in the representation of the sights and sounds of London in book VII generally, are rendered in breathlessly asyndetic enumerations crowding in upon each other in what seems an enactment of complexity, an attempt performatively to suggest the feeling of being overpowered by these impressions. Moreover, book VII with its rendering of

London as a "monstrous ant-hill on the plain" (Wordsworth VII, l. 149) once more makes clear the moral complexities and the ethical judgements inseparable from the representation of "those labyrinths" (Wordsworth VII, l. 185).[20]

A second key text which makes use of the labyrinth *topos* and technique is "Wandering Rocks", the most centrally 'urban' chapter of *Ulysses*. In the famous scheme for *Ulysses*, in which he indicated a "Scene", "Hour", "Symbol", "Art", "Technique", etc., for each chapter, Joyce listed "the streets" for "Scene", "citizens" as the "Symbol" and – most important in our context – "labyrinth" as the "Technique" for the "Wandering Rocks" chapter (cf. Gilbert 41). In 19 sections with multiple insertions and cross-references between them, "Wandering Rocks" traces the itineraries of numerous characters through Dublin and highlights the fact that these are mere glimpses into the doings and ramblings of these characters. The maps in the admirably annotated German edition of the novel tracing the characters' wanderings clearly show that this is the chapter with by far the largest number of characters and locations. As Ellmann writes, the aim of this chapter was "to bring the city of Dublin even more fully into the book by focusing upon it rather than on Bloom or Stephen" (1982, 452).[21] It is highly significant in our context of simultaneity that the Linati scheme, another such scheme Joyce provided, names "synchronisms" as a key "Symbol" for this chapter (cf. Ellmann 1986, 186–196).

My final classic example of a labyrinthine text is again Auster's "City of Glass". In the opening passage already, we read that "New York was an inexhaustible space, a labyrinth of endless steps, and no matter how far he walked, no matter how well he came to know its neighborhoods and streets, it always left him with the feeling of being lost" (Auster 4).

As Stefan L. Brandt has persuasively argued, Auster's "City of Glass" also makes use of experiential strategies of creating a labyrinthine text:

> Not only does Auster's detective hero, Quinn, "lose himself" in the maze of buildings and streets. The reader as well becomes lost in the labyrinth of the text. This structural analogy between protagonist and reader is firmly grounded in the aesthetic design of the novel. Notably, Auster builds up a structural analogy between the urban space of the fictional metropolis and the infinite process of deferral of meaning in the postmodern imaginary [...] The sense of existential disorientation experienced by Auster's heroes is shared by postmodern readers.
>
> (2009, 564)

Moreover, the novel makes use of intermedial strategies of representing urban complexity.[22] By tracing Stillman's wanderings through the maze of Manhattan on a map, Quinn finds the itinerary of each day to form a letter (cf. Auster 81–84), with the observed itineraries of days five to thirteen yielding the sequence "OWEROFBAB" (Auster 85). "Making all due allowance for the fact that he had missed the first four days and that Stillman had not yet finished, the answer seemed inescapable: THE TOWER OF BABEL" (Auster 85). In a novel so centrally concerned with questions of incomprehensibility and the impossibility of reading and understanding the city, this is highly – perhaps excessively – significant: Urban itineraries, incompletely observed and leaving no visible trace except in Quinn's notebook, form a fragmented sequence of letters leading to the archetypal signifier of (linguistic) confusion and incomprehension.

This image of a text traced by means of an urban itinerary appears strikingly to literalise de Certeau's notion of urban "walkers [who] follow the thicks and thins of an urban 'text' they write without being able to read it" (93).[23] Here, however, it seems that the role of the ambulatory urban writer-reader is split into Stillman as the writer and Quinn as the reader of the urban text – and with us as readers doubling Quinn's efforts at attempting to comprehend this urban text.

What is more, Auster's text here multiplies complexity by taking recourse to a classic metafictional device: Metafiction, as Mark Currie has noted, almost inherently makes the reader an active participant in the process of the constitution of meaning. In order to do so, it frequently makes explicit not only the act of narration but also that of reading, incorporating into the text "a kind of surrogate author grappling with his ability as a storyteller and with the ability of words to communicate [...] experience" as well as "a surrogate reader trying, as protagonist [...] to make sense of events and to interpret [their] significance in a manner analogous to that of the external reader" (Currie 4). This is precisely the case in "City of Glass".

A related 'experiential' technique, prevalent in modernist fiction, is the 'stream of consciousness' representation of the overpowering sense impression that frequently occurs in combination with the 'filmic' technique of montage. Once more highlighting the affinities between twentieth-century urban environments and contemporaneous developments in literature and the arts, Raymond Williams perceptively stated that "there are decisive links between the practices and ideas of the avant-garde movements of the twentieth century and the specific conditions and relationships of the twentieth-century metropolis" (59; cf. also Alter ix; and Keunen/Eeckhout 57). Rather than cite the inevitable *Ulysses* here, a passage from the very first pages of Alfred Döblin's *Berlin Alexanderplatz* (1929), which needs to be cited at some length, may serve as a case in point:[24]

> He shook himself and gulped. He stepped on his own foot. Then, with a run, took a seat in the car. Right among people. Go ahead. At first it was like being at the dentist's, when he has grabbed a root with a pair of forceps, and pulls; the pain grows, your head threatens to burst. He turned his head back towards the red wall, but the car raced on with him along the tracks, and only his head was left in the direction of the prison. The car took a bend; trees and houses intervened. Busy streets emerged, Seestrasse, people got on and off. Something inside him screamed in terror: Look out, look out, it's going to start now. The tip of his nose turned to ice; something was whirring over his cheek. *Zwölf Uhr Mittagszeitung*, *B. Z.*, *Berliner Illustrierte*, *Die Funkstunde*. "Anybody else got on?" The coppers have blue uniforms now [...] Crowds, what a swarm of people! How they

> hustle and bustle! My brain needs oiling, it's probably dried up. What was all this? Shoe stores, hat stores, incandescent lamps, saloons. People got to have shoes to run around so much; didn't we have a cobbler's shop out there, let's bear that in mind! Hundreds of polished window-panes, let 'em blaze away, are they going to make you afraid or something, why, you can smash 'em up, can't you, what's the matter with 'em, they're polished clean, that's all. The pavement on Rosenthaler Platz was being torn up; he walked on the wooden planks along with the others. Just go ahead and mix in with people, then everything's going to clear up, and you won't notice anything, you fool. Wax figures stood in the show-windows, in suits, overcoats, with skirts, with shoes and stockings. Outside everything was moving, but – back of it – there was nothing! It – did not – live! It had happy faces, it laughed, waited in twos and threes on the traffic islands opposite Aschinger's, smoked cigarettes, turned the pages of newspapers. Thus it stood there like the street-lamps – and – became more and more rigid. They belonged with the houses, everything white, everything wooden.[25]
>
> (1989, 3f.)

In one of the best essays on modernist urban fiction, Bart Keunen discusses *Manhattan Transfer*, which for the present purpose can be regarded as representative of the modernist city novel, and comments on its representation of complexity:

> In a sense, it follows the adage of Gertrude Stein: "composition as explanation." The novel shows that Manhattan is a complex whole of overlapping plots (lives) and crossing paths. The different world models converge in a construction that reveals the complexity of the world. It is not a chaotic complexity but a complicated network of individuals, actions, observations, and situations.
>
> (2001, 435)

However, while Keunen here argues that "[t]he very essence of montage is to represent discontinuous elements within the artificial continuity of narrative development" (2001, 434), I propose a different reading of the function of modernist montage: Though confined by the linearity of print to sequentialise synchronicity, the fundamental processes of paradigmatic selection and syntagmatic combination covert in 'traditional' narrative are here flaunted to counter the "artificial continuity" of print narrative and to suggest or simulate the synchronicity of events. Thus, the chaotic simultaneity and the overwhelming complexity of the urban experience, rather than being glossed over, are flaunted in modernist montage, while the frequently jarring juxtaposition of discontinuous material, which does not allow for an unbroken narrative flow, draws attention both to the selective nature of the episodes recounted and to the convention of sequentialising simultaneity enforced by the genre of print narrative.

In his acute review of *Manhattan Transfer*, D.H. Lawrence already commented on what he perceived as the essentially 'filmic' technique of the novel (cf. 27f.). Similar arguments have been made for *Ulysses*.[26] Modernist urban novels – whether *Petersburg*, *Ulysses*, *Manhattan Transfer* or *Berlin Alexanderplatz* – though not breaking out of the linearity of prose fiction, frequently incorporate techniques from other genres and thus point forward to the intermedial possibilities more fully exploited by 'postmodern' urban fictions.

Breaking Linearity: Hypertext avant la lettre, *Digital Fiction, Typography and the Materiality of the Book*

A further strategy – or rather group of strategies, as the variations are significant – is the attempt to break the linearity of the printed text. This may range from inviting readers to go on reading elsewhere in the book, via recurring phrases in a text which connect different passages in a form of hyperlink *avant la lettre*, typographical strategies of printing a text in several columns, or the segmentation of the book into unnumbered booklets to be arranged at will, all the way to fully-fledged hypertexts – and more recently to attempts to simulate some of the features and effects of hypertext in print narratives.[27] I discuss some of these in some detail in Chapter 3, in my readings of "The Waste Land" and of Norman M. Klein's hypertext docu-fiction *Bleeding Through: Layers of Los Angeles 1920–1986* as two exemplary attempts at representing urban complexities and particularly layers of urban memory.

B.S. Johnson's *The Unfortunates* (1969) is a central example of pre-hypertext non-linear structures. The book, notorious as Johnson's 'book in a box', consists of 27 separately bound chapters ranging from a few lines to 12 pages in length and delivered in unnumbered random sequence, with only the first and last chapters designated as such.[28]

The novel's opening paragraphs already show the interweaving of its major concerns:

> But I know this city!   This green ticket-hall, the long office half-rounded at its ends, that iron clerestory, brown glazed tiles, green below, the same, the decorative hammerbeams supporting nothing, above, of course! I know this city! How did I not realize when he said, Go and do City this week, that it was this city!   Tony.   His cheeks sallowed and collapsed round the insinuated bones, the gums shrivelled, was it, or shrunken [...].
>
> Covered courtyards, taxis, take a taxi, always take a taxi in a strange city, but no, I know this city! The mind circles, at random, does not remember, from one moment to another, other things interpose themselves, the mind's   The station exit on a bridge, yes of course, and the blackened gantries rise like steel gibbets above the Midland red wall opposite.   I should turn right, right, towards the city centre, yes, ah, and that pub![29]
>
> ("First" 1f.; gaps and incomplete sentences original)

Essentially the interior monologue of a narrator who has been sent to an unnamed city (identifiable as Nottingham) to report a football match, the novel covers some eight hours he spends in the city. Superficially, it recounts his itinerary through the city, but mainly uses topographical details and locations encountered along the way as triggers for memories: It is here that one of his closest friends during his early career as a writer, Tony, lived before he died of cancer at the age of 29 in 1964. Appearing in seemingly random, associative order, these are interwoven memories of Tony and the city, recollections of walks taken together or of evenings spent in pubs, but also of Tony's illness and death. The random workings of memory and its triggering by familiar architectural and topographical details of the city are central to the novel, which associatively ranges back and forth between the task of reporting the match and other activities of the day on the one hand and recollections of Tony and his illness, of their earlier friendship, of his death and funeral on the other, suggesting simultaneity and a superimposition of past and present in the mind. Though arguably at least as much an attempt to render emotional complexities and the intricacies of memory, as a novel essentially 'about' Nottingham, this is on some level decidedly also an 'urban' novel. Arguably more so than with most novels, the central narrative strategy of *The Unfortunates*, the subdivision into unnumbered sections to be read in random order, is inseparable from the key thematic concerns: cancer, memory or the city are all fundamentally characterised by randomness, unpredictability, non-linearity, proliferation and a resistance to formal representation (for a fuller discussion, cf. Gurr 2017).

In this sense, the reader's constant need to choose where to go on reading in B.S. Johnson's 'book in a box' points forward to hypertext structures: The negotiation of paradigmatic selection and syntagmatic combination central to any narrative (cf. my argument on the modernist urban novel above) in the representation of urban complexity poses the particular challenge of constantly having to choose which of innumerable simultaneous impressions to record or which of multiple concurrent threads to follow (and in what order).[30] It is precisely the point of hypertext fiction to "expose the[se] dual processes of selection and combination lying at the root of all stories" (Kinder 54) and either not to have to make such choices in the first place (because of techniques such as split-screen) or to leave such choices to the user (cf. especially my discussion of Norman M. Klein's hypertext narrative *Bleeding Through* in Chapter 3).

One of the formally most inventive, non-linear, and 'complex' fictions in recent decades is Danielewski's *House of Leaves* (2000), a novel centrally concerned with the perception of space and with the literary rendering of architectural features of the built environment. The text cites innumerable architects and urban theorists; it contains an eight-page marginal note listing hundreds of architectural monuments (120–134, even pages), another one listing hundreds of major architects (upside down and backwards from 135 to 121, odd pages), a selective bibliography on architecture (152), a wealth of interspersed philosophical meditations on architecture and the perception of space, as well as numerous references to architecture and urban theory, including quotations from Kevin Lynch's *The Image of the City*, with which I opened this chapter (176). With its passages printed in mirror writing, countless footnotes, cross-references, parallel columns, typographical games, different colours, musical notations, photographs, sketches, a vast range of intertextual references, appendices and an (often misleading) index, the novel is a *tour de force* of strategies designed to break linearity, to represent complexity and to stage simultaneity (though the reader is still forced to choose what to read first).

My final example, J.M. Coetzee's *Diary of a Bad Year*, is interesting as a borderline case of an urban novel:[31] With essays on global political, economic and cultural issues printed in the upper third of each page – representing the macro-level, as it were – with the thoughts of the writer of these essays and those of a young woman living in the same apartment block printed in two further layers on each page – representing the urban micro-level – and with multiple echoes and interferences between these levels, the text first of all appears designed to break the linearity normally enforced by printed texts. Though only obliquely concerned with the representation of the city, the text is clearly set in an urban context and with explicit references to the *mores* of the city, especially in the opening and closing pages – "*that is how it is in the big city*" (Coetzee 5; italics original) or "at heart I am a city person" (Coetzee 222) – it is at least a borderline case as a city novel.

Urban Fiction and Narrative Innovation

My last examples tie in with a discussion about the problem of defining 'urban fiction' today. In a world as urbanised as ours, any novel attempting remotely to capture contemporary experience, one might argue, is bound to be in some sense an 'urban' novel.[32] Though this assumption dissolves any meaningful definition of 'urban fiction', a number of my examples which would traditionally only marginally qualify as urban novels, in many ways do display an engagement with urban complexity, if not necessarily as their major theme. Given my survey of strategies in the negotiation of urban complexity and especially of simultaneity, it is not too much to argue that a number of the key literary innovations throughout the centuries owe themselves to the need to adapt writing to the representation of the urban. As I hope to have shown, despite the "intimate relationship between the novel and the city" (Alter ix),[33] especially the simultaneity so characteristic of urban environments poses representational challenges which have brought forth a host of strategies designed nonetheless to represent simultaneity.

Notes

1 The German original reads: "Welche Architektur, welche Massen von Licht und Schatten, welche Kontraste, welche Mannigfaltigkeit des Ausdruckes! Wo fange ich an, wo höre ich auf, mein Auge zu weiden? Wann mich der Maler so bezaubert,

wieviel mehr wird es der Dichter tun! Ich schlage ihn auf, und ich finde – mich betrogen. Ich finde vier gute plane Zeilen, die zur Unterschrift eines Gemäldes dienen können, in welchen der Stoff zu einem Gemälde liegt, aber die selbst kein Gemälde sind" (Lessing XIII, 73).

2 For a few examples, cf. Alter; Balshaw/Kennedy; Barta; Brooker 1996, 2002; Caws; Harding; Lehan; Lenz/Riese; McNamara; Scherpe; Smuda; Teske; Wirth-Nesher; Wolfreys 1998, 2004, 2007. A few observations on urban complexity are to be found, for instance, in Keunen 2007; and Brandt 2009.

3 For the inseparability of urban imaginaries from ethics and politics, cf. Gassenmeier 1989; as well as Gassenmeier/Gurr; and Gurr 2003.

4 Raymond Williams has argued that "the effect of the modern city as a crowd of strangers was identified, in a way that was to last, by Wordsworth" (60); it appears that Denham is at least an important forerunner here.

5 Cf.: "Nor wonder if (advantag'd in my flight,/By taking wing from thy auspicious height)/Through untrac't waies, and airie paths I flie,/More boundlesse in my fancie, then my eie" (Denham, ll. 9–12).

6 For a remarkably comparable example (if diametrically opposed in political orientation) from the Romantic period, cf. Shelley's "Peter Bell the Third" (written 1819 but not published before 1839), which similarly uses asyndetic sequences to suggest the (moral) complexities of London life:

> There is great talk of revolution –
> And a great chance for despotism –
> German soldiers – camps – confusion –
> Tumults – lotteries – rage – delusion –
> Gin – suicide – and Methodism.
> (ll. 27–31).

7 For the opposing optimistic Whig view, cf. especially Addison's *Spectator* essay on "The Royal Exchange" of May 1711, in which he celebrates "this busy multitude of people [...] so rich an assembly of countrymen and foreigners consulting together upon the private business of mankind, and making this metropolis a kind of emporium for the whole earth" (199).

8 For the image of the city as a hotbed of crime in the Restoration and the early eighteenth century, cf. Gassenmeier 1989. For the analogy between the detective's work of reading a crime and the reading of the city, cf. also Teske's chapter "Die Kriminalgattung: Stadterkennen als Detektivarbeit" (223–234).

9 For crime in LA film, cf. for instance Klein 1998 and 2008.

10 For discussions of Lessing's "Laocoon" and its implications for semiotics and intermediality, cf. Koebner; Wellbery.

11 The German original reads: "Wenn es wahr ist, daß die Malerei zu ihren Nachahmungen ganz andere Mittel, oder Zeichen gebrauchet, als die Poesie; jene nämlich Figuren und Farben in dem Raume, diese aber artikulierte Töne in der Zeit; wenn unstreitig die Zeichen ein bequemes Verhältnis zu dem Bezeichneten haben müssen: so können nebeneinander geordnete Zeichen auch nur Gegenstände, die nebeneinander, oder deren Teile nebeneinander existieren, aufeinanderfolgende Zeichen aber auch nur Gegenstände ausdrücken, die aufeinander, oder deren Teile aufeinander folgen" (Lessing XVI, 77f.); cf. also XVII, 87: "What the eye takes in at once, [the poet] slowly tells one after the other and it often happens that when we hear the last we have already forgotten the first" (my translation). The German original reads: "Was das Auge mit einmal übersiehet, zählt [der Dichter] uns merklich

langsam nach und nach zu, und oft geschieht es, daß wir bei dem letzten Zuge den ersten schon wiederum vergessen haben."

12 The German original reads: "weil das Koexistierende des Körpers mit dem Konsekutiven der Rede dabei in Kollision kömmt" (Lessing XVII, 87).

13 The German original reads: "Es bleibt dabei: die Zeitfolge ist das Gebiete des Dichters, so wie der Raum das Gebiete des Malers [...] Mehrere Teile oder Dinge, die ich notwendig in der Natur auf einmal übersehen muß, wenn sie ein Ganzes hervorbringen sollen, dem Leser nach und nach zuzählen, um ihm dadurch ein Bild von dem Ganzen machen zu wollen: heißt ein Eingriff des Dichters in das Gebiete des Malers, wobei der Dichter viel Imagination ohne allen Nutzen verschwendet" (Lessing XVIII, 90).

14 The German original reads: "Homer malet nämlich das Schild nicht als ein fertiges vollendetes, sondern als ein werdendes Schild. Er hat also auch hier sich des gepriesenen Kunstgriffes bedienet, das Koexistierende seines Vorwurfs in ein Konsekutives zu verwandeln [...] Wir sehen nicht das Schild, sondern den göttlichen Meister, wie er das Schild verfertiget" (Lessing XVIII, 93).

15 Nor do I claim that my categories are always mutually exclusive, e.g. visual strategies of representing complexity may well also be experiential in their effect.

16 Though strictly speaking not the same – a labyrinth has no crossing paths and there is no way of 'losing one's way' – the maze and the labyrinth in a vast number of urban texts are frequently used interchangeably to suggest spatial complexity and a sense of being lost.

17 For a discussion of the city as a maze, labyrinth or jungle, cf. also Brandt 2010, 129–134 and 2009, 558–564; Faris; Kelley; Smith 171 *et passim*; Versluys; as well as several essays in Gurr/Raussert. Cf. also de Certeau's reference to the "mobile and endless labyrinths far below" (92) in the passage on the urban voyeur observing the city from above.

18 For a different view cf. Brandt 2009, who sees this as a specifically postmodern phenomenon, arguing that "in postmodern fiction [...] the reader is put in a position where he or she learns about urbanity through a set of liminal experiences manifested in the text" (557).

19 From among the innumerable discussions of London in book VII of *The Prelude*, cf. for instance Gassenmeier 1985, 1996; Gassenmeier/Gurr; Gurr, 2003, 2005; Stelzig; or Williams.

20 For a contemporaneous and comparably additive strategy of representing "all the bustle" of the city, but with the opposite psychological effect of a "fullness of joy at so much *Life*", cf. Charles Lamb's letter to Wordsworth of 30 January 1801, qtd. in Meller/Slogsnat 54 (emphasis original). Cf. also the essays of Lamb and Hazlitt.

21 For the representation of the city in "Wandering Rocks", cf. also Brown.

22 For intermedial strategies, cf. also several contributions in Gurr/Raussert, especially Berit Michel's discussion of word and image relations in Foer's *Extremely Loud and Incredibly Close*.

23 For parallels between the *New York Trilogy* and *The Practice of Everyday Life*, cf. Jarvis 86.

24 As further classic modernist city novels that display comparable strategies of representation, Andrei Bely's *Petersburg* (1913), John Dos Passos's *Manhattan Transfer* (1925), or, as arguably the most radical case, Joyce's *Finnegans Wake* (1939) come to mind.

25 The German original reads: "Er schüttelte sich, schluckte. Er trat sich auf den Fuß. Dann nahm er Anlauf und saß in der Elektrischen. Mitten unter den Leuten. Los. Das war zuerst, als wenn man beim Zahnarzt sitzt, der eine Wurzel mit der Zange gepackt hat und zieht, der Schmerz wächst, der Kopf will platzen. Er drehte den Kopf zurück nach der roten Mauer, aber die Elektrische sauste mit ihm auf den Schienen weg, dann stand nur noch sein Kopf in der Richtung des Gefängnisses [...] In ihm schrie es entsetzt: Achtung, Achtung, es geht los [...] 'Zwölf Uhr Mittagszeitung', 'B.Z.', 'Die neueste Illustrierte', 'Die Funkstunde neu' 'Noch jemand zugestiegen?' Die Schupos haben jetzt blaue Uniformen [...] Gewimmel, welch Gewimmel. Wie sich das bewegte. Mein Brägen hat wohl kein Schmalz mehr, der ist wohl ganz ausgetrocknet. Was war das alles. Schuhgeschäfte, Hutgeschäfte, Glühlampen, Destillen. Die Menschen müssen doch Schuhe haben, wenn sie so viel rumlaufen, wir hatten ja auch eine Schusterei, wollen das mal festhalten. Hundert blanke Scheiben, laß die doch blitzen, die werden dir doch nicht bange machen, kannst sie ja kaputt schlagen, was ist denn mit die, sind eben blankgeputzt [...] Man mischt sich unter die andern, da vergeht alles, dann merkst du nichts, Kerl. Figuren standen in den Schaufenstern in Anzügen, Mänteln, mit Röcken, mit Strümpfen und Schuhen. Draußen bewegte sich alles, aber – dahinter war – nichts! Es – lebte – nicht! Es hatte fröhliche Gesichter, es lachte, wartete auf der Schutzinsel gegenüber Aschinger zu zweit oder zu dritt, rauchte Zigaretten, blätterte in Zeitungen. So stand das da wie die Laternen – und – wurde immer starrer. Sie gehörten zusammen mit den Häusern, alles weiß, alles Holz" (Döblin 1965, 15f.).

26 For a comparative reading of *Ulysses* and *Manhattan Transfer*, cf. Harding. For a comparative discussion of *Petersburg*, *Ulysses* and *Berlin Alexanderplatz*, cf. Barta.

27 For analyses of the implications of the digital form and their repercussions in literary studies from the early 1990s classics to more recent accounts, cf. Aarseth 1994, 1997; Bolter 1991, 2001; Burnett; Ensslin; Hayles; Landow; McGann; Sloane. For a model reading, cf. Michel.

28 Walter Benjamin's notion of urban memory as spatialised, layered, fragmented, disjointed, non-linear and ultimately hypertextual (as discussed in some detail in Chapter 3) is an interesting parallel to B.S. Johnson's representation of urban memory and its topographical anchoring. The parallels with the *Arcades Project* become even more persuasive if one bears in mind the similarities in the strategy of representation: The organisation of Benjamin's material into 36 folders ("Konvolute") and the ensuing non-linear structure is structurally and functionally similar to the 27 separate sections of *The Unfortunates*.

29 Since simple page references are obviously impossible in the case of *The Unfortunates*, it is common to designate the "First" and "Last" sections as such and to refer to the other sections by their opening words.

30 Cf. my discussion above of how Auster foregrounds this problem in "City of Glass".

31 I owe the suggestion that *Diary of a Bad Year* might be considered as an 'urban' novel to Berit Michel.

32 For a related argument, cf. also the brief remarks on the problems in defining 'urban fiction' in an urbanised society in Ickstadt 1991, 164, 171f. Elsewhere in the essay, Ickstadt rightly observes that a number of 'postmodern' writers (he mentions Barthelme, Pynchon and DeLillo) represent the city as "both ubiquitous and immaterial, less an identifiable geographical unit than a linguistic and semiotic space, a network of self-referential signs and systems of communication" (168; for a more detailed discussion, cf. Ickstadt 1988). Cf. also Keunen/Eeckhout.

33 By contrast, Frahm and others have highlighted the "elective affinities between the metropolis and film" (Frahm 182; my translation), suggesting film as the quintessential urban genre suited to representing these complexities.

References

Aarseth, Espen J. *Cybertext: Perspectives on Ergodic Literature*. Baltimore, London: Johns Hopkins University Press, 1997.

Aarseth, Espen J. "Nonlinearity and Literary Theory." *Hyper/Text/Theory*. Ed. George P. Landow. Baltimore: Johns Hopkins University Press, 1994. 51–86.

Addison, Joseph. "The Royal Exchange" [1711]. *The Works of Joseph Addison*. Ed. George Washington Greene. London: G.P. Putnam, 1854. Vol. IV, 198–202.

Alter, Robert. *Imagined Cities: Urban Experience and the Language of the Novel*. New Haven: Yale University Press, 2005.

Auster, Paul. *The New York Trilogy*. London: Penguin, 1990.

Balshaw, Maria, Liam Kennedy. "Introduction." *Urban Space and Representation*. Ed. Balshaw, Kennedy. London: Pluto, 2000. 1–21.

Barnes, Djuna. "The Hem of Manhattan." *The Blackwell City Reader*. Ed. Gary Bridge, Sophie Watson. Malden: Blackwell, 2002. 71–75.

Baron, Xavier, ed. *London 1066–1914: Literary Sources and Documents*. London: Helm Information, 1998. 3 vols.

Barta, Peter I. *Bely, Joyce, and Döblin: Peripatetics in the City Novel*. Gainesville: University Press of Florida, 1997.

Bely, Andrei. *Petersburg* [1913]. Trans. Robert E. Maguire, John E. Malmstad. Bloomington: Indiana University Press, 2018.

Benjamin, Walter. *The Arcades Project*. Trans. Howard Eiland, Kevin McLaughlin. Cambridge, MA: The Belknap Press of Harvard University Press, 1999.

Bolter, Jay David. *Writing Space: The Computer, Hypertext, and the History of Writing*. Hillsdale: Lawrence Erlbaum, 1991.

Bolter, Jay David. *Writing Space: Computers, Hypertext, and the Remediation of Print*. Mahwah: Lawrence Erlbaum, [2]2001.

Brandt, Stefan L. "The City as Liminal Space: Urban Visuality and Aesthetic Experience in Postmodern U.S. Literature and Cinema." *Amerikastudien/American Studies* 54.4 (2009): 553–581.

Brandt, Stefan L. "Open City, Closed Space: Metropolitan Aesthetics in American Literature from Brown to DeLillo." *Transcultural Spaces: Challenges of Urbanity, Ecology, and the Environment*. Ed. Stefan L. Brandt, Winfried Fluck, Frank Mehring. Tübingen: Narr, 2010. 121–144.

Brooker, Peter. *Modernity and Metropolis: Writing, Film and Urban Formations*. Houndmills: Palgrave, 2002.

Brooker, Peter. *New York Fictions: Modernity, Postmodernism, The New Modern*. London: Longman, 1996.

Brown, Richard. "Time, Space, and the City in the 'Wandering Rocks' Episode of Joyce's *Ulysses*." *Joyce's "Wandering Rocks."* Ed. Andrew Gibson, Steve Morrison. Amsterdam: Rodopi, 2002. 57–72.

Burnett, Kathleen. "Toward a Theory of Hypertextual Design." *Postmodern Culture* 3.2 (1993). http://muse.jhu.edu/journals/postmodern_culture/v003/3.2burnett .html.

Caws, Mary Ann, ed. *City Images: Perspectives from Literature, Philosophy, and Film*. New York: Gordon and Breach, 1991.

Coetzee, J.M. *Diary of a Bad Year*. London: Harvill Secker, 2007.

Currie, Mark. "Introduction." *Metafiction*. Ed. Currie. London: Longman, 1995. 1–15.

Danielewski, Mark Z. *House of Leaves*. New York: Pantheon, 2000.

de Certeau, Michel. *The Practice of Everyday Life*. Berkeley: University of California Press, 1994.

Denham, Sir John. "Coopers Hill [Draft III]" [1642]. *Expans'd Hieroglyphicks: A Critical Edition of Sir John Denham's* Coopers Hill. Ed. Brendan O Hehir. Berkeley: University of California Press, 1969. 109–134.

Döblin, Alfred. *Berlin Alexanderplatz: Die Geschichte von Franz Biberkopf*. Ed. Werner Stauffacher. Munich: dtv, 1965.

Döblin, Alfred. *Berlin Alexanderplatz: The Story of Franz Biberkopf*. Trans. Eugene Jolas. New York: Continuum, 1989.

Dos Passos, John. *Manhattan Transfer*. Boston, New York: Mariner, 2000.

Eckardt, Frank. *Die komplexe Stadt: Orientierungen im urbanen Labyrinth*. Wiesbaden: Verlag für Sozialwissenschaften, 2009.

Ellmann, Richard. *James Joyce* [1952]. New and rev. ed. Oxford: Oxford University Press, 1982.

Ellmann, Richard. *Ulysses on the Liffey*. Oxford: Oxford University Press, 1986.

Ensslin, Astrid. *Canonising Hypertext: Explorations and Constructions*. London: Continuum, 2007.

Faris, Wendy B. "The Labyrinth as Sign of City, Text, and Thought." *City Images: Perspectives from Literature, Philosophy, and Film*. Ed. Mary Ann Caws. New York: Gordon and Breach, 1991. 32–41.

Frahm, Laura. *Jenseits des Raums: Zur filmischen Topologie des Urbanen*. Bielefeld: transcript, 2010.

Gassenmeier, Michael. "Faszination und Angst: Anmerkungen zum widersprüchlichen Bild der Großstadt im 7. Buch des *Prelude*." *English Romanticism: The Paderborn Symposium*. Ed. Rolf Breuer, Werner Huber, Rainer Schöwerling. Essen: Blaue Eule, 1985. 67–104.

Gassenmeier, Michael. *Londondichtung als Politik: Texte und Kontexte der City Poetry von der Restauration bis zum Ende der Walpole-Ära*. Tübingen: Niemeyer, 1989.

Gassenmeier, Michael. "Poetic Technique and Politics in Wordsworth's Rendering of His Urban Experience in Book VII of *The Prelude*." *Expedition nach der Wahrheit: Poems, Essays, and Papers in Honour of Theo Stemmler*. Ed. Stefan Horlacher, Marion Islinger. Heidelberg: Winter, 1996. 221–241.

Gassenmeier, Michael, Jens Martin Gurr. "The Experience of the City in British Romantic Poetry." *Romantic Poetry*. Ed. Angela Esterhammer. Amsterdam, Philadelphia: Benjamins, 2002. 305–331.

Gilbert, Stuart. *James Joyce's* Ulysses*: A Study* [1930]. New York: Random House, [2]1952.

Gurr, Jens Martin. "B.S. Johnson, *The Unfortunates*." *Handbook of the English Novel of the Twentieth and Twenty-First Centuries: Text and Theory*. Ed. Christoph Reinfandt. Berlin, Boston: de Gruyter, 2017. 323–343.

Gurr, Jens Martin. "Morality versus Poetics: Conflicting Evaluations of Sense Perceptions in *The Prelude*." *Romantic Voices, Romantic Poetics: Selected Papers from the Regensburg Conference of the German Society for English Romanticism*. Ed. Christoph Bode, Katharina Rennhak. Trier: WVT, 2005. 57–68.

Gurr, Jens Martin. "'Thus strangely did I war against myself': The 'twofold frame of body and of mind' and the Body Politic in Wordsworth's *Prelude*." Gurr. *The Human Soul as Battleground: Variations on Dualism and the Self in English Literature*. Heidelberg: Winter, 2003. 153–172.

Gurr, Jens Martin, Wilfried Raussert. *Cityscapes in the Americas and Beyond: Representations of Urban Complexity in Literature and Film*. Trier: WVT/Tempe, AZ: Bilingual Press, 2011.

Harding, Desmond. "*Ulysses* and *Manhattan Transfer*: A Poetics of Transatlantic Literary Modernism." Harding. *Writing the City: Urban Visions & Literary Modernism*. New York: Routledge, 2003. 97–136.

Hayles, N. Katherine. *Electronic Literature: New Horizons for the Literary*. Notre Dame: University of Notre Dame Press, 2008.

Ickstadt, Heinz. "The City in English Canadian and US-American Literature." *Zeitschrift der Gesellschaft für Kanadastudien* 19/20 (1991): 163–173.

Ickstadt, Heinz. "Kommunikationsmüll und Sprachcollage: Die Stadt in der amerikanischen Fiktion der Postmoderne." *Die Unwirklichkeit der Städte: Großstadtdarstellungen zwischen Moderne und Postmoderne*. Ed. Klaus R. Scherpe. Reinbek: Rowohlt, 1988. 197–224.

Jarvis, Brian. *Postmodern Cartographies: The Geographical Imagination in Contemporary American Culture*. New York: St. Martin's Press, 1998.

Jefferson, Thomas. "Letter to James Madison, December 20, 1787." *The Papers of Thomas Jefferson*. Ed. Julian P. Boyd. Princeton: Princeton University Press, 1955. Vol. XII, 422.

Johnson, B.S. *The Unfortunates* [1969]. New York: New Directions, 2008.

Johnson, Samuel. "London: A Poem in Imitation of Juvenal's Third Satire" [1738]. *Samuel Johnson: A Critical Edition of the Major Works*. Ed. Donald Greene. Oxford: Oxford University Press, 1984. 2–8.

Joyce, James. *Finnegans Wake* [1939]. London: Minerva, 1992.

Joyce, James. *Ulysses*. Ed. Jeri Johnson. Oxford: Oxford University Press, 1993.

Joyce, James. *Ulysses*. Trans. Hans Wollschläger. Ed. Dirk Vanderbeke, Dirk Schulze, Friedrich Reinmuth, Sigrid Altdorf, Bert Scharpenberg. Frankfurt/Main: Suhrkamp, 2004.

Kelley, Wyn. "Pierre in a Labyrinth: The Mysteries and Miseries of New York." *Melville's Evermoving Dawn: Centennial Essays*. Ed. John Bryant, Robert Milder. Kent: Kent State University Press, 1997. 393–405.

Keunen, Bart. "Living with Fragments: World Making in Modernist City Literature." *Modernism*. Ed. Astradur Eysteinsson, Vivian Liska. Amsterdam: Benjamins, 2007. 271–290.

Keunen, Bart. "The Plurality of Chronotopes in the Modernist City Novel: The Case of *Manhattan Transfer*." *English Studies* 82.5 (2001): 420–436.

Keunen, Bart, Bart Eeckhout. "Whatever Happened to the Urban Novel?" *Postmodern New York City: Transfiguring Spaces – Raum-Transformationen*. Ed. Günter Lenz, Utz Riese. Heidelberg: Winter, 2003. 53–69.

Kinder, Marsha. "Bleeding Through: Database Fiction." Norman M. Klein, Rosemary Comella, Andreas Kratky. *Bleeding Through: Layers of Los Angeles 1920–1986*. [DVD and Book]. Karlsruhe: ZKM digital arts edition, 2003. 53–55.

Klein, Norman M. "Bleeding Through." Norman M. Klein, Rosemary Comella, Andreas Kratky. *Bleeding Through: Layers of Los Angeles 1920–1986* [DVD and Book]. Karlsruhe: ZKM digital arts edition, 2003. 7–44.

Klein, Norman M. *The History of Forgetting: Los Angeles and the Erasure of Memory* [1997]. New York: Verso, 2008.

Klein, Norman M. "Staging Murders: The Social Imaginary, Film, and the City." *Wide Angle* 20.3 (1998): 85–96.

Koebner, Thomas, ed. *Laokoon und kein Ende: Der Wettstreit der Künste*. Munich: Edition Text + Kritik, 1989.

Landow, George P. *Hypertext 3.0: Critical Theory and New Media in an Era of Globalization*. Baltimore: Johns Hopkins University Press, 2006.

Lawrence, D.H. "Review of *Manhattan Transfer*" [1927]. *John Dos Passos: The Critical Heritage*. Ed. Barry Main. London, New York: Routledge, 1988. 71–72.

Lehan, Richard. *The City in Literature: An Intellectual and Cultural History*. Berkeley: University of California Press, 1998.

Lenz, Günter, Utz Riese, eds. *Postmodern New York City: Transfiguring Spaces – Raum-Transformationen*. Heidelberg: Winter, 2003.

Lessing, Gotthold Ephraim. "Laokoon oder über die Grenzen der Malerei und Poesie mit beiläufigen Erläuterungen verschiedener Punkte der alten Kunstgeschichte" [1766]. Lessing. *Ausgewählte Werke*. Ed. Wolfgang Stammler. Munich: Carl Hanser, 1959. Vol. III, 1–150.

Lopate, Phillip, ed. *Writing New York: A Literary Anthology*. New York: Washington Square Press, 2007.

Lynch, Kevin. *The Image of the City*. Cambridge, MA: MIT Press, 1960.

McGann, Jerome. *Radiant Textuality: Literature After the World Wide Web*. New York: Palgrave Macmillan, 2001.

McNamara, Kevin R., ed. *The Cambridge Companion to the Literature of Los Angeles*. Cambridge: Cambridge University Press, 2010.

Meller, Horst, Helmut Slogsnat, eds. *London: The Urban Experience in Poetry and Prose*. Paderborn: Schöningh, 1987.

Michel, Berit. "Urban Identity in a State of Flux: Strategies of Representing Simultaneity, Chaos, and Complexity in *Extremely Loud & Incredibly Close*." *Cityscapes in the Americas and Beyond: Representations of Urban Complexity in Literature and Film*. Ed. Jens Martin Gurr, Wilfried Raussert. Trier: WVT/Tempe, AZ: Bilingual Press, 2011. 173–196.

Nabokov, Vladimir. *Lolita* [1955]. Ed. Alfred Appel, Jr. New York, Toronto: McGraw-Hill, 1970.

O Hehir, Brendan. "Topographical Note: Cooper's Hill/Egham, Surrey." *Expans'd Hieroglyphicks: A Critical Edition of Sir John Denham's* Coopers Hill. Ed. O Hehir. Berkeley: University of California Press, 1969. xxiii–xxvii.

Scherpe, Klaus R., ed. *Die Unwirklichkeit der Städte: Großstadtdarstellungen zwischen Moderne und Postmoderne*. Reinbek: Rowohlt, 1988.

Shelley, Percy Bysshe. "Peter Bell the Third." *The Complete Poetical Works*. Ed. Thomas Hutchinson, rev. G.M. Matthews. Oxford: Oxford University Press, 1970. 346–361.

Simmel, Georg. "The Metropolis and Mental Life" [1903]. *The City Cultures Reader*. Ed. Malcolm Miles, Tim Hall, Iain Borden. London: Routledge, [2]2004. 12–19.

Sloane, Sarah. *Digital Fictions: Storytelling in a Material World*. Stamford, CT: Ablex Publishing, 2000.

Smith, Peter F. *The Syntax of Cities*. London: Hutchinson, 1977.

Smuda, Manfred, ed. *Die Großstadt als "Text."* Munich: Fink, 1992.

Stelzig, Eugene. "Wordsworth's Invigorating Hell: London in Book 7 of *The Prelude* (1805)." *Romanticism and the City*. Ed. Larry Peer. New York: Palgrave Macmillan, 2011. 181–195.

Teske, Doris. *Die Vertextung der Megalopolis: London im Spiel postmoderner Texte.* Trier: WVT, 1999.

Versluys, Kristiaan. "New York as a Maze: Siri Hustvedt's *The Blindfold.*" *Postmodern New York City: Transfiguring Spaces – Raum-Transformationen.* Ed. Günter Lenz, Utz Riese. Heidelberg: Winter, 2003. 99–108.

Wellbery, David E. *Lessing's* Laocoon*: Semiotics and Aesthetics in the Age of Reason.* Cambridge: Cambridge University Press, 1984.

Williams, Raymond. "Metropolitan Perceptions and the Emergence of Modernism" [1985]. *The City Cultures Reader.* Ed. Malcolm Miles, Tim Hall, Ian Borden. London: Routlege, [2]2004. 58–65.

Wirth-Nesher, Hana. *City Codes: Reading the Modern Urban Novel.* Cambridge: Cambridge University Press, 1996.

Wolfreys, Julian. *Writing London: The Trace of the Urban Text from Blake to Dickens.* London: Palgrave, 1998.

Wolfreys, Julian. *Writing London 2: Materiality, Memory, Spectrality.* London: Palgrave, 2004.

Wolfreys, Julian. *Writing London 3: Inventions of the City.* London: Palgrave, 2007.

Wordsworth, William. *The Prelude 1799, 1805, 1850.* Ed. Jonathan Wordsworth, M.H. Abrams, Stephen Gill. New York: Norton, 1979.

Film

The Naked City. Dir. Jules Dassin. USA, 1948.

3 Palimpsests, Rhizomes, Nodes

Texts as Structural and Functional Urban Models

That formal innovation directly results from the need to do justice to urban complexity can also be shown for the two exemplary texts discussed in this chapter: I here use Eliot's "The Waste Land" as the quintessential Modernist city poem and Norman M. Klein's *Bleeding Through*, one of the most ambitious early twenty-first-century attempts at using digital media to represent the city, to outline the ways in which texts function as structural and functional models *of* the city. Both texts, I will argue, make innovative use of textual strategies of simulating palimpsestic and rhizomatic urban structures to simulate cities as spatialised and layered memory.

Urban Memory and the Structural Analogies between 'City' and 'Text': "The Waste Land" and Benjamin's *Arcades Project*

Here, too, we can begin by juxtaposing two passages: The first is again Kevin Lynch's discussion of urban simultaneity in *The Image of the City*:

> At every instant, *there is more than the eye can see, more than the ear can hear*, a setting or a view waiting to be explored. Nothing is experienced by itself, but always in relation to its surroundings, the sequences of events leading up to it, the memory of past experiences.
>
> (1f.; my emphasis)

The second passage is from Michael Coyle's essay on "The Waste Land":

> The sense of meaning escaping one on every side, the sense that at any given point *there is more going on than the reader can take in*, is integral to the experience of the poem.
>
> (166; my emphasis; cf. also Lamos 111 *et passim*)

Taking these corresponding observations on the excess of simultaneous semiosis in both city and text as a point of departure, this chapter sets out to read Modernist urban poetry and poetics in the light of roughly contemporary early urban studies.

In particular, I propose to read "The Waste Land" side by side with Walter Benjamin's *Arcades Project*, which has received an astonishing amount of critical attention in urban studies (and elsewhere) in the last 20 years as arguably *the* paradigmatic text on urban modernity. I want to focus on the urban texture of both texts, particularly with regard to how they represent layers of urban memory. While there are, of course, innumerable readings of the city in "The Waste Land" and a few scholars, such as Bowen, Martindale (1995), Perloff or Yang, have suggested Benjamin as a relevant analogy, the connection between urban and literary textures has hardly been elucidated.[1] Though one would think it should long have been clear that Coyle is right in arguing that "The Waste Land" "is a poem where the most important things happen on the level of form" (163), most readings engaging with the poem's view of the city, such as for instance Day, Johnston (155–181), Thormählen (123–140), and Versluys (172–191), do so more or less mimetically on the content level and essentially ask 'what does it say about London?'. In one of the few attempts to explain the urban texture of Eliot's text, McLaughlin (183), for instance, states that "Eliot's poem is richly overcrowded with 'ethnographic moments' offering the reader [...] an objective correlative for urban overcrowding". However, this notion is not extended in any significant way in an essay that otherwise hardly considers poetic strategies at all. One of the best discussions of the urban texture of "The Waste Land" is Wolfreys's, which, however, takes an approach entirely different from mine and only mentions Benjamin in passing, suggesting differences rather than similarities (cf. 221).

My particular focus in reading Eliot and Benjamin side by side will be on Benjamin's notion of "superposition". The underlying view of the city as a palimpsest and the notion of layered spatialised memory this entails, I believe, accord well with the poetics of Modernist urban poetry (I here discuss "superposition" and "palimpsest" together; Chapter 4 then suggests a distinction and proposes different usages). "The Waste Land", I will argue, is the quintessential poem of urban memory, because the text in its layering of structures and meanings resembles the urban fabric itself.

I will first comment on the more or less simultaneous origin and development of Modernist poetics in the decades around 1900 and of urban studies and particularly of urban sociology as a field of study. How, we may ask, does Eliot's text – and by implication, Modernist urban poetics – situate itself in an ongoing discussion of 'the urban' as the dominant locale of people's lives in a period of dramatic urbanisation? I will then point out a number of analogies between "The Waste Land" (1922) and Benjamin's *Arcades Project* (1927–1940) in terms of their negotiation of urban complexities; I will here especially look at the representation of layered and spatialised urban memory in palimpsestic structures. Finally, I will very briefly comment on how this ties in with questions of transnational poetics in the period of Modernism.

The Modern City and the Origin of Urban Studies

In an enlightening essay on the rise of urban sociology, Ilja Srubar outlines what he calls "the formation of sociological inquiry by means of metropolitan perception" (37; my translation). The underlying point that sociology is essentially and originally an 'urban' discipline is hardly new, but his discussion of the importance of the city in the formation of sociology as a discipline is nonetheless still enlightening. Srubar speaks of the "four decades around 1900" as the formative period of (urban) sociology, mentioning Durkheim, Tönnies, Weber, Simmel, Kracauer and Benjamin as key exponents (38; my translation). That some of them – including Benjamin – also wrote *after* 1922 is not an issue here. In short, without positing an influence in either direction, I propose that key concepts in urban studies – especially those of its roughly contemporaneous early exponents – might more systematically be employed in discussing Modernist city poetry. Parallels between central concepts in early urban studies on the one hand and the formal as well as thematic concerns of both British and American Modernist city poetry on the other hand are hardly surprising, one might argue: Both made similar observations on a related subject, the modern city. Raymond Williams and others have of course commented on the "decisive links between the practices and ideas of the avant-garde movements of the twentieth century and the specific conditions and relationships of the twentieth-century metropolis" (Williams 13; cf. also Bradbury 96; Long 144; Sharpe/Wallock). Poetry as a condensed form of expression – and especially Modernist poetry with its characteristic strategies of compression – it seems, lends itself to rendering the density and intensity of encounters, social ties and palimpsestic structures characteristic of the modern metropolis.

A few examples will suffice to establish the connection between Eliot's text and the roughly contemporary observations on key urban phenomena in early urban studies: In his influential 1903 essay "The Metropolis and Mental Life", Simmel speaks of the "*intensification of nervous stimulation* which results from the swift and uninterrupted change of outer and inner stimuli" and the "rapid crowding of changing images, the sharp discontinuity in the grasp of a single glance, and the unexptectedness of onrushing impressions [as] the psychological conditions which the metropolis creates" (13; italics original). The result, Simmel famously argued, is an intellectualised, indifferent, blasé attitude of the urbanite, who reduces other city dwellers to their particular function in a given situation and no longer engages with them as full personalities. The resulting sense of alienation and isolation in the crowd is a familiar sentiment in modernist city poetry, not least in "The Waste Land". In this vein, one might think of the "crowd flow[ing] over London Bridge", where "each man fixed his eyes before his feet" (ll. 62, 65). Simmel's notions entered Anglophone urban discourses by means of Robert E. Park's influential essay "The City: Suggestions for the Investigation of Human Behavior in the City Environment" published in 1915 as one of the founding essays of the Chicago School of urban sociology. Park here clearly shows the influence of Georg Simmel, with whom he had studied for a while around the turn of the century.

In one of the best discussions of the connection between Modernist form and the texture of the modern city, in which Eliot is only mentioned in passing, Sharpe and Wallock state:

> City and style, object and evocation quickly take on aspects of one another as the urban environment shapes an aesthetic perception, which in turn

> produces a new form of vision of the city. The city is the locus of modernism, and each aspect of city life seems to generate or demonstrate a characteristic of this artistic movement – multiplicity of meaning, loss of sequential or causal connection, breakdown of signification, and dissolution of community.
>
> (5)

> One of the most useful ways of studying the city envisions the urban landscape as a form analogous to that of a literary composition.
>
> (11)

What we might want to trace, they thus suggest, are structural parallels between urban and literary fabrics and textures. However, while Sharpe and Wallock propose to study how the city functions like a text, I aim to show how a text can function like the city in its layering of meanings.[2]

The City and Urban Memory in Eliot and Benjamin: Collage, Palimpsest, Superposition

I do not, of course, posit any kind of influence, but I do want to suggest 'elective affinities' between "The Waste Land" and Benjamin's *Arcades Project*, which are remarkably similar in their aesthetics of representing urban textures and particularly urban memory as well as in the structures and patterns of representation they deploy. Both the *Arcades Project* and "The Waste Land" are essentially topographical: "*The Waste Land* is a London poem" (Martindale 1995, 114) – Long even goes so far as to argue that the "Modernist, fragmented city is virtually the poem's protagonist" (145; cf. also Sharpe/Wallock 6) – while Benjamin is centrally concerned with Paris. Moreover, both take essential cues from Baudelaire as arguably the first truly 'urban' poet.

While analogies with Benjamin's work have occasionally been suggested (cf. Bowen; Martindale 1995; Perloff; Yang), critics have not yet discussed what I regard as the most illuminating parallels: Martindale mentions Benjamin in connection with Eliot's technique of citation and fragmentation and points out parallels in the technique of montage, arguing that "*The Waste Land* comes closer, in its uses of fragmentation, to the writings of Walter Benjamin" (1995, 131); Perloff similarly focuses on the poetics of citation (cf. 24–49). Her analysis of Benjamin's *Arcades Project* is one of the most intriguing short discussions, though I believe Perloff does slightly overstate the 'poeticity' of the work. Finally, in an insightful essay, Yang ties her discussion of "The Waste Land" to some of Benjamin's preoccupations – the media, representations of the urban, Baudelaire, and the *flâneur* as an urban figure – and does refer to "The Waste Land" as "an example of the city archive" (204). However, she does not provide a reading of its historical layering in the light of Benjamin's urban epistemology and palimpsestic urban memory as conceptualised in the *Arcades Project*.

Let me comment on a few structural parallels, the *tertium comparationis* being the texture of the modern metropolis both texts seek to convey. *The*

Arcades Project, Das Passagen-Werk, which Benjamin worked on between 1927 and his death in 1940, though the first notes and suggestions go back to the early 1920s, is a vast collection of about 1,000 pages of some 3,500 quotations and thoughts on the nineteenth-century arcades in Paris, organised into 36 folders or sections ["Konvolute"] and a number of essays and outlines. The text is quintessentially a work of *fragmentary historiography* (rather than a *fragmentary work of historiography*), proceeding as it does, not discursively, but by means of the suggestive juxtaposition and montage of quotations from over 800 different sources, ranging from police reports to Baudelaire and from snippets of observation to more or less aphoristic remarks on methodology. Perloff appropriately describes Benjamin's technique as an "astonishing piling up of quoted passages" (25) and suggestively states that

> the repeated juxtapositions, cuts, links, shifts in register [...] conspire to produce a poetic text [...] The most sober documentation [of] police edicts regulating prostitution in 1830 [...] is placed side by side with an extract from Baudelaire or Rimbaud.
>
> (43)

As Benjamin noted himself, "[t]his work has to develop to the highest degree the art of citing without quotation marks. Its theory is intimately related to that of montage" (458; all references are to the 1999 English edition).

In a way remarkably similar to this type of montage, Eliot's urban montage in "The Waste Land" also makes use of various types of distinctly 'urban' text – pub conversations, street scenes, domestic conversations in various social classes, snippets from popular songs, the language of business transaction, etc. This type of urban montage allows both texts to do justice to what urban sociologist Gerald D. Suttles has called "the cumulative texture of local urban culture" (283), defining "local urban culture" as "a vast, heritable genome of physical artifacts, slogans, typifications, and catch phrases" (284). He speaks of some cities – and both Paris and London would, of course, be supreme examples – as places that "have a lot of such culture" (Suttles 284). Suttles further mentions

> songs that memorialize [...] great streets or side streets, homes once occupied by the famous or infamous, a distinctive dialect or vocabulary, routine festivals or parades [...] dirty lyrics, pejorative nicknames [...] celebrated wastrels, and so on.
>
> (284)

In addition to the built environment, then, the layering of *immaterial* urban memory can also be conceptualised as a palimpsest: Thus, particular neighbourhoods may be characterised by a dense layering of memories, anecdotes, urban legends triggered by established festivities, parades or specific buildings such as long-existing pubs or restaurants, which may be associated with legendary local figures formally or informally memorialised in street names, memorial plaques or drinking songs, poems, or nicknames.

This sequence of examples appears striking in the context of both "The Waste Land" and the *Arcades Project*, which both also use such trivia to suggest local texture. Interestingly, Suttles argues that these items of local culture are richly interconnected in the minds of community residents in that they mutually evoke each other. The "mnemonic relatedness" (Suttles 294) of such items seems strikingly familiar to readers accustomed to the textures of Eliot's and Benjamin's urban evocations.

In his discussion of the *Arcades Project*, Irving Wohlfahrt links Benjamin's practice to contemporary developments in the arts and speaks of "Benjamin's [...] hypothesis that the montage technique of the avantgarde points towards the form of presentation necessary today for a material philosophy of history" (266; my translation). In a related vein, Bolle comments on the "constellation of thousands of building blocks of text which are used in an attempt to translate the order of the city into the syntax of a historiographic text" (2010, 19; my translation). In our context of textualising the city, it should be noted that the German title *Passagen-Werk* – in contrast to the English *Arcades Project*, where this connection is lost – by virtue of the ambiguity of '*Passagen*' as both 'arcades' and 'passages (of text)' suggests a convergence of urban and textual structures that is profoundly resonant in Benjamin's *opus magnum* (cf. also Bolle 2010, 19).

In the *Arcades Project*, the complex structure of the urban fabric with its multiple interconnections is represented in a strongly non-linear form, a hypertext *avant la lettre* (cf. Bolle 2010, 22; Perloff 31–38). There are, for instance, multiple cross-references and some 30 different symbols marking thematic clusters *across* the different folders. This system of internal cross-references instead of a linear presentation strongly invites a kind of hypertextual reading following certain threads or thematic strands; Bolle here speaks of a "network-like reading" (2010, 25; my translation; cf. also Bolle 2005).

The device of recurring phrases in a text suggesting non-linear connections between different parts is also apparent in "The Waste Land". Though a number of critics have commented on the analogies between hypertext and modernist collage writing, citing "The Waste Land" as an example (cf. Barrett; Bolter 1991, 131; Gray; Yang 190, 199),[3] the exact way in which the structure of "The Waste Land" appears to leave behind linearity and to mimic urban complexity, as I see it, has not really been pointed out. One might begin with the archetypal 'city' passage:

> Unreal City,
> Under the brown fog of a winter dawn,
> A crowd flowed over London Bridge, so many,
> I had not thought death had undone so many.
> Sighs, short and infrequent, were exhaled,
> And each man fixed his eyes before his feet.

Flowed up the hill and down King William Street,
To where Saint Mary Woolnoth kept the hours
With a dead sound on the final stroke of nine.
(Eliot 1974b, ll. 60–68)

This passage is referred to again twice in the course of the text, the first time in "The Fire Sermon": "Unreal City/Under the brown fog of a winter noon" (Eliot 1974b, ll. 207f.) and again, more cryptically but unmistakably, in the final "What the Thunder Said":

Falling towers
Jerusalem Athens Alexandria
Vienna London
Unreal.
(Eliot 1974b, ll. 373–376)

Though Coyle briefly comments on some of the characteristic repetitions, he reads them as part of "a poetic texture that challenges readers to look for pattern and [calls] attention to the very processes of interpretation" (163). While this is certainly reasonable, it does not do justice to the specific way in which meanings are being overlaid and multiplied in the text. Gray correctly, I believe, discusses these internal links as functioning in analogy to "anchor links" on websites (237), though he appears to me to overstate the 'digital' nature of the text.

The repetition of characteristic phrases, it seems, for its function depends on Eliot's technique of extreme condensation enabled by the multiple allusions: In only a few words of quotation or allusion, all the associations connected to a given intertext and frequently even its original contexts are imported into the poem and add to its semantic potential. Here, of course, it is the familiar allusion to Dante's *Inferno* in lines 63 and 64 (cf. Eliot's own note, Eliot 1974b, 81) – and thus the familiar *topos* of London as the 'infernal city' they invoke – which are carried on into the further "Unreal City" passages (for London as an infernal place, among many other examples, cf. Denham's "Coopers Hill" (1642); Wordsworth's *The Prelude* (1805/1850); Shelley's "Peter Bell the Third" (1819); Thomson's "The City of Dreadful Night" (1874); or Phillips's "A Nightmare of London" (1913)).

The text, then, not only superimposes levels of the history of London – and of writing *about* London – upon one another, but in a sense makes London the successor of previous cities of empire – "Jerusalem Athens Alexandria/Vienna London" (Eliot 1974b, ll. 374f.). The apocalyptic lines invoking the "[f]alling towers" (l. 373) of a sequence of cities destroyed or threatened with destruction at some point in their history are here overlaid with the infernal associations invoked by the mere repetition of "unreal". The technique appears to be the following: Incisive allusions create additional levels of meaning which are then channelled into further passages by means of suggestive repetition, an effect that is also achieved, for instance, with the Philomel associations established in "A Game of Chess", where the phrase "by the barbarous king/So rudely forced" (ll. 99f.) and the "Jug Jug" (l. 103) of the nightingale's song are established, which are later recalled in "The Fire Sermon" (ll. 203–206). This double effect on the one hand provides a means of leaving behind the linearity of print; on the other hand, it suggestively allows for an extreme multiplication and condensation of meaning appropriate to the representation of complexity in the modern city.

A further parallel between Eliot's and Benjamin's texts lies in the fact that both "The Waste Land" and – even more centrally – the *Arcades Project* foreground a distinct *flâneur* perspective on the metropolis. The importance of the *flâneur* of course is reinforced by the prominent role Baudelaire as the quintessential nineteenth-century city poet plays in both texts: In Benjamin's work, the folder on Baudelaire makes for about one-fifth of the entire text, and Baudelaire is a constant presence throughout; but Baudelaire also repeatedly features in the central "Unreal City" passage, not least in the notorious direct quotation of "You hypocrite lecteur! – mon semblable,– mon frère!" from the opening poem of *Les Fleurs du Mal* (Eliot 1974b, l. 76).[4] For both Benjamin and Eliot, Baudelaire was a major figure in attempting to comprehend and represent the modern city; Benjamin even owed central concepts of his historiography and cultural critique to Baudelaire's poetics (cf. Bolle 2010, 38; cf. also Bowen 31f.). What is more, the sentiment of being lost and isolated in the crowd that is central to the "Unreal City" passage in "The Waste Land" is one that Benjamin is fundamentally concerned with: "[The *flâneur*] is the solitary and lonely man in the crowd, who knows about his solitariness and loneliness" (Hassenpflug 2006, 10; my translation). The sense of observing disconnected scenes of urban life that we hardly ever witness from beginning to end but rather, as the *flâneur* might, in glimpses, contributes to a *flâneur* perspective in "The Waste Land", and Michael Coyle appropriately argues that "the poem positions us as that artist-as-spectator-of-modern-life whom Charles Baudelaire called the *flâneur*" (159; cf. also Yang 196). It might even be argued that the poem's central consciousness Tiresias, a "mere spectator [and] yet the most important personage in the poem",[5] as Eliot refers to him in his note on l. 218, is in fact a type of timeless *flâneur* through the ages: Like Benjamin's *flâneur*, Tiresias, in a form of superposition – i.e. the synchronous perception of different layers of the past – is simultaneously aware of anything that ever happened in any given space and even across different spaces.

How, in addition to suggesting "the cumulative texture of local urban culture" (Suttles 283) and its memorialisation, do these observations relate to the poetics of urban memory? In the *Arcades Project*, Benjamin develops a notion of the interpenetration of different layers of time and of their simultaneous co-presence in urban space, a phenomenon he refers to as "superposition" (172, 418, 854 *et passim*). This concept is never set out discursively in any coherent way by Benjamin; thus, what Bolle (2000, 413) states about Benjamin's notion of historical cognition, namely that it has to be re-constructed from a large number of fragments scattered throughout the *Arcades* book, is also true of his notion of "superposition" and the reading of the layers of meaning in urban history. Isabel Kranz has here spoken of "Parallelstellenexegese", the need for a synoptic reading of numerous parallel passages (115). My reading of Benjamin's notion of "superposition" is indebted to Dieter Hassenpflug, who has explored its implications for urban semiotics. Hassenpflug summarises the idea as follows:

> [Superposition is] the ability to remember the new – for instance by regarding present urban elements as elements of a spatialised memory and, in so doing, as anticipations of prospective urban realities [...] The technique of superposition points to history which is preserved in the elements of cities.
>
> (2011, 54)

Given a certain frame of mind – and Benjamin clearly characterises this frame of mind as that of a *flâneur* – this simultaneous co-presence can be perceived and understood by an urban observer. He even speaks of this "interpenetration and superposed transparency" of different times in a given space as the "perception of space [unique to] the flâneur" (Benjamin, 546): "Thanks to this phenomenon, anything that ever potentially happened in a space is perceived simultaneously. Space winks at the flâneur: 'Well, whatever may have happened here?' " (Benjamin 418; translation modified; cf. also 4, 390, 392, 418, 462, 841, 854, 879f.). Thus, "superposition" refers to both the temporal layering and to the ability to perceive it; Hassenpflug even refers to it as a "technique" (2011, 54).

In an excellent discussion of Benjamin's view of modernity in the *Arcades Project*, Brüggemann speaks of two types of modernity, represented by Breton and Le Corbusier, of which the latter conceives of the metropolis as a space of "geometrical order and functional separations [...] absolutistically related to the present", while the former regards it as "a memory and image space of mutually overlaying and interpenetrating periods" (595; my translation).[6] Though he does not comment on Benjamin's concept of "superposition" here, it lies close at hand in the notion of the city as a time-spanning space of layered memory, an understanding which clearly anticipates all the still current notions of the 'city as palimpsest'[7] (while I here treat superposition as a variety of the palimpsest, I distinguish between the two in Chapter 4).

The remarkably similar way in which the structure of "The Waste Land" suggestively establishes a layered texture of urban memory again partly depends on the combination of extreme condensation by means of multiple allusions with the repetition of key phrases which connect different sections of the text. However, the textual equivalent of the palimpsestic layering of memory as spatialised in the city is primarily achieved through the layering of texts from different periods, as in the layering of Spenser's pastoral view of the river Thames into contemporary London in "The Fire Sermon" ("Sweet Thames, run softly, till I end my song", Eliot 1974b, ll. 176, 183f.), of Ophelia's parting words into the pub conversation (l. 172), or in the sudden appearance of a combatant from the Punic Wars in the crowd on London bridge (l. 70).

This collapsing of past and present into a timeless continuum in "The Waste Land" effectively suggests the layers both of physically built urban fabric (where, for instance, an underlying medieval layout is still visible in even the most heavily bombed and rebuilt European city; cf. Chapter 4) and of memory in the contemporary city. In this context, it is remarkable that classical scholars have also pointed out the use of "palimpsestic superimposition" (Martindale 1995, 137) as a poetic technique in the work of Eliot's revered idol Virgil – they cite, for instance, the passage in which Aeneas walks over sites of later Roman grandeur in book VIII of the *Aeneid* (for a more detailed reading, cf. Martindale 1993, 50–52; Mattheis/Gurr; and Reeves 13 *et passim*).

If we follow Martindale's distinction between two "models for our understanding of the past, the first historical and diachronic, the second archaeological and synchronic" (1995, 117), the notion of the past in "The Waste Land" clearly adheres to the 'synchronic camp'. Martindale appropriately refers to "Eliot's theory of poetry [as] in part an 'archaeological' one, in terms of recessive layers of meaning [which are] brought to simultaneous life" (1995, 116, cf. also 115).

This "archaeological and synchronic" notion of the co-presence of the past in the present suggests a philosophy of history according to which, as we later read in the opening of "Burnt Norton", "all time is eternally present" (Eliot 1974a, l. 4). However, nearer the time of writing "The Waste Land", Eliot famously outlined this view in "Tradition and the Individual Talent", where he defines what he calls "the historical sense":

> [The historical sense] involves a perception, not only of the pastness of the past, but of its presence; the historical sense compels a man to write not merely with his own generation in his bones, but with a feeling that the whole of the literature of Europe from Homer and within it the whole of the literature of his own country has a simultaneous existence and composes a simultaneous order.
>
> (1975, 38; for Eliot's notion of literary tradition in the light of the palimpsest, cf. Dillon 37 and 61)

Though we should be wary of uncritically reading into "The Waste Land" Eliot's aesthetics as outlined in the essay (which appears to be far more aesthetically conservative than his practice especially in "The Waste Land"), I find this a remarkably close textual equivalent to the notion of "superposition" and the presence of the past in the physical urban environment as Benjamin outlines it. Thus, although the largely negative evaluation of the city from Eliot's early poetry onwards (cf. Gordon 19; Versluys 173) contrasts with Benjamin's more positive views, the textual strategies of attempting to simulate urban textures and the layering of urban memory are strikingly similar (for a discussion of political and ideological parallels and differences, cf. Gurr).

Judging from such parallels, the experience of the modern metropolis with its diversity, heterogeneity and complexity, and particularly with the palimpsestic layering of urban memory characteristic of the European city – an experience that appears to have been remarkably similar across different modern metropolises central to the Modernist endeavour, whether Paris or London, Berlin or Vienna – appears to have engendered comparable aesthetic responses highlighting the affinities between literary textures and the urban environments they respond to and model.

Rhizome and Superposition in Hypertext Docu-Fiction: Norman M. Klein's *Bleeding Through: Layers of Los Angeles 1920–1986*

How does one represent, synchronically as well as diachronically, the complexity of Los Angeles, city of Hollywood myths and inner-city decay, of ceaseless self-invention and bulldozed urban renewal, of multi-ethnic pluralism and ethnic ghettos, a city where both the promises and problems of 'America' have crystallised to the present day? For, while the discourses of urban utopia and urban crisis with all their contradictory ideological implications, of course, are as old as the concept of the 'city' itself (cf. Gassenmeier; Mumford; Teske), Los Angeles has always been imagined in particularly polarised ways:

> According to your point of view, Los Angeles is either exhilarating or nihilistic, sun-drenched or smog-enshrouded, a multicultural haven or a segregated ethnic concentration camp – Atlantis or high capitalism – and orchestrating these polarized alternatives is an urban identity thriving precisely on their interchangeability.[8]
>
> (Murphet 8)

Los Angeles, of course, has long been a centre of attention for urbanists as well as for scholars of urban planning and of cultural representations of the city. It has been the subject of innumerable studies, the locale for countless novels, documentary films and particularly of countless feature films.[9] However, one of the most impressive renderings of the complexities of twentieth-century Los Angeles, and surely one of the most ambitious attempts to do justice to these complexities by presenting a wealth of material in a highly self-conscious form of hypertext, is Norman M. Klein's multimedia docu-fiction *Bleeding Through: Layers of Los Angeles 1920–1986*.[10]

Bleeding Through, which combines a 37-page novella with a multimedia documentary DVD[11] on twentieth-century Los Angeles, is based on the fictitious story of Molly, who moved to LA in 1920 when she was 22 and whose life and times the narrator of the novella attempts to chronicle.[12] The question whether or not she killed her second husband Walt (or had him killed) at some point in 1959 serves as a narrative hook to launch the reader and user of the DVD on a quest through layers of twentieth-century Los Angeles. Thus, as the cover blurb appropriately notes, *Bleeding Through* is "a loosely constructed documentary underlying a flexible literary journey, it is an urban bricolage held together by the outline of a novel spanning sixty-six years".[13]

I will here argue that *Bleeding Through* makes full use of the opportunities afforded by the digital medium to represent the complexity, multiplicity and dynamics of the city in a way no other medium could.[14] I will first establish the contexts for an analysis of Klein's multimedia documentary by outlining the key findings of his 1997 monograph *The History of Forgetting: Los Angeles and the Erasure of Memory*, on which *Bleeding Through* is based to a considerable extent. *The History of Forgetting*, however, also provides the context for *Bleeding Through* in another sense: The flaunted self-reflexivity of Klein's distinctly non-academic and often highly literary work and its attempts at creating a non-linear textuality also highlight the problems of representing the complexity of the city in any 'traditional' linear form, whether in print or in a documentary film. These problems of representation demonstrably lead to the non-linear format of multimedia hypertext in *Bleeding Through*. By outlining the relationship between the novella and the documentary and by highlighting some of the features and design principles of the interactive DVD, I will then show how *Bleeding Through* re-presents the complexity of twentieth-century Los Angeles by taking us on a revisionist tour of its history since the 1920s and by pointing out the extent to which fictitious urban imaginaries – the innumerable *films noirs*, detective films and thrillers set in LA – have shaped perceptions of the city and even the city itself. I will then more explicitly point out the aesthetic and political implications of the multimedia format, of what one might call 'interactive multi-medial docu-fiction in hypertext'. Deploying the narrative and aesthetic strategies of hypertext documentaries, *Bleeding Through* can be shown to employ rhizomatic structures both to do justice to urban structures and to provide a radically subversive, anti-hegemonic view of twentieth-century Los Angeles. Finally, I will argue that the emphasis on urban layers and the frequent overlay montage of older and more recent photographs that is one of the most characteristic features of *Bleeding Through* literalises Benjamin's notion of the "interpenetration and superposed transparency" of different temporal layers referred to as "superposition" (546).

Establishing Contexts: The Problems of Representing Urban Complexity in Klein's History of Forgetting

Klein's 1997 monograph *The History of Forgetting: Los Angeles and the Erasure of Memory* is itself highly unusual in its mix of genres: Parts I and IV are scholarly studies of twentieth-century urban planning in LA and of the impact of filmic representations on the urban imaginary of the city; Part II is the imaginative recreation of the perspective on the city of a Vietnamese immigrant in a novella of some 65 pages (2008, 151–215), while Part III is a collection of creatively essayistic "docufables" (2008, 217–243).[15] Klein names as one of his key themes "the uneven decay of an Anglo identity in Los Angeles, how the instability of white hegemonic culture leads to bizarre over-reactions in urban planning, in policing, and how these are mystified in mass culture" (2008, 17).

Referring to what is surely the most drastic urban redevelopment project in twentieth-century Los Angeles, Klein states that "Bunker Hill [became] the emblem of urban blight in Los Angeles, the primary target for redevelopment downtown from the late twenties on" (2008, 52). The Bunker Hill Urban Renewal Project, begun in the 1950s and extending until as late as 2012, brought the virtually total razing of a neighbourhood, the flattening of the hill and the building of the high-rise buildings now popularly regarded as constituting 'Downtown LA'. Similarly, Klein comments on the razing of the "old Chinatown, old Mexican Sonora [...] the old Victorian slum district, and other *barrios* west of downtown, [which] were leveled, virtually without a trace" (2008, 97). Commenting on an eerie commonality of all these twentieth-century urban renewal projects in LA, Klein writes:

> [E]xcept for Chinatown, every neighborhood erased by urban planning in and around downtown was Mexican, or was perceived that way (generally, they were mixed, often no more than 30% Mexican) [...] While East L.A. may *today* seem the singular capital of Mexican-American life in the city, the mental map was different in the forties. The heartland of Mexican-American Los Angeles was identified as sprawling west, directly past downtown, from north to south. Bunker Hill was identified as "Mexican" by 1940, like Sonoratown just north of it [...] and particularly Chavez Ravine.[16]
>
> (2008, 132f.)

In *The History of Forgetting* as well as in a number of essays, Klein further shows how the urban imaginary of Los Angeles has been shaped by images of the city in film, from *noir* to *Blade Runner* and beyond, creating "places that never existed but are remembered anyway" (2001, 452), even arguing that the ideology of *noir* and neo-*noir* films, these "delusional journeys into panic and conservative white flight" also help "sell gated communities and 'friendly' surveillance systems" (1998, 89).

More immediately, *Bleeding Through* – though the details do not all fit – is clearly based on one of the short docufables in Part III of *The History of Forgetting*: In a mere three pages, "The Unreliable Narrator"[17] (230–233) tells the story of 93-year-old Molly Frankel, who moved to the city in the 1920s, ran a shop for decades and rented out most of her spacious Victorian house in Angelino Heights to a large Mexican family. Towards the end of the text, the experimental and tentative nature of these musings is pointed out by self-reflexively sketching a genealogy in a number of references both to the tradition of the unreliable narrator and to accounts of the constructedness of historiography and memory since the eighteenth century: "the Münchhausens and Uncle Tobys [...] German and Central European fiction after 1880 [...] the absent presence that in Michelet's words are 'obscure and dubious witnesses' (1847) [...] the broad crisis of representation in cinema" (Klein 2008, 233).

A similar concern with forms of representation is apparent in the chapter entitled "The Most Photographed and Least Remembered City in the World" (247–262) in *The History of Forgetting*. Klein here comments on previous fictional films and documentaries seeking to record the history of ethnic Los Angeles, such as Kent MacKenzie's *The Exiles* (1961) or Duane Kubo's *Raise the Banner* (1980) and the way in which even these well-intentioned films evade the issue of the razing of ethnic neighbourhoods (cf. 2008, 248f.): "The twin beasts that erased much of downtown – racist neglect and ruthless planning – leave only a faint echo in cinema, because generally one will distract the other, or because cinema, by its very apparatus, resembles the tourist imaginary" (2008, 249). Klein here speaks of the "utter instability of cinema as a formal record, and the fact that audiences enjoy this paramnesiac sensation, as memory dissolves [...] The layering of erasures is essential to moving the narrative along, to its simultaneity, its unreal solidity, its anarchic orderliness" (2008, 253).

Anticipating the self-conscious concern with narrative form in *Bleeding Through*, Klein notes in *The History of Forgetting* that when he began to write about the twentieth-century transformations of Los Angeles, he "noticed that [his] scholarship was beginning to resemble fiction" and speaks of the "crossed identity" fostered by this type of writing, "[making] the scholar both reader and character within the same text" (2008, 6f.). Even more directly linking the arrangement of a wealth of materials to the writing of fiction, he comments: "In many ways the materials I have assembled look like research gathered by a novelist before the novel is written, before the writer turns the contradictions into a character-driven story" (Klein 2008, 7). In a highly revealing footnote, he further comments on his concern with form:

> I am trying, with as much modesty as possible, to identify a form of literature that is not simply "hybridized", or "de-narratized", and certainly not deconstructed – not a blend of others but a structure in itself, a structure that is evolving [...] By structure, I mean *how to generate alternatives within the text itself, within the style itself.*[18]
>
> (Klein 2008, 20, note 10; italics original)

In *The History of Forgetting*, Klein even points forward to *Bleeding Through* by employing – if only half-seriously – the techniques of hypertext. In a short section entitled "Brief Interruption" in the "Introduction", in a reference to theories of memory and forgetting, he states: "The only solution for this introduction is a kind of hypertext (click to page 301). For the reader also interested in memory theory [...] I have included an Appendix [...] Read it now or read it later, whenever is suits you" (Klein 2008, 14).[19] *The History of Forgetting* in its frequently scrupulous and highly self-conscious concern with narrative form thus clearly points forward to *Bleeding Through*.[20]

Bleeding Through*: Multimedia Docu-Fiction on the Erasure of Multi-Ethnic Los Angeles*

While *The History of Forgetting* addresses more directly the perversions of city planning driven by greed and racism, *Bleeding Through* tackles them more obliquely if more experientially. It does so by juxtaposing two formats: the 'traditional' narrative of Klein's novella on the one hand and a multimedia

DVD on the other hand. The documentary is thus held together by the underlying story of Molly and her life in LA between 1920 and 1986.

Klein's constantly self-reflexive 37-page novella "Bleeding Through" has a highly self-conscious first-person narrator who tells the story of Molly and – just as centrally – his attempts to reconstruct it:

> I couldn't trust any of her stories. Not that her facts were wrong. Or that she didn't make an effort. [But] she'd fog out dozens of key facts. Whenever I noticed, she would blow me off, smiling, and say, "So I lose a few years" [...] But there were seven memories in the years from 1920 to 1986 that were luminously detailed.[21]
>
> (10)

It is these seven memories of key stages of Molly's life around which the novella and the DVD are structured, and which serve to explore 66 years of developments in the city.

Set largely within the three-mile radius near downtown LA in which Molly spent most of her life, the documentary deals with neighbourhoods such as Boyle Heights, Bunker Hill, Chavez Ravine, Chinatown and Echo Park, the disappearance of which was chronicled in *The History of Forgetting*. As the narrator explains here, this area was the site of the most drastic urban renewal projects in the country continuing over decades: "Hundreds of buildings gone: that could just as easily have been caused by carpet bombing, or a volcano erupting in the central business district" (BT 12). The same area around downtown, however, is also the centre of a filmic universe: "Inside those three miles, under the skyline dropped by mistake into downtown ten years ago [in the 1980s] more people have been murdered in classic Hollywood crime films than anywhere else on earth" (BT 12).[22]

The documentary database includes hundreds of images, maps, newspaper clippings, drawings and sketches, historical film clips and (for copyright reasons[23]) film snippets recognisably re-enacting key scenes of famous LA films merely by repeating the camera movements in basically empty streets in the original locations, but without actors.[24] Furthermore, there are numerous interviews with long-term residents, sometimes elaborate captions, as well as narrative commentary by Norman Klein.[25] Klein's video commentary frequently gives clues as to the story behind the disappearance of Molly's husband Walt, which adds a playful dimension of detective game to the navigation experience, because, such is the underlying fiction, the point of navigating *Bleeding Through* in the first place is to act as a detective on the hunt for such clues. However, as the narrator of the novella comments, "[t]he journey through the evidence is more exciting than the crime itself. We want to see everything that is erased to make the story legible" (BT 37). In the novella, the narrator outlines the structure and function of the DVD as follows:

> The structure works like this: [...] Each tier [of the DVD] comments on a specific medium that tries to make the city intelligible as it erases,

> collectively forgets, survives from day to day. The history of forgetting is a distraction from the basic reality of urban life in Los Angeles, its quotidian power of survival.
>
> (BT 42)

The first "tier" of the documentary DVD, "The Phantom of a Novel: Seven Moments", structured around the seven key moments of Molly's life in LA between 1920 and 1986, is dominated by historical photographs of people and places in the neighbourhoods surrounding Bunker Hill. Thumbnails of these photographs are arranged in random sequence and can be selected by the user; alternatively, the user can go through the photo archive by enlarging each photo to almost the size of the screen and then continuing either with the photograph on the left or on the right. Making full use of the technical possibilities, the sequence of photographs is not fixed but rather randomly brought up from the archive. Additionally, with each phase of Molly's life, there is a short narrative comment by Norman Klein in a window in the corner – a commentary that can be opened and closed by the user. The narrator of the novella describes this first tier as "a visual, interactive radio program [...] a kind of modern novel on a screen with hundreds of photos and Norman as narrator. You might say they are also a docu-fictional movie" (43).

Tier 2, "The Writer's Back Story", which the narrator of the novella describes as "more like a contextualization" (43), is largely made up of newspaper clippings and establishes the context of other people and places more loosely connected to Molly's story. It collects newspaper clippings covering events and developments occurring during Molly's life, with references to the prohibition and illegal distilleries, the ban on interracial marriages in the state of California in a 1932 newspaper clipping, the controversial reception of a 1941 anti-Semitic speech by Charles Lindbergh, the deportation of Japanese Americans during the Second World War, illicit gambling, the McCarthy era with its Red Scare and the building of air-raid shelters – frequently interspersed with innumerable sensationalist clippings reporting murders in Los Angeles. Additionally, explanatory captions beneath newspaper clippings and photographs contextualise developments, with comments, for instance, on the ambivalent views of Chinatown in the 1920s as both "an exotic place in the popular imagination" and a place "considered as an eyesore, as more brown and black races converged at the Plaza" (DVD 2:1).

Tier 3, "Excavation: Digging Behind the Story and its Locale", is described in the novella as "the aporia of media itself" (BT 43). In five sections, it offers a wealth of further material, here arranged thematically rather than chronologically. There is a section entitled "People Molly Never Met But Would Make Good Characters in Her Story", featuring randomly arranged interviews with twelve residents (including Norman Klein) of these neighbourhoods who comment on their experiences within the social and ethnic developments in twentieth-century LA, the Zoot Suit Riots, fear of violent police officers, ethnic festivities, anti-Communist witch-hunts during the McCarthy era, the 1947 murders of Elizabeth Short – the "Black Dahlia" – and of Bugsy Siegel, or the treatment of Japanese Americans during the Second World War. Largely consisting of film and video sequences, it is a "vast 'ironic index' of what Molly left out, forgot, couldn't see. It samples from the back-story that gets lost when the movie or novel is made legible" (BT 43). It is also described as:

> a meta-text (not a deconstruction). It is the structure of what cannot be found, what Molly decided to forget, what Molly never noticed, what passed before her but was lost to us. It is proof that no novel or film (documentary or fiction) can capture the fullness of how a city forgets, except by its erasures.
>
> (BT 38f.)

Thus, neither the novella nor the DVD are to be regarded as a higher-level commentary one on the other; they are mutually complementary: Just as the DVD can be seen as a vast exploration of the themes outlined in the novella, the narrative frequently comments on the contents of the DVD: "Next day, I went into a newspaper morgue, looking for articles on Walt's disappearance. Instead, I found fifty ways to kill a man between 1959 and 1961 (along with five suicides). I've scanned all the articles into a database for you" (BT 24). In the novella, the fictional story of Walt's disappearance is constantly related to current developments chronicled on the DVD, tying the wealth of documentary material back to the underlying quest narrative: "Among police photos, I find what should be Walt's body [...] Then I discover that on the same day, the downtown editor cancelled photos about racist crimes, particularly the railroading of blacks and Latinos" (BT 25).

With Molly as its protagonist, *Bleeding Through* shifts attention from hegemonic white males and draws attention to the role of minorities in LA's complex history: Molly, "a twenty-something girl from a Jewish home in the Midwest" (DVD 1:1; cf. also BT 13), is herself a newcomer and an outsider when she arrives in the city in 1920. As Bénézet points out, "[t]hrough Molly, Klein articulates a gendered and minority-oriented revision of the city's history" (69).

From the very beginning, both the novella and the DVD characterise Molly's neighbourhood as a multi-ethnic one.[26] Much of the material centres on transformations in twentieth-century multi-ethnic LA, whether in references to "Brooklyn Avenue with its famous mix of Jews and Mexicans, Japanese and other 'swart' young men" (BT 15; cf. also 40) to "restrictions against the black community on Central Avenue, especially when by 1924 membership of the Klan reached its highest number ever" (BT 30), to the tearing down of Chinatown for Union Station (built in 1939), to the history of mixed Japanese and Mexican neighbourhoods, with a Japanese American family man running a Mexican grocery store (cf. DVD 3:1), the 1943 Zoot Suit riots, the Watts rebellion, or the turning of Little Tokyo into "Bronzeville" during the Second World War, when African Americans and Mexicans moved into the area while the Japanese Americans were held in deportation camps away from the West Coast (cf. BT 22).

The drastic changes imposed by radical urban development projects in areas such as Bunker Hill may well be seen as the central theme of the documentary DVD. The section "Collective Dissolve: Bunker Hill", in film sequences from Kent McKenzie's 1956 documentary *Bunker Hill* and *The Exiles* (1961), maps as well as photographs from the 1890s to the 1960s attempts to recreate Bunker Hill before the massive demolition programme that cleared the area for what is now regarded as 'downtown' LA. A long sequence from McKenzie's *Bunker Hill* refers to the Community Redevelopment Agency's major plan to relocate 8,000 residents of the neighbourhood, to demolish all buildings and to sell the land and have modern office and apartment complexes built (cf. DVD 1:6). This chapter of the DVD also displays images from 1959 and 1960 showing the large-scale demolition of Bunker Hill. A sequence from Gene Petersen's 1949 film "... And Ten Thousand More [housing units]" also refers to the problem of 'slums' in LA and the need for urban development. This sequence is captioned "The myths of urban blight".[27] Similarly, the photograph of a model "Redevelopment Study for Bunker Hill, March 22, 1960" is captioned "Cooking statistics to justify tearing down Bunker Hill" (DVD 1:6). Indeed, statistics on the housing situation and living conditions in Bunker Hill appear systematically to have been distorted in order to win public support for the demolition of this predominantly Mexican neighbourhood. In the caption underneath a sequence from McKenzie's *The Exiles*, the fact that "this was a brown and black identified downtown center" is explicitly identified as "one of the reasons it was torn down" (DVD 3:3).

In the interview section, residents comment on racial segregation in LA. Japanese American Bill Shishima recounts his experience of having to leave Los Angeles in May 1942 as an 11-year-old to be interned away from the coast with his family; retired African American fire-man Arnett Hartsfield reports coming to Los Angeles in 1929, "when we couldn't even cross Washington Boulevard on Central Avenue [because of segregation]" (DVD 3:1). Finally, Esther Raucher recalls her experience of first coming to downtown as a white child and of staring at African Americans: "As a child [...] I don't think I'd seen a black person [...] That's how segregated the city was that you would never see a black person" (DVD 3:1). Tying such developments to the underlying story of Molly, a clip from Jeremy Lezin's 1975 documentary *A Sense of Community* with references to illegal immigrants working in LA is captioned "With each year, Molly felt the massive immigration from Latin America change the rules in her world" (DVD 1:7).

All in all, in keeping with *The History of Forgetting*, *Bleeding Through* thus shows how twentieth-century Los Angeles, in the process of becoming increasingly multi-ethnic demographically, continued to erase the visible traces of this diversity in favour of a de-ethnicised all-American look and feel modelled on the needs of a largely white elite and enforced by representing ethnic LA along the lines of the paranoid and implicitly racist aesthetic of innumerable *noir* murder films. It remains to be shown that the attempt at an open, non-hierarchical and anti-hegemonic representation of these complexities is closely tied to the non-linear and decentred form of the multimedia hypertext documentary.

Archival Database Fiction and Questions of Form: Nodes, Rhizomes and the Media-Historical Moment of 2003

The experience of navigating *Bleeding Through* is a fundamentally contradictory one: On the one hand, by making sophisticated use of the technological possibilities of the multimedia database, the fast-paced, multidimensional, overpowering, non-hierarchical, multi-faceted documentary recreates the urban experience of twentieth- or even twenty-first-century LA. On the other hand, there is a nostalgic quality to the experience, which partly arises from the use of vintage photographs, film clips and newspaper clippings which appear to work against the grain of the high-tech mode of presentation – in keeping with Klein's views expressed in *The History of Forgetting* on the constant self-reinvention of the city and the concomitant memoricide of previous layers of its history. However, while these aesthetic and experiential implications of the form are worth noting, the more momentous implications of the form are its implicit politics, which elegantly complement the more explicit political commentary also packaged into *Bleeding Through*.

Repeated references to the editorial decisions that went into the compilation of the material, the frequently self-reflexive narrator of the novella as well as the meta-narrative[28] titles of the DVD's three "tiers" – 1: "The Phantom of a Novel: Seven Moments", 2: "The Writer's Back Story", 3: "Excavation: Digging Behind the Story and its Locale" – already point to the fact that this documentary database fiction self-reflexively foregrounds its own narrative constructedness. This is continued throughout the DVD. In between the interviews with eleven other residents of the central LA neighbourhoods, Klein in interview clips comments on his thoughts on Molly, on the writing of the novella, as well as on his own first coming to Los Angeles:

> When we began these interviews [...] we were continually locating details that were half remembered, badly remembered or often forgotten and lost and couldn't possibly be known to her. [...] And it seems that we became almost more interested in locating what she couldn't find, what she had to forget, what she couldn't locate [...] It's such a great pleasure to not be constrained simply by the legibility of the story [...] The complexity becomes such a great pleasure. It's such a pleasure noticing what she wouldn't have noticed [...] So in a way the absences become much more present in these interviews than anything else.
>
> (DVD 3:1)

Postmodern literary and filmic explorations of the city, it is true, have already dissolved distinctions between genres, between fiction and discursive exploration; they have self-reflexively highlighted the ambiguous role of the writer or film-maker as both observer and participant in urban interactions; they have highlighted the dissolution of traditional views of the city and have frequently attempted to make the city itself legible as a text; they have set out formally to represent the multiplicity, polyphony and fragmentation of the city through multiple, polyphonic and fragmented textuality (for some of these tendencies cf. Teske). Similarly, in keeping with the views on the narrativity and constructedness of historiography in the work of Hayden White, Michel de Certeau and others, many recent documentaries constantly foreground artifice, subjectivity, etc.[29] Furthermore, precisely the fact that the documentary needs to be manipulated by the individual viewer for anything to be visible at all further reminds us of the mediality and the constructedness of what we are witnessing. The medium thus constantly draws attention to itself – in contrast to much traditional documentary film-making which relies on the reality effect of suggesting that what we see is somehow evident and can hardly be questioned. Hence the paradox inherent in much documentary film-making that is meant to be anti-hegemonic, subversive, etc. but through its very narrative form frequently cannot help being suggestive and (since the viewer is essentially passive[30]), imposes a view of the world. *Bleeding Through*, however, in contrast to even the most advanced filmic documentaries, which still inescapably rely on the linearity of film, makes full use of the digital medium to break linearity. Thus, while documentaries, which are originally meant for collective viewing, induce forms of collective medial experience, the effect of *Bleeding Through* specifically relies on a highly individual experience. The constant need to 'do' something in the process of navigating *Bleeding Through* – all clips are very short, hardly anything happens without being triggered by the user, who is essentially assigned the role of a detective in search of the truth – then, not only foregrounds the mediality, narrativity and construction of the material, it also activates the viewer. In keeping with the promise of the medium,[31] the non-linear presentation of the material thus precludes closure, stimulates the discovery of knowledge rather than imposing it and thereby fosters learning without being explicitly didactic.

The non-linear structure of *Bleeding Through* and its dual function of both simulating urban textures *and* of empowering viewers, might be characterised in terms of what Christoph Bode has called "future narratives". Bode designates as a "future narrative"[32] any narrative that describes more than one potential continuation in a given situation and thus does not – as most narratives do – present a development as having already happened in the past and as no longer allowing for different outcomes. Rather, "future narratives" in Bode's sense portray the future as being open and subject to intervention. The decision points at which different future developments are possible are referred to as "nodes". In *Bleeding Through*, the numerous points at which users of the DVD have to make decisions about how and where to continue appear to simulate the nodes and decision points in the city. However, while in most of the cases Bode refers to, the future is at least potentially open for the protagonist of a "future narrative", there is no such openness for Molly as the protagonist – her story is clearly represented as having happened in the past. For the user, however, who becomes the protagonist of the quest through the material, the choices that need to be made do suggest an open future.

Moreover, the aesthetic and political implications of the form can fruitfully be accounted for with reference to the concept of rhizomatic structures.

As proposed by Deleuze and Guattari (7–13), rhizomes are characterised by the principles of "connectivity", "heterogeneity", "multiplicity", "asignifying rupture", "cartography" and "decalcomania".[33] If, as Burnett has argued, "[h]ypertext is rhizomorphic in all its characteristics" (28) – and Klein's work makes full use of the medium – *Bleeding Through* may be characterised as fully rhizomatic, with all the non-totalising and anti-hegemonic implications Deleuze and Guattari famously ascribe to rhizomatic discourses. Thus, the multimedial, multivocal, multi-perspectival, interactive, non-sequential and highly self-reflexive experience of navigating *Bleeding Through* brings out "traits that are usually obscured by the enforced linearity of paper printing" (Burnett 3) and, like hypertext generally, serves to undercut, liquefy and question established and hegemonic representations with their frequently unquestioned dichotomies and "*hierarchies violentes*" (Derrida 56).

As Marsha Kinder argues in her short essay in the booklet of *Bleeding Through*, "database narratives [are] interactive structures that resist narrative closure and expose the dual processes of selection and combination lying at the root of all stories" (54).[34] *Bleeding Through* is narrative 'enough' so as to create interest and curiosity, but it flaunts its constructedness and constantly requires users to select from a wealth of narrative items and, by means of a succession of such choices, consciously to perform themselves the acts of selection and combination usually hidden behind the surface of conventional narrative. Database fictions, in flaunting the arbitrariness of such choices and enabling users to choose differently next time (but never exactly to retrace their steps), are potentially subversive purely in their form in that they expose as a construction and fabulation what narrative traditionally represents as a given. By making each journey through the material necessarily a different one – and by thus presenting what is merely material for a story as subject to change and human intervention – these narratives also contribute to the activation and mobilisation of the user in ways that even the most advanced self-reflexive fiction – which is still subject to the unchangeable linearity of print – cannot achieve (cf. also Kinder 54).

True to the 'democratic form' of hypertext digital media, *Bleeding Through* already by means of its very form serves to deconstruct hegemonic constructions of history by constantly drawing attention to the medial, discursive, constructed nature of such conceptions. As a user, one is never allowed to forget this is a revisionist, anti-hegemonic, at times polemical re-construction of a repressed, alternative Los Angeles.[35]

However, while *Bleeding Through* thus helps to counter the memoricide induced by urban planning in LA, the question remains to what extent a cultural product which so centrally relies on the individual, the solitary user for its experiential form of negotiating central urban issues and which thus inherently forgoes any chance of fostering a sense of community can ever be truly subversive. Although extremely advanced at the time conceptually and in the programming of the interface, in its implied optimism about the liberating potentials of hypertext, the work in retrospect seems characteristic of the media-historical moment of its origin in 2002/2003. Klein himself in an essay written in 2007 but only published in 2017, states that "[f]or media narratives, I have lost my faith in chance techniques, in hypertext, in neo-minimalism, in clicking and clacking to your own adventure …" (2019b, 260f.; open-ended sentence in original).[36] What the digital format allows for in unique ways, however, is the suggestive visualisation of urban layers as implied in the title of *Bleeding Through: Layers of Los Angeles 1920–1986.*

Urban Layers: Memory, Superposition, Archive

In *Bleeding Through*, the changes in twentieth-century Los Angeles are rendered in a fascinating if oblique way in the frequent pairings of an old photograph and a recent one taken from exactly the same angle; some of these are made to blend into one another in fascinating overlay montage.[37] Thus, there is a pair of photos taken on the corner of Spring and Main Street in the 1920s and today, in which a shop sign "D.W. Wong Co. Chinese Herbs" disappears and a billboard advertising Green River Bourbon morphs into a billboard advertising a $7,000,000 lottery draw in Spanish (cf. DVD 1:2). In another of these morphs, juxtaposing 1941 Main Street with a contemporary image, "Fond's Pants Shop" on 655 Main Street (with "Ben's Barber Shop" and "Adams Radios & Appliances" next to it) turns into "Dongyang Machine Co." (cf. DVD 1:3). A further morph overlays a 1943 image of City Hall as clearly the tallest building among a few small shops in small two-storey buildings with a modern image of City Hall surrounded by anonymous corporate glass-and-steel blocks; yet another pair of photographs morphs the area around the South Hill Street funicular "Angels Flight", with buildings around six floors in height, into the present-day high-rise towers of downtown.

This representation of urban layers and their superimposition and interpenetration strongly suggests Benjamin's notion of "superposition". Given the radical changes in twentieth-century Los Angeles, in which older layers of the city were frequently "leveled, virtually without a trace" (Klein 2008, 97), Benjamin is a strong presence in the text (cf. Klein 2019a), although he is not explicitly mentioned in *Bleeding Through*. In its major source, *The History of Forgetting*, however, Benjamin is explicitly referred to several times.[38] The book even includes a six-page speculative piece, "Noir as the Ruins of the Left" (233–240), in which

> Benjamin does not commit suicide; instead, he takes a boat to New York and winds up among the German emigrés. Being too much of a scholar of the city streets, he elects not to live in the Pacific Palisades, not to bow at the feet of Thomas Mann […] Benjamin moves instead to Boyle Heights […] [He writes] fifty pages of notes for a Los Angeles *Passagenwerk*, nothing as elaborate as what Benjamin planned to write on the Parisian arcades.
>
> (Klein 2008, 233–235)

Thus, if *The History of Forgetting* provided an archaeology of twentieth-century LA as the *Arcades Project* did for nineteenth-century Paris, then

Bleeding Through in its non-linear presentation of a broad range of materials even in terms of form approximates Benjamin's representational strategies in the *Arcades Project*, if in an early twenty-first-century format. In this vein, the overlay montages as arguably one of the most suggestive features of *Bleeding Through* simulate the "interpenetration and superposed transparency" of different temporal layers that Benjamin refers to as "superposition" (546). The argument both *The History of Forgetting* – explicitly – and *Bleeding Through* – implicitly – make is that even layers that are gone "without a trace" (Klein 2008, 97) matter to the city because they matter to the people who continue to live there and who do remember.

This memorial potential of Klein's medial configuration of the city is particularly due to its hypertextual structure. In order to conceptualise this archival and memorial function of literary and cultural production, one might draw on a conception that shares the exact media-historical moment of *Bleeding Through*, namely Moritz Baßler's notion of the archive (2003/2005).[39] Baßler defines the archive as follows:

> We will use the term archive to designate [...] the sum of all texts of a culture available for an analysis. In the archive, these texts are accessible without being hierarchized. The archive is a corpus of texts. Within this corpus, passages equivalent to each other can be marked with a search request, as it were. These passages form an intertextual *structure of equivalence.*
>
> (196; my translation)

Following George P. Landow's notion of a "convergence of contemporary critical theory and technology" (subtitle), Baßler then suggests that this theory of textuality, of intertextuality and of text–context relations might quite literally be translated into a methodology of contextualising cultural analysis based on data-processing technology (cf. 294). Thus, he refers to the cultural archive in the sense of such a totality of available texts as a "full-text database" (Baßler 293; my translation) accessible by means of search requests and organised in the manner of a hypertext. Indeed, Baßler's entire terminology and methodology suggest a view of the cultural archive as the collection of heterogeneous and not necessarily contemporary texts in a synchronic, non-hierarchically ordered hypertextual database. This 'archive', it is easy to see, will fulfil an important function in maintaining and shaping cultural memory. This notion, tied as it seems to a specific media-historical and technological moment, appears to be literalised in *Bleeding Through*.

In sum, both "The Waste Land" and *Bleeding Through* function as structural and functional models of urban complexity. However, spatial and temporal structures latent in "The Waste Land" are flaunted in *Bleeding Through*: Spatially, Eliot's proto-hypertextual, nodal structures serving to represent the non-linearity of urban environments become Klein's fully hypertextual structures. Temporally, where "The Waste Land" uses layered intertextual patterns to suggest "the presence of the past" and the "simultaneous existence"

(Eliot 1975, 38) of different urban layers in a form that *functionally* simulates what Benjamin calls "superposition", *Bleeding Through* uses the digital medium to *literalise* Benjamin's notion of "superposition" in a form of overlay montage to represent the interpenetration of these layers.

Notes

1 For a survey of literary strategies of textual urban simulation see Chapter 2.
2 The notion of the city as a text to be read appears to have originated with Ludwig Börne's *Schilderungen aus Paris* (1822–1824); for approaches to 'reading' the city, cf. also Alber; Eco; and Gottdiener/Lagopoulos; for an insightful collection of essays, cf. Hassenpflug/Giersig/Stratmann; for an application, cf. Hassenpflug 2010.
3 It is hardly a coincidence that "The Waste Land" has prompted numerous hypertext versions on the web, allowing readers to read the text and the numerous intertexts side by side.
4 We can thus speak of the transnational migration of the *flâneur* sensibility, with a direct lineage from Poe's "The Man of the Crowd", set, interestingly, in London, via Baudelaire, who not only translated Poe but also saw him as a major influence, to transatlantic Eliot on the one hand and to Benjamin's deeply Francophile *Arcades Project* on the other hand.
5 The fact that Tiresias appears virtually in the exact middle of the poem, line 218 of 434, adds to this significance.
6 The German original reads: "absolutistisch auf die Gegenwart bezogen [...] ein Wahrnehmungsraum geometrischer Ordnung und funktionaler Trennungen" [Corbusier] vs. "[ein] Gedächtnis- und Bild-Raum einander überlagernder und durchdringender Zeiten und Zeit-Räume" [Breton] (Brüggemann 595).
7 For an excellent recent discussion of the urban palimpsest, cf. Mattheis; for various aspects of the 'city as palimpsest' notion, cf. Assmann; Butor; Freud 16–18; Harvey 66; Hassenpflug 2006, 2011; Huyssen; Martindale 1995; Sharpe/Wallock 9; Suttles.
8 This passage is also cited in Bénézet 56.
9 From among the innumerable studies cf. for instance Davis; Fulton; Klein 2008; Murphet; Ofner/Siefen; Scott/Soja; Soja 1996a, 1996b and 2000.
10 Largely written by Klein and programmed by Rosemary Comella and Andreas Kratky, it was co-produced by The Labyrinth Project at the Annenberg Center for Communication at the University of Southern California and the ZKM – Zentrum für Kunst und Medien – Karlsruhe.
11 References to the novella, where this source is not clear, will be abbreviated BT, references to the DVD will be given by tier and chapter.
12 For the connections between Molly's story and the material on the cultural history of LA cf. also the additional texts in the *Bleeding Through* booklet by Klein's collaborators on the project, Comella 59; Kinder 54f.; Kratky 60; Shaw 52.
13 Klein's collaborator Rosemary Comella calls it "a sort of stream-of-consciousness interactive bricolage-documentary overlaying a fictionalized story based on a real person" (59).
14 Though a digital database narrative like *Bleeding Through* would now, in the year 2020, almost certainly be set up as a website, the fact that it was placed on a DVD in 2003 only matters to my argument insofar as a DVD is essentially 'complete' and cannot be added to, whereas a web-based presentation would potentially be enlarged and built upon, possibly even in a curated form with further materials being supplied by users.

15 In his "Outline" in the "Introduction", Klein sets out his plan for the book as follows: "In the chapters that follow (Part I), I will examine the map of what is left out in downtown Los Angeles, how urban myths (social imaginaries) have been used as public policy. In the second part, I present a docu-novel, (or novella) based on Vietnamese immigrants who live in areas affected by these policies. In the third part, I present docufables from other residents in these communities, particularly about how their memories are affected by public traumas: drive-by shootings, racist neglect, policies toward immigrants, the Uprising of 1992, and so on. And in the final parts, I examine how literature and other media use techniques of the 'unreliable narrator,' and how the corporate uses of 'unreliable' memory are transforming the cultures of Los Angeles" (2008, 17).

16 Klein also refers to the "policy of shutting out downtown to non-whites [...] since the 1920s" (2008, 132).

17 "Unreliable Narrators" is also the title of a chapter in the novella (BT 26–34).

18 Cf. also Klein 2008, 7: "There are clear signs that both critical theory and cultural studies have generated what amounts to a new category of literature (as yet unnamed). What names there are sound a bit early in the cycle right now, clearly not what this (genre?) might be called ten years from now: docu-novels, 'mockumentaries', false autobiographies, public autobiography; 'faction'; phonebooks or chatlines as variations of personal essay; public autobiography; 'witnessing' [...] historiographic metafiction. I would rather not add more labels. Instead, I'll stick to the term 'history'. That is problematic and fictive enough already".

19 Elsewhere in the "Introduction", he refers to the effect of his strategies of representation in the book as those of "digital simulations", "special effects, a morphing programme in slo-mo, when the simulation is naked, when the tiger is obviously three frames away from turning human" (16). This morphing of one image into the other is precisely one of the most impressive features of *Bleeding Through*.

20 On the other hand, establishing a connection between the contextual material on Molly's story on the DVD and *The History of Forgetting*, the narrator of the novella comments on "numerous characters in the background [of Molly's story] who may show up, but certainly will appear in future volumes of *The History of Forgetting*" (29; cf. also 32).

21 The "preface" on the DVD, readable above a vintage photograph of downtown LA with City Hall still by far the tallest building, similarly makes clear the central principle of this "cinematic novel archive" (Klein 2001, 453) and already highlights its major concerns: "An elderly woman living near downtown has lost the ability to distinguish day from night. Rumors suggest that decades ago, she had her second husband murdered. When asked, she indicates, quite cheerfully, that she has decided to forget all that: 'I lose a few years.' Three miles around where she is standing, more people have been 'murdered' in famous crime films than anywhere else in the world. Imaginary murders clog the roof gutters. They hide beneath coats of paint. But in fact, the neighborhoods have seen something quite different than movie murders; a constant adjustment to Latinos, Japanese, Filipinos, Jews, Evangelicals, Chinese. What's more, in the sixties, hundreds of buildings were bulldozed. And yet, pockets remain almost unchanged since 1940."

22 The novella refers to "290 murder films [...] shot no more than five minutes from Molly's house" (BT 31). The narrator later states that "[s]ince the Seventies, murders have been relocated a few blocks west, because gunfire looks more ironic underneath the L.A. skyline at night, seen best from the hills in Temple-Beaudry" (BT 37).

23 For this cf. Comella's short essay on the "making of" *Bleeding Through*; cf. especially 58.
24 The re-shot sequences of films such as *Falling Down*, *Heat*, *Training Day*, *Chinatown*, *The Last Boy Scout*, *T-Men*, *Omega Man*, *DOA*, *To Live and Die in L.A.* are frequently iconic scenes with the downtown towers looming in the background. In addition, this section also features maps of LA pointing out key locations used in these films.
25 The narrator of the novella (whom one is likely to have identified as "Norman Klein") refers to his materials as follows: "I have about a thousand photographs and newspaper articles, over two hundred relevant movies on file, and over twenty interviews, along with hours of interviews with Norman Klein; and hundreds of pages of text" (27; cf. also 33, 38, 42, 43). The narrator comments on the way the documentary is to be perceived: "I turned toward my research on Molly's life, as if I could edit her sensations into a story that was symphonic in some way, or contrapuntal [...] I could gather data for Molly's story, and embed it like bots under the skin: newspaper clippings, historical photographs, and patches of interviews. Then I could assemble my assets into a vast database, for a search engine that could be selected according to the senses" (BT 11).
26 In his insert narrative accompanying the DVD preface, Klein refers to a family of "Latino's renting downstairs" in Molly's house.
27 On the discourse of crisis and the frequently disastrous consequences of large-scale restructuring plans in LA cf. also Soja 1996a.
28 For the concept of metanarrative as distinct from metafiction cf. Fludernik; Nünning.
29 For a discussion of these tendencies in recent documentaries cf. for instance Aitken; Hohenberger; Nichols.
30 I am aware, of course, that the tradition especially of British cultural studies has long pointed out the viewer's active role in the constitution of meaning of TV, film and other forms of popular culture; for a discussion of the productive role of the viewer cf. especially Winter. Nonetheless, the constant need for active manipulation and the flaunted non-linear and hypertextual nature of the programme in contrast to the reception of even the most experimental, fragmentary, 'postmodern' – but ultimately still 'fixed and invariable' – documentary film is bound to have consequences for the constitution of meaning.
31 Cf. my discussion of the media-historical moment of 2003 and the optimism about the potentials of digital formats in this chapter.
32 "Future narrative" is a term coined by literary scholar Christoph Bode (Bode/Dietrich). The present outline is strongly indebted to the introduction to Bode/Dietrich.
33 For a discussion of the rhizomatic nature of hypertext along the lines of these characteristics, cf. Burnett.
34 Bénézet's allegedly original coinage of the term "database narrative" and her claim to harmonise what were previously regarded as the incompatible formats of narrative and of database (cf. 56f.) are hardly as original as she claims – she here merely follows Marsha Kinder's essay "Bleeding Through Database Fiction" which already attempts a synthesis based on her reading of *Bleeding Through: Layers of Los Angeles 1920–1986* (cf. especially 54). Curiously, much of what Bénézet somewhat pretentiously presents as the results of "[her] analysis" (63) is explicitly stated in Klein's text or the accompanying essays or is blatantly obvious anyway: "There are many reasons that may have led Klein and his team to privilege a recombinant

poetics. My analysis suggests that the presentation of an openly multifaceted, critical, and self-reflexive creation was one important motivation" (63).

35 I discuss activist scholarship and its dual function as descriptive model *of* and prescriptive model *for* urban development in more detail in Chapter 5.

36 In a laudatory 2003 review of *Bleeding Through*, Helfand (n.p.) insightfully commented on the "digital revolution's promise of new literary forms" and the "brief blossom and fade [of the 'experiments in online interactive fiction']" and – speaking of the "many unfulfilled dreams" of the genre, regards *Bleeding Through* as living up to the promises of the form's technological possibilities. For analyses of the technological and literary implications of the digital form and their repercussions in literary studies, cf. especially the classic studies by Aarseth; Burnett; Ensslin; Gaggi; Hayles; Landow; McGann; or Sloane. Most of these studies date from the early 1990s to the years shortly after 2003.

37 For the use of such techniques in city films, particularly in Pat O'Neill's LA film *Water and Power* (1989) cf. MacDonald 232–234.

38 It may be interesting to note that, although it is centrally concerned with urban layers, the term "palimpsest" is not used a single time in the entire volume of *The History of Forgetting*. For a differentiation between palimpsest and superposition, cf. Chapter 4.

39 This was developed in a postdoctoral project (*Habilitation*) completed in 2003 and published as a monograph in 2005.

References

Aarseth, Espen J. *Cybertext: Perspectives on Ergodic Literature*. Baltimore, London: Johns Hopkins University Press, 1997.

Aitken, Ian, ed. *Encyclopedia of the Documentary Film*. New York: Routledge, 2005.

Alber, Reinhold. *New York Street Reading – Die Stadt als beschrifteter Raum: Dokumentation von Schriftzeichen und Schriftmedien im Straßenraum und Untersuchung ihrer stadträumlichen Bedeutung am Beispiel New York*. Tübingen: Self-published, 1997.

Assmann, Aleida. "Geschichte findet Stadt." *Kommunikation – Gedächtnis – Raum: Kulturwissenschaften nach dem "Spatial Turn."* Ed. Moritz Csàky, Christoph Leitgeb. Bielefeld: transcript, 2009. 13–27.

Barrett, James. "The Waste Land: Collage, Hypertext, and the Nodes of Meaning." (2005). www.scribd.com/doc/9699678/The-Waste-Land-Collage-Hypertext-and-the-Nodes-of-Meaning.

Baßler, Moritz. *Die kulturpoetische Funktion und das Archiv: Eine literaturwissenschaftliche Text-Kontext-Theorie*. Tübingen: Francke, 2005.

Bénézet, Delphine. "Recombinant Poetics, Urban *Flânerie*, and Experimentation in the Database Narrative: *Bleeding Through: Layers of Los Angeles 1920–1986*." *Convergence: The International Journal of Research into New Media Technologies* 15.1 (2009): 55–74.

Benjamin, Walter. *The Arcades Project*. Trans. Howard Eiland, Kevin McLaughlin. Cambridge, MA: The Belknap Press of Harvard University Press, 1999.

Benjamin, Walter. *Das Passagen-Werk*. Ed. Rolf Tiedemann. Frankfurt/Main: Suhrkamp, 1992. 2 vols.

Bode, Christoph, Rainer Dietrich. *Future Narratives: Theory, Poetics, and Media-Historical Moment*. Berlin, Boston: de Gruyter, 2013.

Bolle, Willi. "Geschichte." *Benjamins Begriffe*. Ed. Michael Opitz, Erdmut Wizisla. Frankfurt/Main: Suhrkamp, 2000. 2 vols. Vol. I, 399–442.

Bolle, Willi. "Die Metropole als Hypertext: Zur netzhaften Essaystik in Walter Benjamins 'Passagen-Projekt'." *German Politics & Society* 23.1 (2005): 88–101.

Bolle, Willi. "Metropole & Megastadt: Zur Ordnung des Wissens in Walter Benjamins *Passagen*." *Urbane Beobachtungen: Walter Benjamin und die neuen Städte*. Ed. Ralph Buchenhorst, Miguel Vedda. Bielefeld: transcript, 2010. 17–51.

Bolter, Jay David. *Writing Space: Computers, Hypertext, and the Remediation of Print*. Mahwah: Lawrence Erlbaum, [2]2001.

Bolter, Jay David. *Writing Space: The Computer, Hypertext, and the History of Writing*. Hillsdale: Lawrence Erlbaum, 1991.

Bowen, John. "The Politics of Redemption: Eliot and Benjamin." *The Waste Land*. Ed. Tony Davies, Nigel Wood. Buckingham: Open University Press, 1994. 31–54.

Bradbury, Malcolm. "The Cities of Modernism." *Modernism: 1890–1930*. Ed. Malcolm Bradbury, James McFarlane. New York: Pelican, 1976. 96–104.

Brüggemann, Heinz. "Passagen." *Benjamins Begriffe*. Ed. Michael Opitz, Erdmut Wizisla. Frankfurt/Main: Suhrkamp, 2000. 2 vols. Vol. II, 573–618.

Burnett, Kathleen. "Toward a Theory of Hypertextual Design." *Postmodern Culture* 3.2 (1993). https://muse.jhu.edu/article/27387.

Butor, Michel. "Die Stadt als Text." *Perspektiven metropolitaner Kultur*. Ed. Ursula Keller. Frankfurt/Main: Suhrkamp, 2000. 169–178.

Comella, Rosemary. "Simultaneous Distraction: The Making of *Bleeding Through: Layers of Los Angeles 1920–1986*." Norman M. Klein, Rosemary Comella, Andreas Kratky. *Bleeding Through: Layers of Los Angeles 1920–1986* [DVD and Book]. Karlsruhe: ZKM digital arts edition, 2003. 56–59.

Coyle, Michael. "'Fishing, with the arid plain behind me': Difficulty, Deferral, and Form in *The Waste Land*." *A Companion to T.S. Eliot*. Ed. David E. Chinitz. Chichester: Wiley-Blackwell, 2009. 157–167.

Davis, Mike. *City of Quartz: Excavating the Future in Los Angeles*. Brooklyn: Verso, 2006.

Day, Robert A. "The 'City Man' in *The Waste Land*: The Geography of Reminiscence." *PMLA* 80.3 (1965): 285–291.

Deleuze, Gilles, Felix Guattari. "Introduction: Rhizome." *A Thousand Plateaus*. Trans. Brian Massumi. London, New York: Continuum, 2004 [[1]1987]. Vol. 2 of *Capitalism and Schizophrenia*. 2 vols. 1972–1980. 3–28. [Trans. of *Mille Plateaux*. Paris: Editions de Minuit, 1980].

Denham, Sir John. "Coopers Hill [Draft III]" [1642]. *Expans'd Hieroglyphicks: A Critical Edition of Sir John Denham's* Coopers Hill. Ed. Brendan O Hehir. Berkeley: University of California Press, 1969. 109–134.

Derrida, Jacques. *Positions*. Paris: Les Editions de Minuit, 1972.

Dillon, Sarah. *The Palimpsest: Literature, Criticism, Theory*. New York: Continuum, 2007.

Eco, Umberto. "Function and Sign: The Semiotics of Architecture." *Signs, Symbols, and Architecture*. Ed. Geoffrey Broadbent, Richard Bunt, Charles Jencks. Chichester: Wiley, 1980. 11–69.

Eliot, T.S. "Burnt Norton" [1935]. Eliot. *Collected Poems: 1909–1962*. London: Faber & Faber, 1974a. 189–195.

Eliot, T.S. "Tradition and the Individual Talent" [1919]. *Selected Prose of T.S. Eliot*. Ed. Frank Kermode. London: Faber & Faber, 1975. 37–44.

Eliot, T.S. "The Waste Land" [1922]. Eliot. *Collected Poems: 1909–1962*. London: Faber & Faber, 1974b. 61–86.

Ensslin, Astrid. *Canonising Hypertext: Explorations and Constructions*. London: Continuum, 2007.

Fludernik, Monika. "Metanarrative and Metafictional Commentary." *Poetica* 35 (2003): 1–39.

Freud, Sigmund. *Civilization and Its Discontents*. Trans. Peter Gay. New York: Norton, 1984.

Fulton, William. *The Reluctant Metropolis: The Politics of Urban Growth in Los Angeles*. Baltimore: Johns Hopkins University Press, 2001.

Gaggi, Silvio. *From Text to Hypertext: Decentering the Subject in Fiction, Film, the Visual Arts, and Electronic Media*. Philadelphia: University of Pennsylvania Press, 1997.

Gassenmeier, Michael. *Londondichtung als Politik: Texte und Kontexte der City Poetry von der Restauration bis zum Ende der Walpole-Ära*. Tübingen: Niemeyer, 1989.

Gordon, Lyndall. *Eliot's Early Years*. Oxford: Oxford University Press, 1977.

Gottdiener, Mark, Alexandros Ph. Lagopoulos, eds. *The City and the Sign: An Introduction to Urban Semiotics*. New York: Columbia University Press, 1986.

Gray, Will. "Mashup, Hypertext, and the Future of *The Waste Land*." *The Waste Land at 90: A Retrospective*. Ed. Joe Moffet. Amsterdam: Rodopi, 2011. 227–244.

Gurr, Jens Martin. "The Modernist Poetics of Urban Memory and the Structural Analogies between 'City' and 'Text': *The Waste Land* and Benjamin's *Arcades Project*." *Recovery and Transgression: Memory in American Poetry*. Ed. Kornelia Freitag. Newcastle: Cambridge Scholars Publishing, 2015. 21–37.

Harvey, David. *The Condition of Postmodernity: An Inquiry into the Origins of Cultural Change*. Oxford: Blackwell, 1989.

Hassenpflug, Dieter. "Once Again: Can Urban Space be Read?" *Reading the City: Developing Urban Hermeneutics/Stadt lesen: Beiträge zu einer urbanen Hermeneutik*. Ed. Dieter Hassenpflug, Nico Giersig, Bernhard Stratmann. Weimar: Verlag der Bauhaus-Universität, 2011. 49–58.

Hassenpflug, Dieter. *The Urban Code of China*. Basel: Birkhäuser, 2010.

Hassenpflug, Dieter. "Walter Benjamin und die Traumseite der Stadt." Hassenpflug. *Reflexive Urbanistik: Reden und Aufsätze zur europäischen Stadt*. Weimar: Verlag der Bauhaus-Universität, 2006. 7–22.

Hassenpflug, Dieter, Nico Giersig, Bernhard Stratmann, eds. *Reading the City: Developing Urban Hermeneutics/Stadt lesen: Beiträge zu einer urbanen Hermeneutik*. Weimar: Verlag der Bauhaus-Universität, 2011.

Hayles, N. Katherine. *Electronic Literature: New Horizons for the Literary*. Notre Dame: University of Notre Dame Press, 2008.

Helfand, Glen. "Read Only Memory: A New Interactive DVD Mines Provocative Layers of Storytelling." *San Francisco Chronicle*, 18 September 2003. www.sfgate.com/news/article/Read-Only-Memory-A-new-interactive-DVD-mines-2588147.php.

Hohenberger, Eva, ed. *Bilder des Wirklichen: Texte zur Theorie des Dokumentarfilms*. Berlin: Vorwerk 8, ^{3}2006.

Huyssen, Andreas. *Present Pasts: Urban Palimpsests and the Politics of Memory*. Palo Alto: Stanford University Press, 2003.

Johnston, John H. *The Poet and the City: A Study in Urban Perspectives*. Athens, GA: University of Georgia Press, 1984.

Kinder, Marsha. "Bleeding Through: Database Fiction." Norman M. Klein, Rosemary Comella, Andreas Kratky. *Bleeding Through: Layers of Los Angeles 1920–1986* [DVD and Book]. Karlsruhe: ZKM digital arts edition, 2003. 53–55.

Klein, Norman M. "Absences, Scripted Spaces and the Urban Imaginary: Unlikely Models for the City in the Twenty-First Century." *Die Stadt als Event: Zur Konstruktion Urbaner Erlebnisräume*. Ed. Regina Bittner. Frankfurt/Main: Campus, 2001. 450–454.

Klein, Norman M. "Bleeding Through." Norman M. Klein, Rosemary Comella, Andreas Kratky. *Bleeding Through: Layers of Los Angeles 1920–1986* [DVD and Book]. Karlsruhe: ZKM digital arts edition, 2003. 7–44.

Klein, Norman M. *The History of Forgetting: Los Angeles and the Erasure of Memory* [1997]. New York: Verso, 2008.

Klein, Norman M. "Personal Conversation with J.M. Gurr" [on *Bleeding Through and Walter Benjamin*]. 8 June 2019a.

Klein, Norman M. "Spaces Between: Traveling Through Bleeds, Apertures, and Wormholes Inside the Database Novel" [2007]. *Tales of the Floating Class: Writings 1982–2017: Essays and Fictions on Globalization and Neo-Feudalism*. Los Angeles: Golden Spike Press, 2019b. 257–280.

Klein, Norman M. "Staging Murders: The Social Imaginary, Film, and the City." *Wide Angle* 20.3 (1998): 85–96.

Klein, Norman M., Rosemary Comella, Andreas Kratky. *Bleeding Through: Layers of Los Angeles 1920–1986* [DVD and Book]. Karlsruhe: ZKM digital arts edition, 2003.

Kranz, Isabel. *Raumgewordene Vergangenheit: Walter Benjamins Poetologie der Geschichte*. Munich: Fink, 2011.

Kratky, Andreas. "How to Navigate Forgetting." Norman M. Klein, Rosemary Comella, Andreas Kratky. *Bleeding Through: Layers of Los Angeles 1920–1986* [DVD and Book]. Karlsruhe: ZKM digital arts edition, 2003. 60–61.

Lamos, Colleen. *Deviant Modernism: Sexual and Textual Errancy in T.S Eliot, James Joyce, and Marcel Proust*. Cambridge: Cambridge University Press, 1998.

Landow, George P. *Hypertext 3.0: Critical Theory and New Media in an Era of Globalization* [1992]. Baltimore: Johns Hopkins University Press, 2006.

Long, Michael. "Eliot, Pound, Joyce: Unreal City." *Unreal City: Urban Experience in Modern European Literature and Art*. Ed. Edward Timms, David Kelley. Manchester: Manchester University Press, 1985. 144–157.

Lynch, Kevin. *The Image of the City*. Cambridge, MA: MIT Press, 1960.

MacDonald, Scott. "Ten+ (Alternative) Films about American Cities." *The ISLE Reader: Ecocriticism, 1993–2003*. Ed. Michael P. Branch, Scott Slovic. Athens, GA: University of Georgia Press, 2003. 217–239.

Martindale, Charles. "Ruins of Rome: T.S. Eliot and the Presence of the Past." *Arion* 3.2–3 (1995): 102–140.

Martindale, Charles. *Redeeming the Text: Latin Poetry and the Hermeneutics of Reception*. Cambridge: Cambridge University Press, 1993.

Mattheis, Lena. *Translocal Narratability in Contemporary Anglophone Fiction*. Dissertation manuscript, University of Duisburg-Essen, 2019.

Mattheis, Lena, Jens Martin Gurr. "Superpositions: A Typology of Spatiotemporal Layerings in Buried Cities." *Buried Cities*. Special Issue of *Literary Geographies* (forthcoming).

McGann, Jerome. *Radiant Textuality: Literature After the World Wide Web*. New York: Palgrave Macmillan, 2001.

McLaughlin, Joseph. *Writing the Urban Jungle: Reading Empire in London from Doyle to Eliot*. Charlottesville: University Press of Virginia, 2000.

Mumford, Lewis. *The City in History: Its Origins, its Transformations, and its Prospects*. London: Secker & Warburg, 1961.

Murphet, Julian. *Literature and Race in Los Angeles*. Cambridge, New York: Cambridge University Press, 2001.

Nichols, Bill. *Representing Reality: Issues and Concepts in Documentary*. Bloomington: Indiana University Press, 1991.

Nünning, Ansgar. "On Metanarrative: Towards a Definition, a Typology, and an Outline of the Functions of Metanarrative Commentary." *The Dynamics of Narrative Form: Studies in Anglo-American Narratology*. Ed. John Pier. Berlin, New York: de Gruyter, 2005. 11–58.

Ofner, Astrid, Claudia Siefen, eds. *Los Angeles: Eine Stadt im Film/A City on Film: Eine Retrospektive der Viennale und des Österreichischen Filmmuseums, 5. Oktober bis 5. November 2008*. Marburg: Schüren, 2008.

Park, Robert E. "The City: Suggestions for the Investigation of Human Behavior in the City Environment." *The American Journal of Sociology* 20.5 (1915): 577–612.

Perloff, Marjorie. *Unoriginal Genius: Poetry by Other Means in the New Century*. Chicago: University of Chicago Press, 2010.

Phillips, Stephen. "A Nightmare of London." Phillips. *Poems and Dramas*. London: Lane, 1913. 49.

Reeves, Gareth. *T.S. Eliot: A Virgilian Poet*. Houndmills: Palgrave Macmillan, 1999.

Scott, Allen J., Edward W. Soja, eds. *The City, Los Angeles and Urban Theory at the End of the Twentieth Century*. Berkeley: University of California Press, 1997.

Sharpe, William, Leonard Wallock. "From 'Great Town' to 'Nonplace Urban Realm': Reading the Modern City." *Visions of the Modern City: Essays in History, Art, and Literature*. Ed. Sharpe, Wallock. Baltimore: Johns Hopkins University Press, 1987. 1–50.

Shaw, Jeffrey. "The Back Story: Reformulating Narrative Practice." Norman M. Klein, Rosemary Comella, Andreas Kratky. *Bleeding Through: Layers of Los Angeles 1920–1986* [DVD and Book]. Karlsruhe: ZKM digital arts edition, 2003. 52.

Shelley, Percy Bysshe. "Peter Bell the Third." *The Complete Poetical Works*. Ed. Thomas Hutchinson, rev. G.M. Matthews. Oxford: Oxford University Press, 1970. 346–361.

Simmel, Georg. "The Metropolis and Mental Life" [1903]. *The City Cultures Reader*. Ed. Malcolm Miles, Tim Hall, Iain Borden. London: Routledge, [2]2004. 12–19.

Sloane, Sarah. *Digital Fictions: Storytelling in a Material World*. Stamford, CT: Ablex Publishing, 2000.

Soja, Edward W. "Exopolis: The Restructuring of Urban Form." Soja. *Postmetropolis*. Oxford: Blackwell, 2000. 233–263.

Soja, Edward W. "Los Angeles, 1965–1992: From Crisis-Generated Restructuring to Restructuring-Generated Crisis." *The City, Los Angeles and Urban Theory at the End of the Twentieth Century*. Ed. Allen J. Scott, Edward W. Soja. Berkeley: University of California Press, 1996a. 426–462.

Soja, Edward W. *Thirdspace: Journeys to Los Angeles and Other Real-And-Imagined Places*. Oxford: Blackwell, 1996b.

Srubar, Ilja. "Zur Formierung des soziologischen Blickes durch die Großstadtwahrnehmung." *Die Großstadt als "Text."* Ed. Manfred Smuda. Munich: Fink, 1992. 37–52.

Suttles, Gerald D. "The Cumulative Texture of Local Urban Culture." *American Journal of Sociology* 90.2 (1984): 283–304.

Teske, Doris. *Die Vertextung der Megalopolis: London im Spiel postmoderner Texte*. Trier: WVT, 1999.

Thomson, James. "The City of Dreadful Night." Thomson. *The City of Dreadful Night and Other Poems*. London: Reeves and Turner, 1880. 1–55.

Thormählen, Marianne. *The Waste Land: A Fragmentary Wholeness*. Lund: CWK Gleerup, 1978.

Versluys, Kristiaan. *The Poet in the City: Chapters in the Development of Urban Poetry in Europe and the United States (1800–1930)*. Tübingen: Narr, 1987.

Williams, Raymond. "The Metropolis and the Emergence of Modernism." *Unreal City: Urban Experience in Modern European Literature and Art*. Ed. Edward Timms, David Kelley. Manchester: Manchester University Press, 1985. 13–24.

Winter, Rainer. *Der produktive Zuschauer: Medienaneignung als kultureller und ästhetischer Prozess*. Munich: Quintessenz, 1995.

Wohlfahrt, Irving. "Die Passagenarbeit." *Benjamin-Handbuch: Leben – Werk – Wirkung*. Ed. Burkhardt Lindner. Stuttgart: Metzler, 2006. 251–274.

Wolfreys, Julian. "'Concatenated words from which the sense seemed gone': *The Waste Land*." Wolfreys. *Writing London 3: Inventions of the City*. London: Palgrave, 2007. 191–244.

Wordsworth, William. *The Prelude 1799, 1805, 1850*. Ed. Jonathan Wordsworth, M.H. Abrams, Stephen Gill. New York: Norton, 1979.

Yang, Carol L. "*The Waste Land* and the Virtual City." *The Waste Land at 90: A Retrospective*. Ed. Joe Moffet. Amsterdam: Rodopi, 2011. 187–210.

4 Reversing Perspectives

Urban Memory in Built and Literary Post-Industrial Cities[*]

Introduction: A Post-Industrial Palimpsest?

In 1988, 26 years after the Opel car plant (for decades the largest employer in the city of Bochum in Germany's long-time industrial heartland, the Ruhr region) opened in 1962, and 26 years before it closed in 2014, the following print ad appeared as part of an image campaign for the Ruhr region (cf. Figure 4.1).

While the caption, "Bochum macht auch ohne Kohle Kohle", puns on a double meaning of 'Kohle' as the German word for both 'coal' and, colloquially, 'money', thus stating that "Bochum also makes money without coal", the

Figure 4.1 "The past, the present and the future of Bochum" in a 1988 print ad.

Source: Motif from the image campaign "Ein starkes Stück Deutschland" commissioned by the Kommunalverband Ruhrgebiet, now Regionalverband Ruhr (KVR/RVR). Reprinted with permission of the RVR (KVR 64).

opening of the accompanying text reads: "This image is as symbolic as it is meaningful. The shaft tower reflected on the Opel stands for the past, the car for the present and the future of Bochum" (KVR 64; my translation).[1]

This image and the text strike a chord that will resonate through much of my discussion in this chapter. We can begin with a banal observation: To an observer in 1988, especially an observer who knew that the Opel plant was literally built on the site of a former coal mine, this image must indeed have seemed highly symbolic, suggesting a successful transformation from a city of coal to a city with a bright future in car manufacturing. However, it must have meant something very different to an observer in 2014, when the plant in Bochum closed. A very poignant image it must have been then. All I want to take from the ad at this point is the notion that an observer's knowledge of a site's previous functions or its later history makes a difference.

This chapter continues the investigation of urban layers and further explores the notions of palimpsest, superposition and rhizome and their analytical yield for literary urban studies, but it reverses perspectives in a double sense: It does not begin with the text, but with the city – here an urban region – and it attempts to apply the concepts outlined in the previous chapters – palimpsest, superposition, rhizome – first to physical sites and only then to literary texts representing them. In doing so, it seeks to address the question of how concepts from literary urban studies can help understand the real-world city. Second, it also asks to what extent such concepts – usually applied to 'old' European cities such as Rome, Berlin, London, Paris or St. Petersburg – also fit post-industrial cities.

The Ruhr region as a polycentric post-industrial region made up both of cities dating back to the Middle Ages (such as Dortmund and Essen) and of cities that only came into being as mining settlements in the nineteenth century (such as Oberhausen and Gelsenkirchen), lends itself to exploring further the connection between city and text and to demonstrating the ability of literary texts to represent the unique characteristics and specificities of a city or metropolitan region. If one takes criteria such as the size and population of a conurbation, its political and administrative function and role for the country as a whole, its administrative and economic structure (monocentric vs. polycentric) as well as – with polycentric regions – the relative size of the cities within the region or their degree of interconnection, then the Ruhr region is indeed unique among the world's conurbations (for a comprehensive recent account of the region, cf. Farrenkopf *et al.*): It neither contains the country's largest cities (like the Randstad in the Netherlands, which, with Amsterdam, Rotterdam, The Hague and Utrecht, politically, economically and in population size represents most of the country), nor is the Ruhr region dominated by one city (as is the case with the English Midlands, otherwise a partly comparable post-industrial region, dominated as it is by Birmingham as by far the largest city) – other differences could be pointed out to distinguish the region from any other conurbation in the world. What especially sets the Ruhr region apart from most post-industrial regions is the way it has handled deindustrialisation: Though long plagued by above-average unemployment and many of the social and economic problems of structural transformation, the Ruhr – in contrast to regions especially in Britain or the United States – has seen a remarkable long-term concerted effort of the national government, the state government of North Rhine-Westphalia and of the large industrial corporations and associations to manage the transition, to attempt to limit the social costs of structural transformation and to offer a perspective to employees in declining industries.[2] Moreover, structural transformation has been understood as a comprehensive effort also encompassing the built environment of cities. All in all, the transition has, despite its persisting problems, been fairly successful in comparison with other regions.

In thinking about what literary urban studies can contribute to an understanding of key issues here, the notion of the "knowledge of literature" (*sensu* Hörisch; cf. Chapter 1) may be helpful again. Especially with structurally and historically so unique a conurbation as the Ruhr region, a region with so much 'local colour', a type of modelling that privileges the specific as opposed to the quantifiable and the aggregate may yield insights otherwise unavailable. This time taking our cue from selected characteristic sites in the region, we may ask how established concepts work for them before inquiring into literary strategies that may do justice to the spatial and temporal complexities of the region.

This chapter first briefly discusses how the notion of the palimpsest can and cannot help an understanding of layers of memory in post-industrial regions and especially the Ruhr region. It then returns to Walter Benjamin's notion of "superposition" from the *Arcades Project*. I want to argue, and this may be somewhat counter-intuitive, that it lends itself especially to post-industrial regions, more so than the notion of the palimpsest. I want to illustrate this point by means of three sites in the Ruhr region and then want to trace it in two of the most ambitious literary texts on layers of the Ruhr region, Jürgen Link's *Bangemachen gilt nicht auf der Suche nach der Roten Ruhr-Armee* (2008) and Jörg Albrecht's *Anarchie in Ruhrstadt* (2014).

My approach in this chapter is thus comparable to what Bertrand Westphal (2011) has called "geocriticism", an analysis which prioritises not the individual text but a specific geographical site as it is represented in numerous texts from different periods, producing what Westphal calls "stratigraphic" accounts of these sites (141; cf. also Prieto 20f.; for related approaches cf. Tally; Prieto; and Finch). Thus, texts here still primarily function as models *of* the urban, though the primary interest here is with the individual site.[3]

Cities as Palimpsests: All Cities?

In discussions of the Ruhr region and its specificities, it seems that spatial relations are discussed far more than are temporal layers. Even where the titles of books suggest a *temporal* focus, they are often predominantly concerned with space. Thus, *Schichten einer Region* (2011), literally "Layers of a Region", surely one of the most important and impressive attempts at understanding the specificities of the region, by its title primarily suggests *temporal* layers. However, although the question of how the region reached its present-day form is often referred to, it is overwhelmingly concerned not with temporal layers but with spatial configurations. The subtitle, "Kartenstücke zur *räumlichen* Struktur des Ruhrgebiets" (my emphasis), "Maps on the *Spatial* Structure of the Ruhr Region", already makes this very clear. Similarly, we may take one of the most ambitious attempts at doing justice to the complexities of the region in fiction, Jürgen Link's 2008 novel *Bangemachen gilt nicht auf der Suche nach der Roten Ruhr-Armee: Eine Vorerinnerung*. The title and especially the subtitle "Eine Vorerinnerung", literally "a pre-recollection" or "a pre-memory", does suggest temporal layers – and the novel does very subtly engage with temporal layers, but at least in the reception of the book – and even in the author's own pronouncements on it – the focus has overwhelmingly been on the rhizomatic nature of the Ruhr region and thus on its *spatial* characteristics (cf. Heidemann; cf. also Ernst; Lachmann; Link 2011).

While there is no reason to criticise this tendency, this observation may serve as a point of departure for reflections on the representation of temporal layers in post-industrial cities. The suggestion in both cases, the scholarly study *Schichten einer Region* by Reicher *et al.* as well as Link's novel – and this is true of many more – seems to be that post-industrial regions have a history that is too short to be conceptualised in terms of the palimpsest. As a case in point, we may take Aleida Assmann's 2009 essay "Geschichte findet Stadt". When she suggests that "[f]or many European cities, the term 'palimpsest' imposes itself" (18),[4] the cities she mentions (Gdansk, Kaliningrad, Riga, Wrocław, Berlin) are all 'old' European cities, and a post-industrial city would look decidedly odd in this list. So, what about post-industrial cities?[5]

If a palimpsest in the literal sense is a piece of paper or parchment, which (in times when writing material was scarce) was written on more than once, in such a way that at least one erased older layer is (partly) legible – or can be made legible – underneath a later one, what does it mean to say – as is so common in urban studies – that cities are palimpsests? Many contemporary European cities, even ones that have been heavily bombed or have seen several successive phases of demolition and rebuilding, can be regarded as palimpsests if, for instance, an underlying medieval layout is still visible in the circular form of present-day roads around the city centre, in the location and shape of streets which may still trace a winding way around buildings long gone, or in the presence of churches from eight or more centuries ago, churches that might each in turn be seen as palimpsests if they have gone through various phases of enlargement, redesign and modernisation.

Take the case of the city of Essen, where the present-day layout of the city still follows the early nineteenth-century layout of the old city, which follows, in fact, the medieval layout of the city (cf. Figure 4.2).[6] Given this persistence of older layers, I here want to argue that – in contrast to a suggestion in many urban studies arguments – the notion of the palimpsest does also fit post-industrial cities, but that the palimpsest concept leaves a lot of things unaddressed.

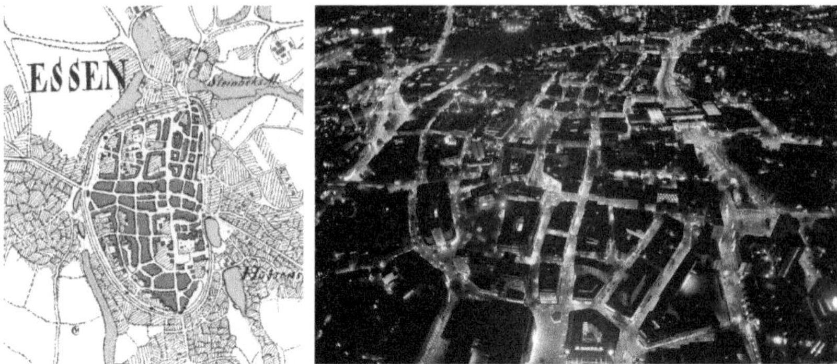

Figure 4.2 The inner city of Essen as a palimpsest – the small town centre in 1803 and the shape of the present-day inner city in an aerial photograph.

Source: Amt für Geoinformation, Vermessung und Kataster, Stadt Essen (4.2a); www.blossey.eu (4.2b).

Thus, for post-industrial cities with a long pre-industrial history, the notion of the palimpsest may work just as well as for any other city. However, what the notion of the palimpsest leaves out or at least does not fully do justice to, is the role of the observer, the role an observer's awareness of earlier layers, plays for an understanding of a specific site. In post-industrial cities with their numerous erasures, over-writes and radical redevelopments, these older layers are often not visibly 'present' as the concept of the palimpsest implies, which suggests that, while layers may no longer be legible, they are at least still visible or can be made visible again. This is where a more precise differentiation between the notion of the palimpsest and Benjamin's notion of "superposition" becomes helpful (for an initial discussion of "superposition", cf. Chapter 3).

Walter Benjamin and "Superposition"

What Benjamin allows us to do is to conceptualise the connection between memory and the built environment. Benjamin's notion of "superposition", the interpenetration of different layers of time and of an observer's awareness of their simultaneous co-presence in urban space, is particularly pertinent here (1999, 172, 418, 546, 854 *et passim*). If, as Fran Tonkiss has argued, "[t]he relationship of memory to space operates *somewhere* between the landmarks of the official city and the footfalls of the solitary subject" (120; my emphasis), it is the concept of "superposition" that allows us more precisely to locate and conceptualise this "somewhere". As we have seen, Benjamin defines "superposition" as "the interpenetrating and superposed transparency of the world of the flâneur" (1999, 546, 854).[7] Elsewhere, he then uses a truly wonderful phrasing that captures very precisely the importance of an observer's knowledge: " 'The colportage phenomenon of space' is the flâneur's basic experience. Thanks to this phenomenon, everything that has potentially taken place in this [space] is perceived simultaneously. Space winks at the flâneur: What do you think may have gone on here?" (Benjamin 1999, 418f.).[8]

Thus, "superposition" refers to both temporal layering and to the ability to perceive it. According to this understanding, different historical layers superimpose themselves onto the same space if only an observer is in the right state of mind to perceive them. It is important to note that this type of perception is possible even if the space no longer offers any points, traces or clues to which these layerings can be anchored. Thus, while a palimpsest would be expected physically to contain the different levels and to have them at least partially visible, the notion of "superposition" allows for a *remembered presence*: What matters is what an observer knows, remembers or associates with a site. The following passage from the *Arcades Project* in another characteristically Benjaminean formulation that is as poetic as it is incisive, makes clear the role of this knowledge to the perception of urban space:

> That anamnestic intoxication [and this is anamnesis in the medical sense of knowing about a pre-history, the pleasure, the intoxication of having these levels simultaneously present] in which the flâneur goes about the city not only feeds on the sensory data taking shape before his eyes but often possesses itself of abstract knowledge – indeed, of dead facts – as something experienced and lived through. This felt knowledge travels from one person to another, especially by word of mouth. But in the course of the nineteenth century [this refers to the literature on Paris, of course], it was also deposited in an immense literature [...] Wouldn't he, then, have necessarily felt the steep slope behind the church of Notre Dame de Lorette rise all the more insistently under his soles if he realized: here, at one time, after Paris had gotten its first omnibuses, the *cheval de renfort* was harnessed to the coach to reinforce the other two horses.[9]
>
> (1999, 417)

The past of a site does not necessarily have to be physically seen to be remembered and to inform an observer's perception.

We may ask, however, whether this notion of superposition *has* to be related to 'irrational' states like dream and intoxication (cf. Benjamin's argument that superposition is also the mode of perception characteristic of the "hashish eater" (1999, 841)): Brüggemann speaks of superposition as the "signature of a hallucinatory mode of perception" (584) – but does that have to be so? Can we not – more systematically than Dieter Hassenpflug (2006, 2011) has done – understand superposition as a method of urban analysis? As Brüggemann argues (cf. 592f.), this rationalisation is precisely what Benjamin himself was concerned with.[10]

For the urban planner and for anyone trying to understand the historical fabric of the city, "superposition", in addition to the involuntary perception of historical layers, can then also refer to a conscious approach or even 'technique'. Thus, the ability to perceive how an ensemble of modern buildings in its location and cubature fits into its environment of historical buildings and possibly even 'cites' a pre-war building that might have stood on the same plot – and thus the ability to perceive the continuing presence of the past in the palimpsestic layering of the built environment – is crucial for any planning effort in the same environment (cf. Hassenpflug 2011, 54).

Urban Layers: Selected Sites in the Ruhr Region

As we will see in my examples of selected sites in the Ruhr region, the connection between the built environment and layers of memory in post-industrial cities is not a mechanical one. We need to know what we are seeing to see it properly. The awareness of different levels of time is tied to a perceiving consciousness and what it knows. I here use three exemplary sites in the Ruhr region to discuss forms of layering before I turn to literary representations of layered urban memory. Let me begin with Mark 51°7,[11] the site of the former Opel plant in Bochum so poignantly referred to as "the future of Bochum" in my opening image from 1988 (cf. Figure 4.3).

The oldest layer on or near the site is Haus Laer, a mansion dating back to the early tenth century (~930) and up to the present day surrounded by meadows and farmland (cf. Figure 4.4). Tellingly, 'Laer' – also the name of the Bochum district Laer named after it – is from Old High German 'lahari', meaning 'meadow', which points to the fact that this was originally fertile agricultural land.

Figure 4.3 Mark 51°7, the site of the former Opel plant, in May 2020 with (from top to bottom) medieval Haus Laer, the new DHL logistics centre, the former Opel admin building and a remaining mine building of coal mine Dannenbaum.

Source: www.blossey.eu.

Figure 4.4 Haus Laer, a mansion partly dating back to the tenth century, adjacent to the Mark 51°7 site.

Source: J.M. Gurr (2019).

Figure 4.5 Former administration building and payroll office of coal mine Dannenbaum, now housing community centres and educational facilities.

Source: J.M. Gurr (2019).

Secondly, at least since the eighteenth century, this was also a mining site, known since the later nineteenth century as "Zeche Dannenbaum". The mine closed in 1958 during the first phase of the coal crisis. What is left today at the edge of the site is a former administration building including the former payroll office, which now houses community centres and welfare organisations (cf. Figure 4.5).

Historically the next layer is that of car manufacturing; as we saw earlier, the Opel plant opened in 1962 and closed in 2014. Today, Mark 51°7 is a major construction site (cf. Figure 4.6).

Virtually the only building that is left of the Opel plant is the former central administration building, now protected under conservation, which houses

Figure 4.6 The site of Mark 51°7 in October 2019 (the former Opel admin building is on the right).
Source: J.M. Gurr (2019).

offices and a number of high-tech and training institutions. Since 2017, the site has been home to a major DHL logistics hub and to several high-tech firms; Ruhr-University Bochum will have research facilities there.

If one now stands next to the former admin building of Zeche Dannenbaum and looks south-south-east, the view includes the remaining mining building, the former Opel admin building, the new DHL logistics centre and, in the distance, at least potentially Haus Laer (cf. Figure 4.7).

The overlay of infrastructures from different periods in this site is truly striking. Thus, when the closing of the Opel plant was imminent already, a 2013 report by the City of Bochum on impediments to redevelopment of the site stated:

> The site of the [Opel] plant I is traversed by the so-called Isabella adit [a drainage drift]. The pit water flowing out of this adit supplies the moat of Haus Laer. This water supply by means of the Isabella adit is secured by water rights. To secure the site's surface against sink-holes, the adit and the mining tunnels branching off from it would have to be filled, which would end the supply of the moat with pit water.[12]
>
> (Bürgerinformationssystem der Stadt Bochum; my translation)

Thus, in a curious assemblage of infrastructures characteristic of many post-industrial sites, the site of Mark 51°7 has an eighteenth-century mining adit running underneath the twentieth-century Opel plant and supplying the moat of a tenth-century medieval mansion – and twenty-first-century developers of the site have to take care to secure these mining infrastructures so they do not

Figure 4.7 View of Mark 51°7, mining building, Opel admin building and DHL logistics hub; Haus Laer is at least potentially visible behind the logistics building.
Source: J.M. Gurr (2019).

literally collapse underneath new developments on the site. This site, it seems, is a case where it makes perfect sense to speak of a palimpsest.

A second site in the Ruhr region that lends itself to exploring the suitability of the palimpsest concept is Herne Crange. This is the site of the Cranger Kirmes, one of the world's largest entertainment fairs going back to a fifteenth-century horse fair. The large fairground borders on the early twentieth-century industrial Rhine-Herne Canal, the eighteenth-century village of Alt-Crange and the fifteenth-century mansion of Haus Crange. On the site, there are the fenced-in remains of a shaft of former coal mine "Unser Fritz", named after Emperor Frederick III (cf. Figures 4.8a, b, c, d).

Looking east across the fairground in times outside the August fair (moving from foreground to background and from left to right), one sees in one view the fairground, the remains of shaft V of coal mine "Unser Fritz", the eighteenth-century village of Alt-Crange, the remains of fifteenth-century mansion Haus Crange and a number of twentieth- and twenty-first-century manufacturing and storage buildings at the back and to the right (cf. Figure 4.9).

It seems to me that the notion of the palimpsest has limited explanatory value here, because it leaves largely unclear how these layers overlap. There appears to be very little actual erasure, writing over and layering and little shining through or reminder of the old in the new. However, there is in fact one such reminder: The official mascot of the Crange Fair is pit horse "Fritz", miner's shirt and all, subtly or not so subtly and for eight Euros only reminding pleasure-seekers in the fair that this used to be the site of coal mine "Unser Fritz" (cf. Figure 4.10).

Figure 4.8 Fairground of Cranger Kirmes with adjacent Rhine-Herne Canal (4.8a); inserts (from top to bottom): fifteenth-century mansion Haus Crange (4.8b), eighteenth-century village of Alt-Crange (4.8c) and remains of a mining shaft (4.8d).

Source: www.blossey.eu (4.8a), J.M. Gurr (4.8b, c, d).

Figure 4.9 Fairground of Cranger Kirmes with different historical layers visible. Source: J.M. Gurr (2019).

Figure 4.10 Pit horse "Fritz", mascot of Crange Fair in traditional miner's shirt. Source: Stadtmarketing Herne GmbH.

Finally, if there was any doubt just how Benjaminesque the district of Wanne-Eickel in the city of Herne can be, one could take present-day Mozartstraße in Wanne, an early twentieth-century Art Nouveau residential street just off Bahnhofstraße, Wanne's main shopping street. This is a street that has seen more fashionable days, as its by no means unambitious architecture asserts (cf. Figure 4.11).

One may wonder, however, about the function of the pilasters and empty support capitals on the façades. In fact, present-day Mozartstraße used to be the Kaiserpassage – literally the Emperor's Arcade – and had an Art Nouveau cast-iron and glass roof until the late 1920s (cf. Figure 4.12).

Figure 4.11 Façades in present-day Mozartstraße in Herne.
Source: Gerd Biedermann (2020).

Figure 4.12 Kaiserpassage in Herne (now Mozartstraße), about 1910.
Source: Stadtarchiv Herne.

The glass roof was dismantled around 1928, because too much pigeon dirt and coal dust impossible ever to clean were soiling the glass roof and kept out too much light. What remained were the pillars and capitals and other roof supports. Figure 4.13 shows what the corner buildings at the entrance to the street look like today.

Therefore, if one happens to be a *flâneur*, a hashish eater or otherwise inclined to perceive layers of the urban, if, in Benjamin's inimitable wording, one feels that "space winks at [the observer], asking whatever may have happened here" or whatever may have been here, one may have a perception somewhat like the one suggested in Figure 4.14.

Here, too, it seems that the notion of the 'palimpsest' is far less meaningful than that of Benjamin's "superposition" with its implications of an observer's knowledge and a 'remembered presence'.

Figure 4.13 Corner buildings of present-day Mozartstraße in Herne.
Source: Gerd Biedermann (2020).

Figure 4.14 Overlay montage of present-day Mozartstraße with Kaiserpassage glass roof, suggesting Benjamin's notion of "superposition".
Source: Gerd Biedermann, Stadtarchiv Herne (original images); overlay montage: Daniel Bläser, www.dbgrafik.de.

Layered Memory in Ruhr Literature

This section is not centrally concerned with the way in which literary texts function like palimpsests in Genette's sense of references to earlier texts (1997), though, as I have shown in Chapter 3 with regard to "The Waste Land", the layering of texts brought about by such references does, of course, lend itself to suggesting layers of the city. Thus, intertextual references can be one strategy of suggesting historical layers. What I *am* concerned with here is the question to what extent and how literary texts on post-industrial cities represent these cities as historically layered.

As a case in point, we might take Jürgen Link's 2008 novel *Bangemachen gilt nicht auf der Suche nach der Roten Ruhr-Armee: Eine Vorerinnerung*. The title translates into something like "Don't Be Intimidated in Search of the Red Ruhr Army: A Pre-Memory", the Red Ruhr Army being a reference to the left-wing workers' army which, since March 1920, defended the early Weimar Republic against reactionary and anti-republican forces after the right-wing Kapp-Putsch.

In over 900 pages, the text on the one hand is a fictionalised (if sometimes thinly veiled) collective biography of a group of 'old leftists', "non-renegade members of the 68 generation"[13] (Link 2008, 881; my translation) in the Ruhr region from the 1960s to the early 2000s. On the other hand, it is an attempt at representing the complex topography of the Ruhr region in a structurally and conceptually – and often stylistically – highly complex novel:

> The route changes in its combinations of bits of *autobahn* and alleged short-cuts, that is labyrinthically curving residential neighbourhood streets or transition roads from the last suburb of the previous Ruhr city to the 1st suburb of the next; traffic jams increase or intermittently decrease in parallel with construction noise and the economic situation; the airstream of the cars in front of you whirls up shreds of tabloid papers from the ditch and sometimes a completely empty car with flashing alarm lights stands on the right curb [the sentence continues for eight more lines].
>
> (Link 2008, 28; my translation)

> The Turkish colleague had to brake hard: right on this stretch of commercial street through which we then had to commute on our way to work, felt reminded of France every time: broad and splendid it went on for several 100 metres straight on and slightly uphill between glaring and pleasantly renovated façades in all sorts of Krupp styles: from Krupp Romanesque via Krupp Gothic all the way to Krupp Renaissance and Krupp Baroque, in which large shop windows flashed, façades, and nothing behind them [again, the sentence continues for several more lines]. In the evenings, as is typical of the Ruhr region, such brightly lit neighbourhoods with shop windows and shiny tube station entrances abruptly alternated with gloomy stretches, where, to the left and to the right, there were still fields, before it just as abruptly became bright again, but this time as if we had entered the inside of a production site, where bright lights were supposed to protect a mix of new plastic halls and old brick buildings against gangs of burglars.[14]
>
> (Link 2008, 37f.; my translation)

In an interview, but also in an essay on his own novel, Link comments on the function of these complex structures as follows: "The Ruhr region is one of the very few conurbations that are structured like a rhizome" (Heidemann n.p.).[15] Thus, in keeping with the original biological meaning of the term 'rhizome' as a multifariously interconnected network of roots, the concept as established by Deleuze and Guattari also designates a web of interconnections without a tree-like hierarchy (cf. also Chapter 3). As an organisational structure in which, to put it simplistically, 'everything is connected to everything else', as a symbol of a non-hierarchical organisation of knowledge, such a decentralised structure also implies a moment of resistance against dominant, authoritarian and hierarchical forms of organising knowledge and of exercising power.

Thus, it is not least on the micro-level of its individual endlessly meandering sentences that the novel simulates the heterogeneous *spatial* structures, layers and interdependencies of and in the region. Yet, as the above passage with its reference to a succession of "Krupp styles" makes clear, the novel also subtly engages with *temporal* layers, both in such individual passages and in its overall structure, which frequently includes so-called "simulations", often highly political projections of the future from previous decades, which are then explicitly or implicitly checked against actual developments as they *did* take place. However, the palimpsestuous nature of the region, its spatialised layered memory, is arguably even more centrally represented through the individual and collective recollections of the protagonists and in the forms and locations in which these recollections physically manifest themselves and through which, in turn, they are kept alive and are invoked.

A recurring image that is in keeping with the frequent references to the region's mining past is that of consciousness and memory as functioning in layers that are explicitly referred to as the levels of a mine, for instance in a reference to "all five levels of our pit of consciousness" (Link 2008, 398; my translation):

> though in that brief moment of saturation before falling asleep we may have felt an insight flit through our brains – during our walks through the colliery grounds, again and again, a further clarity of insight had temporarily come into our heads, accompanied by multivocal simultaneous awareness of the various levels in our heads, sometimes almost down to the lowest, the 5th level.[16]
>
> (Link 2008, 398; my translation; cf. also 711, 721)

This understanding of consciousness and of memory, it seems, is indebted to Benjamin's notion of "superposition", just as Benjamin is a strong presence generally: In addition to being mentioned explicitly several times, Benjamin is also present in references to the vaulted glass constructions of shopping centres, to the novel itself as a "Konvolut" (Benjamin's term for the folders into which the material of the *Arcades Project* is sorted), or in striking invocations of his theory of memory and the perception of the past in the built environment:

> It had to be possible, we thought, somehow to come up with tricks to suddenly change direction in the official track of time and in the precarious hovering, if only briefly, to be able to see future correspondences between

> present and past moments of hovering. Here we somehow had a half-baked version of Benjamin in mind.[17]
>
> (Link 2008, 239; my translation; for further references and allusions to Benjamin, cf. 8, 71, 75, 85, 842–846, 875, 885, 917)

Moreover, the text even provides a version of the hashish-induced perception of superposition, the only variation being, as it were, a more mundane, local-colour form of intoxication: "Most of us had had, on average, three beers and a few shots and from that, from the summer night and from the discussion, we had reached that certain multidimensional or rather polysimultaneous mode of perception" (Link 2008, 484; my translation).[18]

In addition to such small-scale instances of Benjaminean perception, the novel frequently stages the more large-scale layering of the region by referring to the temporal succession of dominant industries on specific sites, not least in numerous references to car manufacturing as the major industry that has taken over from mining. Thus, in the course of the novel, there are some 40 references to "Ruhr-Motor", sometimes also referred to as "Inter-Ruhr-Motor", which is clearly recognisable as a reference to the Opel plants in Bochum. Occasionally, the text even directly refers to the succession of industries on the same site: "'He had been working in mine Gneisenau Two [...] where now there is plant 3 of Ruhr Motor'" (Link 2008, 370; my translation).[19] This passage is also telling in its use of specific place names: "Zeche Gneisenau" was in fact a coal mine in Dortmund, but it seems to be typical of the novel to obscure, blur or amalgamate concrete place references in order all the more strongly to suggest an overarching 'Ruhr local colour' at the same time.

Finally, the process of putting together the parts of the novel, which appears to have been written over a period of some 30 years between the mid-1960s and the mid-1990s, is frequently referred to as "*Endmontage*" (final assembly), a term suggesting not only modernist techniques of montage, but even more so industrial assembly, and especially car manufacturing (for the 1995 "*Endmontage*" in the novel, cf. Link 2008, 425, 698, 817, 888, 917 *et passim*).[20] Thus, even the self-reflexive comments on the work of finishing the novel take the form of highly topical references to industry and manufacturing, and even more specifically to car production. In sum, Link's novel thus lends itself to exemplifying both the importance of temporal layers *and* the analytical value of Benjamin's notion of "superposition" for a "stratigraphic" reading (*sensu* Westphal) even and especially of post-industrial cities.

A less experimental form of suggesting temporal layers in the Ruhr region is explored in Jörg Albrecht's pop-inspired 2014 novel *Anarchie in Ruhrstadt*. The novel develops an over-the-top version of a future for the Ruhr region after the state government essentially gives it up and leaves it to its own devices in the year 2015. Satirically exaggerating the hype of the creative industries and the hope in their urban development potentials – a hype then arguably at a peak in late-comer regions like the Ruhr – the novel portrays a Ruhr region in which a committee of creatives takes over and develops each Ruhr city into a remarkably homogenous hot spot for *one* specific branch of the creative industries, with, for instance, Essen as the hub of film and TV production, Dortmund as the fashion centre and Wesel as the centre of creative writing. While the satirical representation of trends in urban development would be worth exploring, I am here concerned with the representation of temporal layers in a novel that, in numerous prolepses and analepses, non-chronologically extends over a period between 2014 and 2044.

Throughout the novel, representations of temporal layering abound:

> From some part of her memory the appropriate images now rise up: The Committee of Creatives, seven heads around thirty, who, back in 2015, in an incredibly cheeky and incredibly charming act had declared takeover of government for the entire region, the foundation of one city from 53 cities [...] The pictures from the Committee of Creatives in 2015 on the hyperwatches cross-fade into different, more current ones.[21]
>
> (Albrecht 7f.; my translation)

These representations frequently highlight phases of economic development in the region and the concomitant stages of urban development from cities shaped by coal mining, steel-making and industrial production to a region shaped by the post-industrial creative economy with its recreational and entertainment infrastructure: "Synthetic lakes where there used to be mines. Shopping malls where there used to be breweries. Marinas where there used to be simply the bank of a river" (Albrecht 33; my translation; cf. also 15, 33, 39, 48, 79, 178, 209, 214, 237 *et passim*).[22]

This also becomes clear in one of the most sustained such reflections during protagonist Rick's visit to "Kloster Kamp", originally a twelfth-century Cistercian monastery, destroyed and rebuilt several times and now maintained in a late-seventeenth-century Gothic-inspired baroque style; the present-day neo-baroque gardens were only begun in the 1980s. This curious amalgamation of styles and their perception by a character in 2044 is rendered as follows:

> Rick Rockatansky [...] now stands on the slope, where he looks down on the baroque terraced gardens of the monastery. The loudspeakers stand right in the terraced gardens, right in this rebuilt piece of baroque, reconstructed at the end of the 20th century – easy to recognize in the then fashionable embedded particles of blue metal. About 1994, Rick thinks, while at the same time he reads an info plate explaining that the original 1740 garden was copied in Sanssouci as early as 1746. Right in this crude mix of centuries which around 1994 people regarded as organic.[23]
>
> (Albrecht 10; my translation)

Here and elsewhere, the layering of different periods is clearly associated with the perception of an individual or of collectives and is explicitly formulated as being based on a character's memories and recollections or even as taking place in a character's consciousness.

One might object that these two examples of Ruhr literature, one by a former professor of German literature (Jürgen Link), one by a novelist with a doctorate in literary studies (Jörg Albrecht), are rather too convenient for my argument. However, in order to show that I have not simply made it too easy for myself by choosing texts by two scholar-writers with an obvious penchant for literary and cultural theory, I turn to a transatlantic example. My final case, here only to be discussed very briefly, is Luis J. Rodriguez's 2005 novel *Music of the Mill.* This is an activist novel on three generations of a Mexican American family working in and affected by the boom and ultimate closing of a steel mill in Los Angeles:

> But in two years, it's over [...] Nazareth Steel Corporation finally declares the closing of its steel-production facility in Los Angeles [...] Around that time [the 1980s], the big plants in tires, steel, auto, meatpacking, weapons production, and aerospace also begin shutting down [...] Los Angeles, the country's second-largest industrial center – after Chicago – [loses all of its major industry] [...] The biggest change is that the mill doesn't exist anymore. It's completely gone [...] Rows of pastel-colored warehouses with semis line most of the old streets – and a shopping mall takes up the west end where the old wire mill used to be [...] Every bridge, skyscraper, ship, tank, car, and public art sculpture with steel in it has the stories, songs, blood, hopes, tears, human limbs at times, of the generations that labored in those mills.
>
> (Rodriguez 192ff.; cf. also 90, 194f., 204, 206; for a more detailed discussion of the novel, cf. Gurr 2008)

Here, too, where any visual trace of a previous layer is "completely gone" and the past is only present in what an observer knows, the palimpsest is hardly an illuminating concept; rather, the notion of superposition, highlighting as it does the knowledge of an observer and thus allowing for a 'remembered presence', seems much more appropriate.

Conclusion: Layered Memory in Post-Industrial Cities

While the notion of the palimpsest, in contrast to what a number of urban studies discussions of the concept imply, does also fit post-industrial cities – especially those that have a significant history before industrialisation, but even those that do not – I argue that Benjamin's notion of "superposition" lends itself to a more nuanced conceptualisation of layered urban memory, because it makes an observer's awareness and knowledge of a site's previous phases, uses, etc. central to an understanding of layered urban memory. Moreover, it allows us very precisely to understand the interplay between the built environment and the way it functions as a form of layered spatialised memory.[24] This is a form of memory which needs to be actualised by an observer, memory which is triggered when, following Benjamin's beautiful formulation, space winks at the observer and asks: "What do you think may have gone on here?"

(1999, 418f.). Benjamin's notion of "superposition", the interpenetration and superimposition of different historical layers in the perception of a subject thus inclined, can be helpful here. This concept, as I hope to have shown, lends itself both to describing the way in which key actual sites preserve a memory of their previous uses *and* the way in which literary texts simulate this layered urban memory. It is especially fruitful for post-industrial regions, because it helps conceptualise the importance of an observer's knowledge of a site's previous layers – layers which, in post-industrial cities with their numerous erasures and overwrites, often have not left any visible trace as the notion of the palimpsest would suggest. Here, too, Westphal's notion of a "stratigraphic" reading (141), which does justice to the complex history of a place by layering different texts, comes to mind as a parallel (cf. also Finch's notion of "deep locational criticism"). In this vein, we can conclude with a final return to the site of the former Opel plant in Bochum. Here is another brief passage from Albrecht's *Anarchie in Ruhrstadt*, published in 2014, the year the Opel plant in Bochum closed after 52 years. In the chronology of the novel, we are in the year 2044.

> The former Häusner quarter [*sic*], which was to fall for Opel,[25] then was occupied and in the end did succumb to the power of the car company in the 1970s [...] In 2014 of all years, the year of [Julieta's] birth, Opel left Bochum forever, leaving behind only the red and white buildings when General Motors withdrew everything from Detroit [...] Now she sees in front of her those red and white ruins of the Opel plant she thought about only seconds ago. There was so much she would have liked to ask them, if she could.[26]
>
> (Albrecht 178f.; my translation)

Finally, let us return to the print ad from 1988, which celebrated the Opel plant as "the future of Bochum". The full text describes the transition from the "mining city to the automotive city" as "one solution" to the structural crisis in the region. What can be observed here is the essence of 'scripting' the future of a city (discussed in more detail in Chapter 7). The campaign here makes use of the prospective power of texts by building on the past to craft a future narrative for the city which attempts to break path dependencies:

> This image is as symbolic as it is meaningful. The shaft tower reflected on the Opel stands for the past, the car for the present and the future of Bochum.
>
> From the mining city to the automotive city – more than 25 years ago, that was one solution to the problems that the decline of coal mining brought with it. Because the Opel plant, erected on two former mining plots in 1962, gave thousands of unemployed miners a new future.
>
> Today, some 17,000 people find employment with Opel. 1,100 fully assembled Kadett cars and 1,900 sets of parts of this automotive bestseller leave the gates of Bochum's state-of-the-art plant every day. To date, Opel has built more than 6 million cars on the Ruhr.

To be sure, in coping with the structural crisis in the Ruhr region, Opel is a particularly spectacular success. But it's not the only one: Numerous newly funded companies, but even more so, the technological reorientation of traditional companies in the region show that the decline in coal and steel is compensated for. Nonetheless: Even with the aid of the latest technologies in chemicals, machine-building, electronics or environmental technologies, the Ruhr region still needs a lot of time, a lot of energy and, above all, a lot of self-confidence.

But it's on the right track: In the Ruhr region, it's now full throttle ahead into the future.[27]

(KVR; my translation)

Notes

* Finding appropriate illustrations for part of this chapter has been possible because the City Archives of Essen and Herne as well as City Marketing Herne have been very helpful and generous with materials. However, I would particularly like to thank Jürgen Hagen, director of Stadtarchiv Herne, who has been extremely kind and supportive, not least by specifically commissioning Gerd Biedermann to take extra photos of present-day Mozartstraße at short notice. I am very grateful to both of them for their help.

1 The German original reads: "Dieses Bild ist ebenso symbolträchtig wie bedeutsam. Der sich auf dem Opel spiegelnde Förderturm steht für die Vergangenheit, das Auto für die Gegenwart und Zukunft Bochums" (KVR). I return to the entire text at the end of this chapter.

2 For an excellent account of deindustrialisation in the United States and its cultural repercussions, cf. Linkon; for comparative perspectives, cf. Sattler 2015, 2016, 2017 as well as her ongoing post-doc project "Ruhr|Detroit: Urban Planning and American Cultural Studies"; for comparative perspectives on old industrial regions, cf. also much of the work of industrial and labour historian Stefan Berger at Ruhr-University Bochum.

3 I am grateful to Lena Mattheis for drawing my attention to Westphal.

4 The German original reads: "Für eine Vielzahl europäischer Städte drängt sich das Bild eines Palimpsests auf."

5 For the city as palimpsest, cf. also Butor; Freud 16–18; Gurr 2015; Harvey 66; Hassenpflug 2006, 2011; Huyssen; Kronshage/Sandten/Thielmann; Martindale; Mattheis; Mattheis/Gurr; Sharpe/Wallock 9; Suttles.

6 The only reason there is no medieval map is because Essen was too insignificant for anyone to want to map it, as my urban geography colleague Hans-Werner Wehling likes to point out.

7 The German original reads: "[Diese] Raumwahrnehmung [...] ist die Durchdringungs- und Überdeckungstransparenz der Welt des Flaneurs" (Benjamin 1992, 678f., 1023). There is also, it is true, a form of *spatial* superposition, overlay or bleed: "If a shoemaker's shop [is] neighbor to a confectioner's, then his festoons of bootlaces will resemble rolls of licorice" (Benjamin 1999, 872). The German original reads: "Ist ein Schusterladen Nachbar einer Confiserie, so werden seine Schnürsenkelgehänge lakritzenähnlich" (Benjamin 1992, 1042). But the more important point for my present purpose is the temporal layering.

8 The German original reads: “Das ‘Kolportagephänomen des Raumes’ ist die grundlegende Erfahrung des Flaneurs [...] Kraft dieses Phänomens wird simultan was alles nur in diesem Raume potentiell geschehen ist, wahrgenommen. Der Raum blinzelt den Flaneur an: Nun, was mag sich in mir wohl zugetragen haben?” (Benjamin 1992, 527).

9 The German original reads: “Jener anamnestische Rausch, in dem der Flaneur durch die Stadt zieht, saugt seine Nahrung nicht nur aus dem, was ihm da sinnlich vor Augen kommt, sondern wird oft des bloßen Wissens, ja toter Daten, wie eines Erfahrenen und Gelebten sich bemächtigen. Dies gefühlte Wissen geht von einem zum andern vor allem durch mündliche Kunde. Aber es hat sich im Laufe des XIX. Jahrhunderts doch auch in einer fast unübersehbaren Literatur niedergeschlagen [...] Musste [der Flaneur] dann nicht wirklich den steileren Anstieg hinter der Kirche Notre Dame de Lorette eindringlicher unter den Sohlen fühlen, wenn er wusste: hier wurde einmal, als Paris seine ersten Omnibusse bekam, das *cheval de renfort* als drittes vor den Wagen gespannt” (Benjamin 1992, 525f.).

10 This was partly, it seems, in response to Adorno’s critique in the famous Hornberg letter of 1935 (cf. Brüggemann 612; for the debate between Benjamin and Adorno, cf. van Reijen).

11 For a discussion of the layers of Mark 51°7, cf. also Heyer.

12 The German original reads: “Die Werksfläche I wird vom sogenannten Isabella-Stollen unterquert. Die über diesen Stollen ausfließenden Grubenwässer dienen der Wasserversorgung der Gräfte von Haus Laer. Die Wasserversorgung über den Isabella-Stollen ist wasserrechtlich gesichert. Zur Sicherung der Tagesoberfläche vor Bruchgefahr müssten der Stollen und abzweigende Abbaustrecken verpresst werden, wodurch die Speisung der Gräfte mit Grubenwasser unterbunden wird” (Bürgerinformationssystem der Stadt Bochum).

13 The novel professes to be “a realistic report on the experiences of a group of non-renegade members of the 68 generation” (Link 2008, 881; my translation); the German original reads: “realistische[r] Erfahrungsbericht einiger nichtkonvertierter 68er”.

14 The German original reads: “Die Route wechselt in ihren Kombinationen von Autobahnstücken und angeblichen Schleichwegen will sagen sich labyrinthisch biegenden Wohnviertelstraßen oder Überbrückungspisten vom letzten Vorort der letzten Ruhrstadt zum 1. Vorort der nächsten, die Staus nehmen weiter zu oder zwischendurch wieder etwas ab parallel mit dem Baulärm und mit der Konjunktur, der Fahrtwind der Wagen vor Euch wirbelt Schlagzeitungsfetzen in der Gosse auf und manchmal steht ein vollständig leeres Auto mit blinkendem Alarmlicht am rechten Straßenrand [der Satz geht noch über acht Zeilen weiter]” (Link 2008, 28).

“Der türkische Kollege musste voll auf die Bremse treten: mitten auf diesem Stück Geschäftsstraße, durch das wir damals pendeln mussten auf dem Weg zur Arbeit, uns jedesmal wieder erinnert an Frankreich: breit und prächtig ging es ein paar 100 Meter schnurgerade und leicht bergauf zwischen knallig und schön renovierten Fassaden in allen möglichen Kruppstilen: von Kruppromanik über Kruppgotik bis hin zu Kruppprenaissance und Kruppbarock, worin überall große Schaufenster blitzten, Fassaden und nichts dahinter, ging es leicht bergauf, scheppernd über die zugegossenen Straßenbahnschienen, gerade wie in den blauen Himmel über der Ruhr hinein, wenn er einmal wieder blau war und sozusagen wild und makaber vollplakatiert mit großen Wolkenfahnen flatternd im Marsch nach Osten. Abends wechselten, wie es typisch im Ruhrgebiet ist, solche hell erleuchteten Viertel mit

Schaufenstern und glitzernden U-Bahn-Eingängen abrupt mit finsteren Abschnitten, wo rechts und links noch Felder waren, bevor es ebenso abrupt wieder hell wurde, aber diesmal wie als ob wir ins Innere eines Werksgeländes geraten wären, wo helle Laternen ein Gemisch aus neuen Plastikhallen und alten Ziegelbauten gegen die Einbrecherbanden schützen sollten" (Link 2008, 37f.).

15 The German original reads: "Das Ruhrgebiet ist eines der ganz wenigen Ballungsgebiete, die wie ein Rhizom strukturiert sind" (Heidemann n.p.).

16 The German original reads: "alle 5 Sohlen unseres Bewusstseinspütts" (Link 2008, 398): "mochten wir dann im kurzen Moment des Sattseins vor dem Einschlafen noch eine Einsicht durch die Gehirne huschen fühlen – so war bei den Spaziergängen im Zechengelände immer wieder zeitweise eine noch zusätzliche Durchblicksklarheit in unsere Köpfe gekommen, wozu ein mehrstimmiges simultanes Bewusstsein der verschiedenen 'Sohlen' in unseren Köpfen gehört hatte, manchmal fast bis auf die unterste, 5. Sohle herab" (Link 2008, 398).

17 The German original reads: "Es musste doch möglich sein, dachten wir, irgendwie Tricks herauszufinden, um in der offiziellen Zeitschneise und in der Kippschwebe [...] plötzlich irgendwie die Richtung umzuschwenken, wenn auch bloß kurz, um künftige Korrespondenzen der gegenwärtigen und vergangenen Schwebemomente in den Blick zu bekommen. Wir hatten dabei irgendwie unausgegoren Benjamin im Kopf" (Link 2008, 239; for Benjamin, cf. also 71, 75, 306f., 842,844, 917, 885).

18 The German original reads: "Die meisten von uns hatten im Schnitt schon 3 Flaschen Bier nebst ein paar Kurzen intus und dadurch sowie durch die Sommernacht und das Diskutieren bereits die einschlägige mehrdimensionale oder besser polysimultane Wahrnehmungsweise erreicht" (Link 2008, 484).

19 The German original reads: "'Der hatte da auf Zeche Gneisenau Zwo gearbeitet [...] wo jetzt Werk 3 von Ruhr-Motor steht'" (Link 2008, 370).

20 For the writing and publication history of *Bangemachen gilt nicht auf der Suche nach der Roten Ruhr-Armee*, cf. also Lachmann (171), who also comments on the term "*Endmontage*".

21 The German original reads: "Aus irgendeinem Teil ihres Gedächtnisses steigen nun die passenden Bilder auf. Das Komitee der Kreativen, sieben etwa dreißigjährige Köpfe, die damals, 2015, in einem unerhört dreisten und unerhört charmanten Akt die Übernahme einer Gesamtregierung für die Gesamtregion erklärten, die Gründung einer Stadt aus dreiundfünfzig Städten. [...] Die Bilder vom Komitee der Kreativen 2015 überblenden auf den Hyperwatches zu anderen, aktuellen" (Albrecht 7f.).

22 The German original reads: "Synthetische Seen, wo vorher Zechen waren. Shopping Malls, wo vorher Brauereien waren. Yachthäfen, wo vorher einfach das Ufer eines Flusses war" (Albrecht 33).

23 The German original reads: "Rick Rockatansky [...] steht nun am Hang, wo er auf die barocken Terrassengärten des Klosters [Kamp] hinabsieht [...] Die Lautsprecher stehen inmitten der Terrassengärten, inmitten dieses wiederaufgebauten Stücks Barock, rekonstruiert Ende des 20. Jahrhunderts – unschwer zu erkennen an den damals modernen blauen Metall-Einsprengseln. 1994, denkt Rick, während er zugleich eine Infotafel liest, die erklärt, dass der Originalgarten von 1740 schon 1746 in Sanssouci kopiert worden sei. Inmitten dieser kruden Mischung von Jahrhunderten, die man zirka 1994 mal als organisch ansah" (Albrecht 10).

24 In other words, it allows us very precisely to locate the "somewhere" in Fran Tonkiss's observation that "[t]he relationship of memory to space operates

somewhere between the landmarks of the official city and the footfalls of the solitary subject" (120).

25 The demolition of the Heusner-Viertel (the actual spelling) was not, in fact, to make room for Opel but for the Bochumer Ring, a ring road that was indirectly of course related to Opel and was part of the infrastructure investment to attract the plant to the city.

26 The German original reads: "Das ehemalige Häusner-Viertel [sic] [von Bochum], das für Opel fallen sollte, dann besetzt wurde und am Ende doch der Macht des Autokonzerns wich in den 1970ern [...] Ausgerechnet 2014, in [Julietas] Geburtsjahr, verließ Opel Bochum endgültig, ließ nur die rot-weißen Bauten zurück, nachdem General Motors von Detroit aus alles abberufen hatte [...] Da sieht sie vor sich jene rotweißen Ruinen des Opel-Werks, an die sie vor Sekunden dachte. Was würde sie die alles gern fragen, wenn sie könnte" (Albrecht 178f.).

27 The German original reads: "Dieses Bild ist ebenso symbolträchtig wie bedeutsam: Der sich auf dem Opel spiegelnde Förderturm steht für die Vergangenheit, das Auto für die Gegenwart und die Zukunft Bochums.

Von der Bergbaustadt zur Automobilstadt, das war hier vor mehr als 25 Jahren eine Lösung der Probleme, die der Rückgang der Kohleförderung mit sich brachte. Denn die Opelwerke, 1962 auf zwei ehemaligen Zechengeländen errichtet, gaben Tausenden von arbeitslosen Bochumer Bergleuten eine neue Zukunft.

Heute finden bei Opel rund 17.000 Menschen Arbeit. 1.100 komplett montierte Kadett und 1.900 Teilesätze dieses automobilen Bestsellers verlassen täglich die Tore des hochmodernen Bochumer Opel-Werks. Bis heute baute Opel über 6 Millionen Autos an der Ruhr.

Sicher, für die Bewältigung der Strukturkrise im Ruhrgebiet ist Opel ein besonders spektakulärer Erfolg. Aber nicht der einzige: Zahlreiche Firmengründungen, aber mehr noch die technologische Neuorientierung traditioneller Revier-Unternehmen zeigen, dass der Rückgang bei Kohle und Stahl kompensiert wird. Nur: Selbst mit Hilfe neuester Technologien in Chemie, Maschinenbau, Elektronik oder Umwelttechnik braucht das Ruhrgebiet noch viel Zeit, viel Kraft und vor allem viel Selbstbewusstsein.

Doch man ist auf dem richtigen Weg: Im Ruhrgebiet geht's jetzt mit Vollgas in die Zukunft."

References

Albrecht, Jörg. *Anarchie in Ruhrstadt*. Göttingen: Wallstein, 2014.

Assmann, Aleida. "Geschichte findet Stadt." *Kommunikation – Gedächtnis – Raum: Kulturwissenschaften nach dem "Spatial Turn."* Ed. Moritz Csàky, Christoph Leitgeb. Bielefeld: transcript, 2009. 13–27.

Benjamin, Walter. *The Arcades Project*. Trans. Howard Eiland, Kevin McLaughlin. Cambridge, MA: The Belknap Press of Harvard University Press, 1999.

Benjamin, Walter. *Das Passagen-Werk*. Ed. Rolf Tiedemann. Frankfurt/Main: Suhrkamp, 1992. 2 vols.

Brüggemann, Heinz. "Passagen." *Benjamins Begriffe*. Ed. Michael Opitz, Erdmut Wizisla. Frankfurt/Main: Suhrkamp, 2000. 2 vols. Vol. II, 573–618.

Bürgerinformationssystem der Stadt Bochum. "Werksflächen der Adam Opel AG, Untersuchungsstatus." 2013, Nr. 20132689.

Butor, Michel. "Die Stadt als Text." *Perspektiven metropolitaner Kultur*. Ed. Ursula Keller. Frankfurt/Main: Suhrkamp, 2000. 169–178.

Deleuze, Gilles, Felix Guattari. "Introduction: Rhizome." *A Thousand Plateaus*. Trans. Brian Massumi. London, New York: Continuum, 2004 [[1]1987]. Vol. 2 of *Capitalism and Schizophrenia*. 2 vols. 1972–1980. 3–28. [Trans. of *Mille Plateaux*. Paris: Editions de Minuit, 1980].

Ernst, Thomas. "Das Ruhrgebiet als Rhizom. Die Netzstadt und die 'Nicht-Metropole Ruhr' in den Erzählwerken von Jürgen Link und Wolfgang Welt." *Literaturwunder Ruhr*. Ed. Gerhard Rupp, Hanneliese Palm, Julika Vorberg. Essen: Klartext, 2011. 43–70.

Farrenkopf, Michael, Stefan Goch, Manfred Rasch, Hans-Werner Wehling, eds. *Die Stadt der Städte: Das Ruhrgebiet und seine Umbrüche*. Essen: Klartext, 2019.

Finch, Jason. *Deep Locational Criticism: Imaginative Place in Literary Research and Teaching*. Amsterdam, Philadelphia: Benjamins, 2016.

Freud, Sigmund. *Civilization and Its Discontents*. Trans. Peter Gay. New York: Norton, 1984.

Genette, Gérard. *Palimpsests: Literature in the Second Degree*. Trans. Channa Newman, Claude Doubinsky. Lincoln: University of Nebraska Press, 1997.

Gurr, Jens Martin. "The Modernist Poetics of Urban Memory and the Structural Analogies between 'City' and 'Text': *The Waste Land* and Benjamin's *Arcades Project*." *Recovery and Transgression: Memory in American Poetry*. Ed. Kornelia Freitag. Newcastle: Cambridge Scholars Publishing, 2015. 21–37.

Gurr, Jens Martin. "The Multicultural Marketing of Urban Fiction: Temporality, Language, Genre, and Readership(s) in Luis J. Rodriguez's *The Republic of East L.A.* and *Music of the Mill*." *E Pluribus Unum: National and Transnational Identities in the Americas/Identidades nacionales y transnacionales en las Américas*. Ed. Sebastian Thies, Josef Raab. Münster: LIT/Tempe, AZ: Bilingual Press, 2008. 263–276.

Harvey, David. *The Condition of Postmodernity: An Inquiry into the Origins of Cultural Change*. Oxford: Blackwell, 1989.

Hassenpflug, Dieter. "Once Again: Can Urban Space be Read?" *Reading the City: Developing Urban Hermeneutics/Stadt lesen: Beiträge zu einer urbanen Hermeneutik*. Ed. Dieter Hassenpflug, Nico Giersig, Bernhard Stratmann. Weimar: Verlag der Bauhaus-Universität, 2011. 49–58.

Hassenpflug, Dieter. "Walter Benjamin und die Traumseite der Stadt." Hassenpflug. *Reflexive Urbanistik: Reden und Aufsätze zur europäischen Stadt*. Weimar: Verlag der Bauhaus-Universität, 2006. 7–22.

Heidemann, Britta. "Das Leben – ein Rhizom: Autor Jürgen Link über Renitenz und Resistenz im Ruhrgebiet. Eine Begegnung am Rande einer Nicht-Metropole." *WAZ*, 25 June 2010.

Heyer, Rolf. "Mark 51°7 – Vom Acker zum Technologiestandort: Strukturwandel in Bochum-Laer." *Die Stadt der Städte: Das Ruhrgebiet und seine Umbrüche*. Ed. Michael Farrenkopf, Stefan Goch, Manfred Rasch, Hans-Werner Wehling. Essen: Klartext, 2019. 552–556.

Hörisch, Jochen. *Das Wissen der Literatur*. Munich: Fink, 2007.

Huyssen, Andreas. *Present Pasts: Urban Palimpsests and the Politics of Memory*. Palo Alto: Stanford University Press, 2003.

Kronshage, Eike, Cecile Sandten, Winfried Thielmann, eds. *Palimpsestraum Stadt*. Trier: WVT, 2015.

KVR/Kommunalverband Ruhrgebiet. *Das Ruhrgebiet packt aus – Zehn Jahre Werbung für eine unerschöpfliche Region*. Essen: Kommunalverband Ruhrgebiet, 1996.

Lachmann, Tobias. "Das Ruhrgebiet in Jürgen Links *Bangemachen gilt nicht auf der Suche nach der Roten Ruhr-Armee: Eine Vorerinnerung.*" *Von Flussidyllen und Fördertürmen: Literatur an der Nahtstelle von Ruhr und Rhein.* Ed. Jan-Pieter Barbian, Gertrude Cepl-Kaufmann, Hanneliese Palm. Essen: Klartext, 2011. 163–185.

Link, Jürgen. *Bangemachen gilt nicht auf der Suche nach der Roten Ruhr-Armee: Eine Vorerinnerung.* Oberhausen: asso, 2008.

Link, Jürgen. "Wie Heimatliteratur am Ruhrgebiet scheitert. Mit einem Blick auf einen autogenen Versuch in narrativer Deterritorialisierung." *Literaturwunder Ruhr.* Ed. Gerhard Rupp, Hanneliese Palm, Julika Vorberg. Essen: Klartext, 2011. 71–89.

Linkon, Sherry Lee. *The Half-Life of Deindustrialization: Working-Class Writing about Economic Restructuring.* Ann Arbor: University of Michigan Press, 2018.

Martindale, Charles. "Ruins of Rome: T.S. Eliot and the Presence of the Past." *Arion* 3.2–3 (1995): 102–140.

Mattheis, Lena. "A Brief Inventory of Translocal Narratability: Palimpsestuous Street Art in Chris Abani's The Virgin of Flames." *Narrative* 26.3 (2018): 302–319.

Mattheis, Lena, Jens Martin Gurr. "Superpositions: A Typology of Spatiotemporal Layerings in Buried Cities." *Buried Cities.* Special Issue of *Literary Geographies* (forthcoming).

Prieto, Eric. "Geocriticism, Geopoetics, Geophilosophy, and Beyond." *Geocritical Explorations: Space, Place, and Mapping in Literary and Cultural Studies.* Ed. Robert T. Tally. New York: Palgrave Macmillan, 2011. 13–27.

Reicher, Christa, Klaus R. Kunzmann, Jan Polívka, Frank Roost, Yasemin Utku, Michael Wegener, eds. *Schichten einer Region: Kartenstücke zur räumlichen Struktur des Ruhrgebiets.* Berlin: Jovis, 2011.

Rodriguez, Luis J. *Music of the Mill.* New York: HarperCollins, 2006.

Sattler, Julia. "Dealing with the Past Spatially: Storytelling and Sustainability in Deindustrializing Communities." *European Journal of American Studies* 10.3 (2015). Special Issue: Sustainability and the City. America and the Urban World.

Sattler, Julia. "Narratives of Urban Transformation: Reading the Rust Belt in the Ruhr." *Urban Transformations in the USA: Spaces—Communities—Representations.* Ed. Sattler. Bielefeld: transcript 2016. 11–26.

Sattler, Julia. "This is (not) Detroit: Projecting the Future of Germany's Ruhr Region." *Why Detroit Matters: Decline, Renewal and Hope in a Divided City.* Ed. Brian Doucet. Bristol: Policy Press, 2017. 157–175.

Sharpe, William, Leonard Wallock. "From 'Great Town' to 'Nonplace Urban Realm': Reading the Modern City." *Visions of the Modern City: Essays in History, Art, and Literature.* Ed. Sharpe, Wallock. Baltimore: Johns Hopkins University Press, 1987. 1–50.

Suttles, Gerald D. "The Cumulative Texture of Local Urban Culture." *American Journal of Sociology* 90.2 (1984): 283–304.

Tally, Robert T., ed. *Geocritical Explorations: Space, Place, and Mapping in Literary and Cultural Studies.* New York: Palgrave Macmillan, 2011. 13–27.

Tonkiss, Fran. *Space, the City, and Social Theory.* Malden, MA: Polity, 2005.

van Reijen, Willem. "Die Adorno-Benjamin-Kontroverse." *Zeitschrift für Philosophische Forschung* 60.1 (2006): 99–121.

Westphal, Bertrand. *Geocriticism: Real and Fictional Spaces.* Trans. Robert T. Tally Jr. New York: Palgrave Macmillan, 2011.

5 Urban Activist Writing and the Transition from 'Models *of*' to 'Models *for*' Urban Developments

This chapter uses a selection of urban activist writings from anti-gentrification and 'right to the city' movements to highlight the transition from texts as 'models of' to 'models for' urban developments. More specifically, it seeks to identify aesthetic strategies of subverting commodification common in such writing in order to point out how such writings both *critically describe current urban developments* and *seek to influence their future course*. Moreover, it highlights a curious paradox in scholarship *on* such activism: Most scholarly work in 'critical urban studies' and on urban activism tends to theorise *for* and *about* these movements and largely ignores how activists themselves conceptually frame their activities, an observation one may find somewhat surprising in the context of a movement so centrally concerned with questions of agency, voice, participation and self-directedness.

'Right to the City' Activism and 'Critical Urban Studies'

Studying what might broadly speaking be subsumed under 'right to the city' activism, it is worth distinguishing between different aims: Is activism directed against gentrification, against concrete building projects or the privatisation of public space, against 'neo-liberal' urban growth policies, foreclosure, the housing crisis or homelessness, or does it more generally advocate the 'right to the city'? Since urban activism has frequently come to crystallise around anti-gentrification movements, the implicit or explicit understanding of gentrification is frequently related to the forms of activism chosen: The emphasis may here be on a demand- or consumption-side understanding ('yuppies or hipsters want to move to the inner city') or the supply or production side ('real estate owners can make more money if they upgrade their property'; for this 'rent gap theory', cf. especially Smith 1979, 1996). Accordingly, the implications for activism will be markedly different: 'Yuppies' – or possibly 'hipsters' – are a far more identifiable target than economic structures and frequently invisible – often corporate – investors. Depending on the concrete target and aim of a specific movement, the types of coalitions will also frequently differ and may involve various constellations of tenants, artists, small shop owners, professionals or leftist groups, and may be organised in local, regional, national or even transnational networks. Moreover, we may heuristically distinguish between three forms of commitment within anti-gentrification movements: (1) community activism (whether explicitly theory-conscious or not), (2) activist or politically committed scholarship, or (3) activist cultural production. As for the degree of explicit engagement with urban theory, we might differentiate between activism and cultural production that (1) appear to make no use of notions borrowed from 'critical urban studies', (2) that implicitly use such notions or appear to be indebted to them, (3) that affirmatively deploy theoretical concepts, (4) that reflexively and critically make use of such concepts, occasionally with the more or less explicit aim to contribute new facets to theoretical discussions. This chapter largely addresses the two latter forms as arguably the more common types: Given the demographics of many activist groups and the frequently academic background of many leading members (cf. Liss 257), it is hardly surprising that anti-gentrification and 'right to the city' movements in the United States, Britain, Germany and elsewhere frequently appear to be highly theory-conscious.[1]

In a 2008 essay in the *New Left Review*, David Harvey captures the essence of what I take 'critical urban studies' to mean here:

> The question of what kind of city we want cannot be divorced from that of what kind of social ties, relationship to nature, lifestyles, technologies and aesthetic values we desire. The right to the city is far more than the individual liberty to access urban resources: it is a right to change ourselves by changing the city [...] The freedom to make and remake our cities and ourselves is, I want to argue, one of the most precious yet most neglected of our human rights [...] At this point in history, this has to be a global struggle, predominantly with finance capital, for that is the scale at which urbanization processes now work [...] Lefebvre was right to insist that the revolution has to be urban, in the broadest sense of that term, or nothing at all.
>
> (23–40)

We can thus conceive of 'critical urban studies' as a broadly coherent tradition of leftist inquiry into the relations between the city and capitalism, questions of marginalisation, power structures and socio-spatial developments, which seeks to point out strategies for alternative urban communities, taking its cues from leading exponents such as Henri Lefebvre, David Harvey, Manuel Castells or Edward Soja. In a 2012 essay, Neil Brenner conveniently identified four key principles of the tradition of 'critical urban studies':

(1) it is interested in theory as such (not just as a tool for practice);
(2) it is reflexive and situationally specific in the sense that it is aware of its local and historical positionality;
(3) it is critical of merely descriptive (or even boosterist) urban studies that "promote the maintenance and reproduction of extant urban formations" (19);
(4) it is interested in the distance "between the actual and the possible", between what is and what might be – the "ultimate goal being a different

city as an expression of a different, just, democratic and sustainable society" (19 *et passim*; cf. also Brenner/Marcuse/Mayer 5 *et passim* and further contributions in their volume).

One can observe that many such movements generally seeking to foster a more equitable, sustainable or democratic society, tend to crystallise around fairly concrete issues such as activities against gentrification, specific building projects, the privatisation of public space, 'neo-liberal' urban growth policies, or protests drawing attention to housing issues in the city.

There have been numerous publications conceptually engaging with what appears to be a surge of anti-gentrification activities and 'right to the city' (*sensu* Lefebvre) movements in the 'neo-liberal city' and especially in the wake of the fiscal crisis beginning in 2008. However, while much of the scholarly interest has been concerned with theorising *about* or *for* such movements, there have been far fewer studies focusing on how these movements themselves conceptually frame their activities. Take as a representative example the rather ambitious collection of essays entitled *Cities for People, not for Profit*, which brings together a number of the major figures in 'critical urban studies'. The editors state as one of their main goals "to contribute intellectual resources that may be useful for those institutions, movements, and actors that aim to roll back the contemporary hypercommodification of urban life, and on this basis to promote alternative, radically democratic, socially just, and sustainable forms of urbanism" (Brenner/Marcuse/Mayer 2). In fact, in the entire volume, Jon Liss's essay on the nation-wide Right to the City (RTCC) Alliance in the United States, largely a report of the organisational efforts and strategies of this group to move beyond traditional community organising, is the only one by an activist rather than by a scholar. This essay is also clearly the odd one out in the collection for being largely devoid of theorising. Addressing the issue of voice and agency, Liss states that the "leadership of NWCOs [New Working Class Organisations] is primarily university-educated, 'middle class', and oppressed nationality" (257) and also comments on conflicts between university-educated middle-class activists and members of the class they are supposedly struggling for (cf. 257).

Case Study I: The 'Mission Yuppie Eradication Project' in 1990s San Francisco

The heuristic categories introduced above and the efficacy – or lack thereof – of specific constellations of actors can be illustrated by means of the "Mission Yuppie Eradication Project" (MYEP) in San Francisco (1998–2000), which, because of the aggressive rhetoric of its posters, gained substantial press coverage (cf. Keating; Solnit/Schwartzenberg 124–128). In the years 1998–2000, when, in the wake of the 'dot.com boom', gentrification became an increasingly pressing issue in San Francisco, protest crystallised in the city's Mission District, traditionally a working-class neighbourhood. In this period, a number of pithily phrased posters called for vandalism against 'yuppie' vehicles and restaurants:

> MISSION YUPPIE ERADICATION PROJECT. Over the past several years the Mission has been colonized by pigs with money. Yuppie scumbags have crawled out of their haunts on Union Street and [in] the suburbs to take our neighborhood away from us [...] They come to party, and end up moving in to what used to be affordable rental housing. They help landlords drive up rents, pushing working and poor people out of their homes [...] This yuppie takeover can be turned back [...] VANDALIZE YUPPIE CARS: BMWs – Porsches – Jaguars – SPORT-UTILITY VEHICLES [*sic*]. Break the Glass – Scratch the Paint – Slash Their Tires and Upholstery – Trash Them All. If yuppie scum know their precious cars aren't safe on the streets of this neighborhood, they'll go away and they won't come back – and the trendoid restaurants, bars and shops that cater to them will go out of business [...] TAKE ACTION NOW.
>
> (Mission Yuppie Eradication Project)

Unsurprisingly, the aggressive rhetoric of the poster is based on a demand-side understanding of gentrification and identifies "yuppie scumbags" as the targets of activism. While this poster does not make explicit use of any theoretical notion (and, though providing a by-the-book description of the process, appears deliberately to avoid the term 'gentrification'), a later poster from 1999 alludes to a key moment of urban protest and thus suggests familiarity with a tradition of theoretically informed activism. Translating a widely known Situationist graffiti from May 1968, "bientôt des ruines pittoresques", it calls for the destruction of what appear to have been iconic 'yuppie' bars and restaurants:

> Soon to be picturesque ruins: During the next major urban riots, we must attack and destroy the following yuppie bars and restaurants in the Mission [...] Beauty Bar [...] Tokyo A Go-Go [...] the corporate-types inside make it look like a scene from a bad '80s movie starring Rob Lowe and Demi Moore [...] Blowfish Sushi [...] a nest of cell phone yuppies and upper middle class privilege [...] Circadia, a Starbucks [...] where virtual humans surf the Internet all day while slurping 7$ coffee drinks [...] There are other places to be targeted – use your imagination. Be creative. Take action. Don't get caught.
>
> (Mission Yuppie Eradication Project)

In a 2007 essay, "A Critique of San Francisco's Mission Yuppie Eradication Project", Kevin Keating, who identifies himself as having been the MYEP's leading activist – partly, it seems, its *only* activist – engages with what he regards as the achievements and limitations of his professedly radical and revolutionary commitment. He comments on the high visibility gained by the aggressive rhetoric of the posters and regards the lack of a dedicated network as the key weakness of his stand-alone initiative. His highly self-conscious assessment needs to be quoted at some length:

> In a de-politicized culture rampaging market forces can't be confronted effectively with conventional political language. So a logical first step in an effort to foment resistance was to cover the walls of the Mission with a thousand photocopied posters calling for working people to resist the bourgeois invasion by vandalizing yuppie cars [...] The posters communicated an extremist message in clear, simple language, avoiding Marxist or anarchist buzz-words. I described the process of gentrification without using the word "gentrification." As the posters hit the walls working people started fighting back [...] And I used the global news media attention focused on the gentrification of the Mission as a soapbox for a larger anti-capitalist perspective [...] The posters succeeded on the basic level that anti-capitalist agitprop efforts should aim at; they helped define a contemporary social problem in clear class conflict terms, and tried to move the fight away from the atomization and powerlessness of the democratic process toward some kind of large-scale direct action. Exactly what form that large-scale direct action would take wasn't clear to me [...] In the face of many decades of failure of a work-within-the-system perspective, and its inability to deliver the goods in both small ways and large, the field is wide open for a wholly different kind of autonomous direct action response, outside of and against the conventional, legitimate decision-making structures of democratic capitalism [...] My focus was too narrow. I concentrated solely on the Mission District. My anti-gentrification effort happened at the high point of my love affair with the neighborhood I live in, and my passion blinded me to opportunities I might have otherwise taken advantage of. I should have exploited media coverage that came my way to get out more of a city-wide message against rent and landlords and the larger issue of housing as a commodity. Under the best circumstances a subversive effort can have a "bleed-through" effect. What starts in one collective conflict between wage slaves and capital can spread or cross-pollinate into other everyday life situations, even ones that don't appear to be related to the initial issue.
>
> (Keating n.p.)

In keeping with these insights, Keating points to the 'dot.com bust' and the recession rather than to any activism to account for the fact that, at the time of his writing (2007), the Mission District was still largely working class and that gentrification had significantly slowed down (for an account of the MYEP, including an interview with Keating, cf. also Solnit/Schwartzenberg 124–128).

Case Study II: Christoph Schäfer's *Die Stadt ist unsere Fabrik/The City is our Factory* and Hamburg's 'Right to the City' Movements

A particularly illuminating example of explicit engagement with 'critical urban studies' in urban activism and especially in what might be termed 'activist cultural production' commenting *on* this phenomenon is to be found in the work of Christoph Schäfer, especially in his *Die Stadt ist unsere Fabrik/The City is our Factory* (2010c), an activist pictorial essay on the history of the urban, detailing especially the 'right to the city' movement in Hamburg, Germany. This text will allow me to think through several questions central to this chapter: How are theoretical concepts in urban studies appropriated and strategically deployed in these representations? To what extent are urban activism and activist cultural production self-reflexive and aware of their own ambivalence and potential for commodification? I will argue that some of the most theoretically informed exponents of these movements are keenly aware of this ambivalence. This awareness surfaces time and again when they ironically and self-reflexively portray theory-inflected urban activism as to some extent the pursuit of an internationally connected urban elite failing to address the concerns of those groups most severely hit by gentrification and exclusion.

Christoph Schäfer has for years been a central figure in Hamburg's "Recht auf Stadt" ['right to the city'] movement, a network of some 25 initiatives working towards affordable housing, the preservation of public space and of urban green spaces, more participation and a more democratic city. He has been called an "embedded artist" of the movement (moderator in Schäfer 2009), and his book demonstrates this role: An ambitious pictorial essay in some 160 drawings, *The City is our Factory* is "a rhizomatic history of the urban" (publisher's blurb) from the first cities thousands of years ago to Hamburg in 2009. In the form of exploratory and annotated drawings and in some 15 pages of more discursive text densely printed in five columns per page,[2] it discusses issues such as the origin and development of urban settlements, the production of space, urban anthropology, the connections between social and spatial developments, urban imaginaries and identities, changing forms of work, participation, bottom-up community organising, gentrification, squatting, the struggle against the privatisation and commercialisation of public space, city branding and marketing, the creative class discourse, or the role of art and artists in urban development.[3] Throughout, the book displays an acute theory-consciousness and familiarity with central concepts of 'critical urban studies' in the sense outlined above. Here, as well as in interviews (cf., e.g., 2010b), Schäfer very adeptly employs, cites and alludes to Benjamin, Heidegger's reading of Hölderlin, Lefebvre, Foucault, Deleuze and Guattari, or Harvey, to Siqueiros and the aesthetics and politics of Mexican *muralismo* and innumerable further directly apposite as well as arcanely related notions and concepts. I here only need to discuss a small selection of issues and their negotiation and will do so focusing on those which lend themselves to highlighting how Schäfer segues from 'model of' to 'model for' the city in his prescriptive commentary and thus best illustrate the poetics and politics of his approach. Schäfer's visual essay is an interesting case of a text that is clearly both a descriptive history of urban developments and thus a 'model of', but also a prescriptive 'model for' in that it clearly voices a view as to desirable future developments.

The more explicitly political sections dealing with the then recent Hamburg initiatives revolve around the intersecting concerns of city branding and imagineering, the attempt at tailoring the city to the needs of the 'creative class', and the privatisation and commercialisation of public space: "Unnoticed at first, something essential began to change in the cities when we started walking around with cardboard cups full of hot milk and coffee. Entire neighbourhoods soon gave you the feeling that you were purchasing a stay permit with your latte" (Schäfer 2010c, 142).

An impressive sequence of drawings explores the connection between 'neo-liberal' urban policies and the loss of urban memory emblematised in the collapse of the Cologne City Archive. On 3 March 2009, the Cologne City Archive, containing millions of documents dating all the way back to the High Middle Ages, collapsed into an open building excavation some 25 metres deep. The collapse, which resulted in two deaths and the damage and partial loss of invaluable historical documents, appears to have been the result of criminal negligence and insufficient construction site security in privatised construction work on a new underground line: "Cologne, March 2009: Suddenly the earth opened up and the entire history of the city disappeared down a hole" (Schäfer 2010c, 152; cf. Figure 5.1). In an interview, Schäfer commented on the collapse as "an almost biblical omen for the end of the neoliberal city model" (2010a, 106; my translation).

In a related vein, Schäfer attacks the way in which the City of Hamburg uncritically deployed Richard Florida's widely debated, reductionist "creative class" policies (cf. Florida) in its urban development strategies in order to target

Figure 5.1 Christoph Schäfer's representation of the Cologne City Archive disaster: "an almost biblical omen".

Source: Schäfer (2010c, 153). Reproduced by permission of Spector Books, Leipzig.

this 'economically desirable' segment of the population. In addition to overstating the contribution of specific forms of culture to an attractive economic milieu, which has led to a socially exclusionist 'latte-macchiatoisation' of parts of the city, the concomitant instrumentalisation of art and artists as well as the gentrification associated with these processes have also met with significant resistance from artists refusing to be commodified as mere location factors conducive to the 'bohemian index' of a city.[4] The connection is captured as follows: "In 2004, Senator of Science Dräger hands out books by Richard Florida in the Hamburg city senate. Florida holds lectures. [Consulting firm] Roland Berger develops 'Hamburg, City of Talent'. Artists leave city" (Schäfer 2010c, 174).

Arguably the central issue in this most topical and specific chapter "Hamburg: Surrounding the 'Expanding City' with Projects" (165–271) in his pictorial essay *The City is our Factory* is that of gentrification, in response to which numerous projects and initiatives have been launched.

In addition to the more conventional flyers, protests, public lectures, performances or squatting, one of the more humorous ideas is the "degentrification kit" (cf. Figure 5.2), a set of items and ideas to "ruin the image of the neighbourhood" so as to scare away investors: "add foreign names to your door bell [...] dry ugly clothing outdoors [the illustration suggests the type of ribbed undershirt popularly known as a 'wife-beater'] [...] [use] broken windows effect foil[5] [...] hang Lidl bag out of your window [...] add satellite dish (or 2, or 3!)" (Schäfer 2010c, 183).[6] The *caveat* "[b]ut watch it – don't

Figure 5.2 Christoph Schäfer's drawing of the "degentrification kit": how to make a neighbourhood unattractive to investors.

Source: Schäfer (2010c, 183). Reproduced by permission of Spector Books, Leipzig.

get too creative [where the creatives are working, rents go up]" (Schäfer 2010c, 183) is characteristic of the constant awareness of the 'anti-gentrifier's dilemma', the insight that even (and especially) resistant cultural production can be commodified.[7]

It is not least the ongoing light-hearted reflections on this ambivalence of activist art and the self-mockery in the awareness of a privileged form of theory sudoku – insights which in no way trivialise the sincerity of the commitment – that make Schäfer's work so compelling. This is especially prominent in the final chapter entitled "The Evening I Would Like to Have on Film". The book here represents the gathering of a group of – apparently privileged – activist friends engaging in clever 'critical urban studies' talk in a place none other than the McDonald's in Hamburg Central Station:

> The evening I'd like to have as a movie began like this: We had arranged to meet with the Utopia Salon & Spa Group at the McDonald's in the central station.[8] We drank lattes and gazed at the tracks. Only 3 people showed up. The conversation revolved around arcades, urbanity, rambling, the promises of a by-gone age as encapsulated in architecture. After a while we left and went on talking as we walked. The evening was dry and warm. It was August 21, 2009.[9]
>
> (Schäfer 2010c, 274)

The corresponding drawing (cf. Figure 5.3) is highly allusive: three figures at a table perched above the platforms and underneath the steel arches of the station architecture reminiscent of the arches of the nineteenth-century Paris arcades memorialised in Benjamin's *Passagen-Werk*.[10]

The ambivalence of subversion and the awareness of the 'anti-gentrifier's dilemma' directly tie in with the questions raised in my initial discussion of voice, agency, privilege and the question of who, given the potential for commodification, ultimately benefits from such activism:

> It was our most radical gestures that could best be made use of. – To increase the value of real estate, to construct new neighbourhood identities. As soon as there was an illegal club somewhere, a cappuccino bar would open next door, followed by a new media agency ... we were management consultants [...] So we had acquired precisely the skills that image capitalism needs – visually literate, consumption-competent truffle pigs ...
>
> (Schäfer 2010c, 132, 134; omission marks original unless indicated as [...])

This is remarkably close to Mayer's thoughts in an essay on some of the key issues in 'right to the city' activism:

> Even though these coalitions do frequently succeed in preventing, or at least modifying crass neoliberal urban development projects, their struggles often end up saving some oases and protected spaces only for the *comparatively privileged protagonists*, spaces which increasingly become

Figure 5.3 Schäfer's allusive and self-reflexive mockery of privileged "critical urban studies" talk in a Benjaminean setting.

Source: Schäfer (2010c, 275). Reproduced by permission of Spector Books, Leipzig.

> *instrumentalized in creative city branding efforts* in the competitive entrepreneurial urban policy game. The chapter thus raises the questions whether the "right to the city" movements in the global North need not relate more directly to the struggles of groups that have been excluded from the model of the neoliberal city.
>
> (64; my emphasis)

What Mayer here notes about the need to "relate" different types of urban struggles to each other is precisely what Mark Purcell has termed a "well-known problem for left politics [...] [the need] to combine local struggles into something larger without reducing each struggle to a homogenous unity" (562). Here, according to Purcell, "[t]he right to the city [*sensu* Lefebvre] can be useful in establishing relations of equivalence among groups in a broad counterhegemonic urban alliance" (571f.).

This need for a broad range of highly diverse urban social movements to march under *one* banner and the 'right to the city' as a claim with such an integrative potential are also a central and recurring subject in Schäfer's account of urban activism in Hamburg:

> *Right to the City*: appropriation, social questions, counter-projects, international, tenant battles, poverty, solidarity, segregation, self-organized spaces [...] Unlikely alliances[11] [...] And there we are [...] a group of left

> activists, from different ethnical and religious backgrounds [...] To come together and fight we use the term *Right to the City*.
>
> (2010c, 236, 190; emphasis original)

In search of 'success factors' for urban activism and activist cultural production, in addition to such organisational issues of community organising, Schäfer in an interview with a German media studies journal also comments on the political implications of artistic form and the choice of media and genres:

> U.B.: Your book is not poly-perspectivist, but functions in a rather linear way from beginning to end, beginning with the history of the city of "Ur" and ending in the urban present.
>
> C.S.: Strictly pseudo-linear [...] I like techniques that compress things. It looks linear, fixed, pigeon-holed, but the brevity also opens up associative possibilities of jumping back and forth. Thus, even if universalism has rightly been criticized, such a schematic representation allows me to relate developments on different continents to each other – and thus also to relativize genealogies such as Eurocentrism. My book claims, first of all, to define fundamentally what a city is, what the urban revolution might be and what it aims at. At the same time, the book works against such linearity; there are constant prolepses and analepses.
>
> (Schäfer 2010b, 119f.; my translation)

Emphasising the processuality and openness of drawing, he further speaks about drawing as an activity in which exploratory doodling, the deliberate putting-to-paper of an idea and the making of a product until the last moment do not have to be mutually exclusive: "A drawing can potentially escape goal-directedness and instrumentalisation until the last second" (Schäfer 2010b, 116). This understanding is developed further in response to a critical question about de-collectivisation and his potential appropriation of drawings originally from and for a political context for his own artistic and economic self-promotion: "I was able to give talks in 'right to the city' contexts with these drawings, using them to illustrate Lefebvre's terms in a different way, thus using them for our exchange. There is no pure form that is entirely free of a potential commodification" (Schäfer 2010b, 122; my translation).

Given this constant exploration of artistic strategies of subversion, the considerable publicity and success achieved by the Hamburg movement, and finally Schäfer's own prominent role in it as an activist, participant observer and "embedded artist" (moderator in Schäfer 2009), a comment on the intersection of activism and cultural production in an earlier section of Schäfer's book might well be read as an oblique remark on his own successful negotiation of these issues: "Some succeeded in connecting their sub-cultural and art practices with the struggles against gentrification" (2010c, 130).

Conclusions

A few tentative conclusions may be drawn based on the above observations: Strategically speaking, it seems that a success factor in urban activism is to achieve what Purcell calls "networks of equivalence [...] counterhegemonic combinations of differentiated but equivalent popular struggles" (562) and what Christoph Schäfer refers to as "*[u]nlikely alliances: Letting disparities co-exist and emphasizing differences even while acting together*" (2010c, 236; emphasis original).

As far as aesthetic strategies in activist cultural production are concerned, they frequently appear to be the result of a keen awareness of the 'anti-gentrifier's dilemma'. But the more theory-conscious and self-reflexive artists and activists also appear to be aware that their own brand of urban activism is occasionally an activity of the privileged rather than of those most directly affected by gentrification and social exclusion. It seems that one of the recurring strategies in response to these dilemmas is a highly self-conscious, extremely reflexive, media-conscious form of experimentalism in cultural production, frequently with fairly explicit claims as to the emancipatory potential of this formally experimental form of presentation. In Schäfer's case, his highly self-conscious formal strategies of undercutting commodification appear to work: His drawings have been used in lectures at MIT and elsewhere and thus furnish material for academic discussions, but they also work as posters, flyers, food for thought in community workshops, etc. Thus, without claiming that Schäfer's work was pivotal in this, the Hamburg 'right to the city' initiative has had a number of very remarkable successes; and as long as activist cultural production can thus be tapped into at various levels – and the kind of deliberately open-ended, exploratory process of drawing seems to lend itself to that – it does have the potential to be instrumental in the kind of urban resistance movement we are concerned with here.

Hence, urban activist writings, whether anti-gentrification pamphlets or activist cultural production,[12] play an important role in the larger framework of this study: In the course of my conceptual trajectories from descriptive 'model of' to prescriptive 'model for' and from literary texts to pragmatic texts, they occupy a half-way position and clearly combine critical commentary with advocacy for a just and equitable urban future. My discussion of this interplay, then, paves the way both for the side-by-side reading of literary and planning texts in Chapter 6 and for the discussion of 'scripts' with their comparable oscillation between descriptive and normative commentary in Chapter 7.

Notes

1 For the city as a location central to the formation of social movements and for a discussion of literature on 'urban social movements' (Lefebvre, Castells, Harvey, etc.), cf. Miller/Nicholls.

2 Like the entire book, these texts are in both English and German.

3 The six chapters are titled as follows: "Lefebvre 4 Kids" (3), "Appropriated Space" (69), "1979: The City is Our Factory" (115), "Black Holes" (151), "Hamburg: Surrounding the 'Expanding City' with Projects" (165), "The Evening I Would Like to Have on Film" (272).

4 Cf. also the much-publicised protest of artists in Hamburg against such endeavours: "Kunst als Protest" from 2009.

5 There is a certain irony here in the reference to Wilson/Kelling's notorious "Broken Windows" essay, in that the 'broken windows theory' is usually vehemently attacked by 'critical urban theory'-inflected urban activism and scholarship, because it has been read as supporting excessive zero-tolerance policing.

6 The phrases appear in a drawing, hence in no particular order; the order is mine.

7 More generally, the 'anti-gentrifier's dilemma' refers to the problem that an awareness of one's own privileged position and even activism against gentrification may not be enough to avoid supporting the process by one's mere presence as someone able to pay higher rents. A pithy literary representation of the issue is to be found in Kiran Desai's *The Inheritance of Loss*: "One evening, Biju was sent to deliver hot-and-sour soups and egg foo yong to three Indian girls, students, new additions to the neighborhood in an apartment just opened under reviewed city laws to raised rents. Banners reading 'Antigentrification Day' had been hauled up over the street by the longtime residents for a festival earlier in the afternoon [...] One day the Indian girls hoped to be gentry, but right now, despite being unwelcome in the neighborhood, they were in the student stage of vehemently siding with the poor people who wished them gone" (49).

8 McDonald's is, of course, a highly contentious place for – broadly speaking – leftist groups to meet; like Coca Cola, it has long been a controversial brand boycotted by some groups and defended by others.

9 Cf. also Schäfer 2010c, 284: "We stopped at a cellar restaurant. A place I had never been before. We got hold of a corner sofa and on went the conversation: Lefebvre and the urban revolution, David Harvey and the urban roots of the fiscal crisis, how a post-crisis urbanisation model might look, the invention of the Bohemian and its totalisation today, the 3D printer and Fab Lab [...] Hours later we left the pub, poisoned with alcohol and nicotine."

10 In the Bergermann interview, Schäfer explicitly speaks of this as "a Benjaminean situation" (2010b, 122; my translation).

11 The terms and concepts appear in a drawing, hence in no particular order; the order is mine.

12 This could also be said of the type of politically committed scholarship I discuss in Chapter 3: Klein's *The History of Forgetting* as a type of activist scholarship as well as *Bleeding Through* as a form of scholarly and activist cultural production similarly combine critical commentary and – at least implicitly – views on alternative, more socially just urban development.

References

Benjamin, Walter. *Das Passagen-Werk*. Ed. Rolf Tiedemann. Frankfurt/Main: Suhrkamp, 1992. 2 vols.

Brenner, Neil. "What is Critical Urban Theory?" *Cities for People, not for Profit: Critical Urban Theory and the Right to the City*. Ed. Neil Brenner, Peter Marcuse, Margit Mayer. London: Routledge, 2012. 11–23.

Brenner, Neil, Peter Marcuse, Margit Mayer, eds. *Cities for People, not for Profit: Critical Urban Theory and the Right to the City*. London: Routledge, 2012.

Desai, Kiran. *The Inheritance of Loss*. London: Penguin, 2006.

Florida, Richard. *Cities and the Creative Class*. New York: Routledge, 2005.

Gurr, Jens Martin. "'All those who know the term "gentrification" are part of the problem': Self-Reflexivity in Urban Activism and Cultural Production." *Resistance: Subjects, Representations, Contexts*. Ed. Martin Butler, Paul Mecheril, Lea Brenningmeyer. Bielefeld: transcript, 2017. 117–133.

Gurr, Jens Martin. "Critical Urban Studies and/in 'Right to the City' Movements: The Politics of Form in Activist Cultural Production." *Resistance and the City: Challenging Urban Space*. Ed. Christoph Ehland, Pascal Fischer. Amsterdam: Brill/Rodopi, 2018. 181–198.

Harvey, David. "The Right to the City." *New Left Review* 53 (2008): 23–40.

Keating, Kevin. "A Critique of San Francisco's Mission Yuppie Eradication Project." 2007. www.infoshop.org/myep/mission-yuppie-eradication-project.

Klein, Norman M. *The History of Forgetting: Los Angeles and the Erasure of Memory* [1997]. New York: Verso, 2008.

Klein, Norman M., Rosemary Comella, Andreas Kratky. *Bleeding Through: Layers of Los Angeles 1920–1986* [DVD and Book]. Karlsruhe: ZKM digital arts edition, 2003.

"Kunst als Protest: Lasst den Scheiß!; Hamburg nur noch als 'Marke', der wir Aura, Ambiente und Freizeitwert verpassen sollen? Das machen wir nicht mit. Ein Künstler-Manifest gegen die Hamburger Kulturpolitik." *Zeit*, 5 November 2009. www.zeit.de/2009/46/Kuenstlermanifest.

Lefebvre, Henri. *The Production of Space* [1974]. Trans. Donald Nicholson-Smith. Oxford: Blackwell, 1991.

Liss, Jon. "The Right to the City: From Theory to Grassroots Alliance." *Cities for People, not for Profit: Critical Urban Theory and the Right to the City*. Ed. Neil Brenner, Peter Marcuse, Margit Mayer. London: Routledge, 2012. 250–263.

Mayer, Margit. "The 'Right to the City' in Urban Social Movements." *Cities for People, not for Profit: Critical Urban Theory and the Right to the City*. Ed. Neil Brenner, Peter Marcuse, Margit Mayer. London: Routledge, 2012. 63–85.

Miller, Byron, Walter Nicholls. "Social Movements in Urban Society: The City as a Space of Politicization." *Urban Geography* 34.4 (2013): 452–473.

Mission Yuppie Eradication Project. www.foundsf.org/index.php?title=Mission_Yuppie_ Eradication_Project.

Purcell, Mark. "To Inhabit Well: Counterhegemonic Movements and the Right to the City." *Urban Geography* 34.4 (2013): 560–574.

Schäfer, Christoph. "The City is our Factory: Politics of Desire and the Production of Urban Spaces between Grande Latte and Park Fiction." Lecture at MIT, 28 September 2009.

Schäfer, Christoph. "Ein biblisches Warnzeichen" [Interview]. *Der Spiegel* 21/2010a. 106.

Schäfer, Christoph. "Maschinen aus Möglichkeiten: *Die Stadt ist unsere Fabrik*" [Schäfer in interview with Ulrike Bergermann]. *Zeitschrift für Medienwissenschaft* 3 (2010b): 115–123.

Schäfer, Christoph. *Die Stadt ist unsere Fabrik/The City is our Factory*. Leipzig: Spector Books, 2010c.

Smith, Neil. *The New Urban Frontier: Gentrification and the Revanchist City*. London, New York: Routledge, 1996.

Smith, Neil. "Toward a Theory of Gentrification: A Back to the City Movement by Capital, not People." *Journal of the American Planning Association* 45.4 (1979): 538–548.

Solnit, Rebecca, Susan Schwartzenberg. *Hollow City: The Siege of San Francisco and the Crisis of American Urbanism*. London, New York: Verso, 2000.

Wilson, James Q., George L. Kelling. "Broken Windows: The Police and Neighborhood Safety." *Atlantic Monthly* (March 1982): 29–38.

6 Narrative Path Dependencies

From Scenario Building in Literary Texts to the Narratology and Rhetoric of Pragmatic Texts

This chapter further seeks to conceptualise the transition from texts as 'models *of*' the city to texts as 'models *for*' the city. More precisely, it develops a theoretical framework for the side-by-side analysis of the real-world functions of literary texts, for instance in scenario building, and of the literary strategies in and functions of pragmatic texts such as planning documents. In doing so, it draws on a number of fields and builds on selected concepts from narratology, the theory of metaphor as developed in the interplay between literary studies and the theory of historiography, research on cognitive models in cognitive linguistics and cognitive anthropology, the history of ideas as well as approaches to text–context relations and *Funktionsgeschichte*.[1] Though I do not wish to add to the wealth of material on text–context relations directly (for a compelling approach, cf. Baßler), a few considerations on the relationship of literature and context are in order. Finally, developing further recent narratological research on planning texts in literary urban studies,[2] the chapter proposes the notion of what I call "narrative path dependencies" in planning texts.

A Caveat: Ambiguity as Blessing or Curse?

If the field of literary urban studies is genuinely interested in a productive exchange with planning studies, as I think it must be, a potential challenge emerges from the very different valuation of ambiguity in both fields: While ambiguity has generally been regarded as a central characteristic of literary texts and has been highly valorised in literary studies, which thrive on ambiguities, it has generally been regarded as a problem in much planning research.[3]

Even though the Latin root "*ambi-*" strictly speaking suggests exactly two meanings, ambiguity may be defined as the phenomenon of a term, an utterance, a text, an image or a concept having several meanings or potential interpretations. The first definition in the *OED* is telling, because it suggests both a neutral to positive as well as a clearly negative evaluation: "Originally and chiefly with reference to language: the fact or quality of having different possible meanings; capacity for being interpreted in more than one way; (also) lack of specificity or exactness" (*OED*, 1a). At the simplest level, many common words in everyday language are ambiguous, words like 'set', 'put' or 'bank' (both as nouns and as verbs) being obvious examples. Visually, the

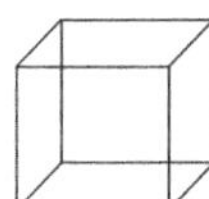

Figure 6.1 The 'Necker cube' as an example of visual ambiguity.
Source: Daniel Bläser, www.dbgrafik.de.

'Necker cube' is a well-known example of ambiguity: It is unclear whether we are looking at the cube from above or from below (cf. Figure 6.1).

Ambiguity may arise at several levels and may have several causes: We might distinguish – at least – between verbal, syntactic and semantic or conceptual ambiguity. Moreover, ambiguity needs to be distinguished from related terms such as ambivalence or contradiction, which, although frequently treated as overlapping or even as synonymous, should be regarded as different categories from diverse fields of intellectual inquiry (for this cf. Berndt/Kammer; Gurr 2017). While 'ambivalence' is originally a psychological or cognitive concept designating a state of indecision, undecidability or unclear evaluation, and 'contradiction' is a notion from logic designating two or more irreconcilable propositions, 'ambiguity' is originally a rhetorical concept (cf. Berndt/Kammer). Thus, ambiguity in a text may be the *result* of attitudinal ambivalence, which manifests itself in unresolved contradictions in the text: For instance, conflicting interests in a planning process may manifest themselves in irreconcilable requirements, which may be understood as the result of attitudinal ambivalence on the part of the authors. In any longer document, ambiguity may also be the result of a sequence of propositions which, each in themselves, are unambiguous but irreconcilable with one another. Thus, even if any individual passage is perfectly clear, the unharmonised concatenation of contradictory passages, as its cumulative effect, may still create an ambiguity of the text as a whole (cf. Gurr 2017 for a detailed discussion of a specific literary example). This sequential type of ambiguity may be the result of ambivalent attitudes on the part of one author, but it is frequently the result of an unsuccessful attempt at harmonising or combining conflicting interests. In a more positive sense, however, ambiguity does not have to be seen as the *result* of, say, an imprecise use of language. Rather, language, and especially literary language, often allows for the resolution, suspension or sublation – one might more critically also speak of the 'glossing over' – of contradictions in a type of deliberate ambiguity (cf. Gurr 2017 for a more detailed discussion).

While most societal fields will generally seek to eliminate or at least to minimise ambiguity – law, medicine or technology come to mind, but the same can be said of the field of planning – scholars of narrative have argued that ambiguity may also foster social cohesion: By allowing more diverse groups of stakeholders to find points of identification, narratives with a certain fuzziness and indeterminacy, those which leave room for interpretation and negotiation, are *more* rather than *less* socially binding than precise narratives, and thus *more* conducive to generating social cohesion and to canvassing public support (cf. Koschorke 349–352 *et passim*). A classic case in point would be programmes of political parties, which, if too specific, could hardly generate broad support across different societal groups and coalitions of interest.

While one will hardly want to suggest that planning documents – let alone legal texts or contracts – should deliberately be ambiguous, it may be helpful to bear in mind this social function of ambiguity. Thus, not only is the tolerance of ambiguity a central ability for individuals to function in complex, highly differentiated social environments. Ambiguous documents – or those which allow different stakeholders complementary, possibly even contradictory means of identification – may even productively function as 'boundary objects' enabling communication and exchange across academic cultures as well as between professionals and laypeople.[4] It seems, however, that contentious issues are here frequently 'postponed' rather than resolved.[5]

Scenarios, Symbolic Action, Emplotment and Cognition: Concepts for the Contextual Reading of Literary and Planning Texts

One of the central functions of literature, according to one understanding, is that it serves as a form of symbolic action, as a social experiment free from the constraints of everyday life – literature as 'de-pragmatised behaviour in rehearsal', which makes it possible symbolically to try out in fiction different scenarios or potential solutions for key societal issues.[6] This is the view formulated, among others, by Kenneth Burke, Dieter Wellershoff, Wolfgang Iser or somewhat more recently in an impressive volume edited by Stefan Glomb and Stefan Horlacher. One classic formulation is Wellershoff's, who spoke of literature as providing "spaces of simulation for alternative behaviour in rehearsal at reduced risk"[7] (57; my translation; cf. also Glomb/Horlacher *passim*). Kenneth Burke's notion of "Literature as Equipment for Living" is a related concept, according to which any work of literature has the social function of being an attempt at naming a situation and coming to terms with it. In this sense, literature can be seen as an assembly of case studies in naming situations and in solving problems, an arsenal of strategies for dealing with situations that is developed in fiction but can lay claim to real-world applicability (cf. Burke; for a convenient summary of his position, cf. the essay "Literature as Equipment for Living" in that volume, 293–304).

What is also helpful to an understanding of texts as models *for* urban developments are the views of Jürgen Link, Winfried Fluck or Hubert Zapf on functions of literature in the system of culture in the sense of a 'history of its functions' ('*Funktionsgeschichte*'; for an overview cf. Gymnich/Nünning; for one influential account, cf. Fluck). Thus, following Zapf's suggestive terminology in his "triadic model of functions" (2002, 63ff.), literature can function as a form of critical cultural diagnosis ("critical meta-discourse"), or as a "reintegrating inter-discourse", which re-integrates into the cultural whole what is otherwise marginalised or repressed. Finally, it is also an "imaginative counter-discourse", which develops alternatives to dominant discourses and processes and which can thus assume a utopian potential (Zapf 2001; cf. also Zapf 2002; and several contributions in Zapf 2008).

It is especially this last function that productively relates to Wellershoff's notion of literature as a 'de-pragmatised rehearsal' (57). But these considerations relate more specifically to the strand of research connected to the 'story turn in planning', which has made central fields of knowledge in literary and cultural studies productive to interdisciplinary urban research. Thus, planning research has for some 20 years now recognised the centrality of narratives to urban planning and urban development (cf. for instance Ameel 2021; Sandercock 2010; Throgmorton 1996, 2003; van Hulst). While in Zapf's suggestive terminology literature functions as an "imaginative counter-discourse", Sandercock in an essay on the "story turn in planning" has in remarkably similar ways stressed the role of narratives in developing and fostering alternative scenarios: "Stories and storytelling can be powerful agents or aids in the service of change, as shapers of a new imagination of alternatives" (Sandercock 2010, 25; cf. also van Hulst 303 *et passim*).

In this vein, storytelling is frequently deployed in ambitious, large-scale urban development projects such as the reuse of former industrial or port areas in order, for instance, to project a *genius loci* or to conjure up a specific type of urbanity. Thus, it is hardly surprising that large-scale urban projects have even specifically commissioned literary texts in order to develop and foster scenarios for future developments of these areas.[8]

More specifically, however, narratives (together with suggestive visualisations) are often used in scenario depictions, which, originally in the field of futures studies (for an overview, cf. Bell), but also in the field of urban development, are frequently used as descriptions of a potential future development (merely sketched or fully fleshed out), usually presented in the form of several alternative possible developments. A high-profile example of four global scenarios for 2050 – including suggestive narratives, visualisation and personalisation through allegedly representative individuals and their lives in 2050 – is provided by consultancy ARUP's 2019 foresight report *Scenarios 2050: Four Plausible Scenarios* (cf. ARUP). More specifically, research on the future of urban mobility frequently works with different scenarios, alternative versions of the future. Project NEMO (New Emscher Mobility; my translation) at the University of Duisburg-Essen, for instance, a project on future mobilities in the Emscher region, works with five scenarios in which (1) rapid technological innovation will have led to largely automated mobility systems ('smart mobility'), (2) a concern with human health and well-being will have led to an emphasis on walkability, bikeability and electrically-powered public transport with an inner-city ban on fossil-fuel vehicles ('healthy city'), (3) inhospitable living conditions in cities will have led to deurbanisation, or (4) the present-day situation continues as it is (commonly referred to as 'business as usual'). Finally, there is also a scenario that combines elements of the other scenarios (5). A frequently formulated scenario not visualised here is one in which drastic environmental degradation will have led to the enforced imposition of radical

Figure 6.2 Visualisation of five scenarios for future urban mobility and settlement patterns.

Source: Reprinted with permission from the New Emscher Mobility Research Project, funded by Stiftung Mercator. Copyright by University of Duisburg-Essen, Institute of Mobility and City Planning (imobis), 2020.

measures ('eco-dictatorship'). Each of these scenarios may be outlined in a short text accompanied by suggestive visualisations (cf. Figure 6.2).

Scenario techniques are usually said to have originated in military strategies during the Cold War, with Herman Kahn of the RAND Corporation combining game theory and fictional stories to devise possible strategies in the face of nuclear threats (cf. Ghamari-Tabrizi). An awareness of possible future developments and their impacts on a given system (a city, a region, the nation-state, the planet as a whole) is clearly crucial to any responsible and circumspect planning and strategy development.

If we regard 'scenario building' and the testing of alternative parameter settings in their impact on a given system as a crucial function of urban systems modelling, an important parallel between literature and planning emerges, and the uses of literature and literary studies for planning purposes become apparent: If literature is regarded as a "space of simulation for alternative behaviour in rehearsal at reduced risk" (Wellershoff 57; my translation; cf. above), literary texts become models *for* the city in a manner that corresponds in interesting ways with planning and decision models.

In the practice of planning, most plans – whether they are master plans for an entire district or plans for an individual building – do not explicitly present alternatives. However, in order to do justice to the fact that planning in democratic societies should never pretend to be without alternatives, but also in order to give stakeholders a genuine sense of involvement, planning might benefit from explicitly formulating alternatives. Thus, planning might work with a limited number of scenarios fleshed out in brief narrative descriptions and suggestive visualisations. These ideally come with considerations of anticipated costs, benefits, impact assessments and other relevant discussions of opportunities and threats.[9]

In addition to their function in allowing for more informed decision-making, scenarios also have a purpose in the context of planning in and for situations of uncertainty. Climate research, for instance, has long realised the need to think in terms of scenarios rather than pretending that developments can be predicted with a high degree of certainty. Thus, different scenarios – whether for demographic developments, climate change and environmental degradation or different technological developments – might also help urban planners to decide what would be meaningful choices ('What would we be doing anyway?/ What would be helpful under any circumstances?'). Thus, thinking in terms of scenarios might help planners to become aware of path dependencies and to remain aware that the closure (potentially) provided by one plan may be the origin of a new planning problem. Scenario techniques can thus aid in developing open-ended, potentially reversible planning solutions in and for conditions of uncertainty.

In order further to conceptualise text–context relations in literary urban studies, I here want to use the notion of 'emplotment', the turning into narrative of concepts, events, oppositions. This is what Paul Ricœur calls "mise en intrigue" (1983, *passim*). According to Ricœur, it is the telling of stories that allows the expression of human experience, of history and of human identity.[10] Narrative, in other words, is an anthropological necessity; we need narrative as a form of making sense of the world: "I see in the plots we invent the privileged means by which we re-configure our confused, unformed, and at the limit mute temporal experience" (Ricœur 1984, I, xi).[11] Literature thus becomes a prime form of appropriation and refiguration of the world and ultimately a form of sense-making. This notion of literature as necessarily a culturally embedded form centrally concerned with human experience might be formulated in terms of what Iser calls "the return of lived reality in the text" (21; my translation).[12]

However fictitious a text is, it cannot help being in some sense mimetic. This connection between text and 'reality' can also be conceptualised in terms of what Stierle calls "connecting worlds in literature" which extend the real world into the realm of the imaginary (176; my translation).[13]

In trying to understand the way in which experience is turned into narrative, I use Hayden White's notion of 'emplotment' (for the following, cf. mainly White 1–42). As one of the most important theorists of narrative, mainly in historiography, but also of fiction, virtually all of White's work can be seen as an attempt to come to terms with the way in which narrative is used to structure and order the representation of experience. In producing such narrative, White argues, there are only four basic plots available: comedy, tragedy, romance and satire. The choice of a plot structure, moreover, also implies the choice of a figure of speech and thought – he analogises them with the established tropes of metaphor, metonymy, synecdoche and irony – and carries an implicit ideology, a way of seeing the world. Drawing on Frye, Pepper and Mannheim, White thus comes up with an extremely complex and sometimes quite schematic, though highly suggestive, combination of these basic plots, of key figures of speech and of ideological implications.

What becomes crucial to me here is the research carried out in cognitive linguistics since the 1980s by George Lakoff, Mark Johnson, Mark Turner, Gilles Fauconnier, Zoltan Kövecses and others.[14] This research has revealed the close connection between figures of speech, figures of thought, human experience and the way in which cognitive patterns shape our understanding of the world. Metaphors and other figures of speech, according to this research *are* figures of thought:

> Metaphors [...] are conceptual in nature. They are among our principle vehicles for understanding. And they play a central role in the construction of social and political reality [...] New metaphors have the power to create a new reality. This can begin to happen when we start to comprehend our experience in terms of a metaphor, and it becomes a deeper reality when we begin to act in terms of it [...] Much cultural change arises from the introduction of new metaphorical concepts and the loss of old ones.
>
> (Lakoff/Johnson 1980, 159, 145)

We construct reality through conceptual metaphors. This research has become far more rigorously and empirically cognitive in recent years (for an excellent overview, cf. Geeraerts/Cuyckens, especially part I, 3–418), and according to an increasingly prevalent view, these figures of speech and thought are often based on human experience and virtually become 'embodied' in the sense that they become hard-wired patterns in the brain.

A related field of research at the intersection of cognitive linguistics and cognitive anthropology is concerned with cognitive or cultural models. These are established concepts of perception and cognition that also shape thought and behaviour. Quinn and Holland in a classic account define cultural models as follows:

> [Culture is understood as] shared knowledge – not a people's customs and artefacts and oral traditions, but what they must know in order to act as they do, make the things they make, and interpret their experience in the distinctive way they do [...] *Cultural models* are presupposed, taken-for-granted models of the world that are widely shared [...] by the members of a society and that play an enormous role in their understanding of that world and their behaviour in it.
>
> (4; italics original; cf. also Kronenfeld 2018, 83–100)

It is one of the central insights of this branch of research that these forms of conceptualising the world are made up of a very limited number of small and comparatively simple building blocks. The "prototypical scenarios" encoded in these simplified models of reality and the applicability of these models to a wide range of situations can help to account for how we acquire knowledge about the world, how we are able appropriately to act in it, and how we can share this knowledge by means of communication (cf. Quinn/Holland 35).

As might be expected – and as Zoltan Kövecses has shown in his excellent 2005 study *Metaphor in Culture* – a number of these metaphorical ways of conceptualising the world are specific to certain cultures, while others are virtually universal and appear in all cultures. This may be indicative of just *how* fundamental these models are. Although strictly speaking, Kövecses is only concerned with metaphorical concepts, these are frequently elaborate and far-reaching enough to qualify as cultural models in the sense I have just outlined.

Even if we eschew the simplistic version of linguistic determinism now largely refuted as being untenable, what all this ultimately means is that patterns of conceptualising the world are deeply rooted and inescapably shape thinking – and writing, for that matter. In a sense, culturally embedded beings that we are, we cannot help sharing a – surprisingly limited – number of figures of thought, cognitive models and plot patterns available to us in negotiating and making sense of reality. Thus, in synthesising these concepts and approaches, I suggest that – by leveraging both the close textual awareness of 'literary studies' and the contextual awareness of 'cultural studies' – the specific form in which a text emplots an issue, in a limited number of basic patterns available, can be used to ascribe certain functions to a text in a given cultural situation. If I thus propose to discuss literary texts and their functions in the system of culture, it is clear that there can be no mechanist scheme in the sense of a one-to-one mapping of one plot pattern or one trope and one ideological view. But White's notion of a correspondence or "elective affinity" between certain figures of thought, "modes of emplotment, and ideological implication" (29 *et passim*), if not used too schematically, can be very illuminating.[15] This is where Ricœur, White, cognitive linguistics and '*Funktionsgeschichte*' can fruitfully be brought together in an attempt to use the narrative patterns and central tropes a text makes use of as a tool in 'cultural diagnosis' or at least in order to ascribe certain functions to a text in a given cultural context. Without wishing to be too apologetic, I do believe that this might be one way of continuing to show that close engagements with individual texts as well as "distant reading" (in Moretti's sense) or "wide reading" (cf. Hallet 2002, 2010) can be fruitfully combined – and that a text-oriented literary studies approach can simultaneously be fruitful in the 'real-world'-oriented field of literary urban studies. Finally, an awareness of the extent to which cognitive models and their emplotment open up or foreclose, suggest or deter from different possible developments may be conducive to more sensitive or circumspect planning and planning communication.

A Key Application: Narrative Path Dependencies

After decades of almost exclusively analysing literary representations of the city – in the sense of primarily descriptive models *of* the city (for a typology of central literary strategies, cf. Chapter 2) – the emerging field of literary urban studies has begun to shift perspectives and to leave the comfort zone: It has begun to engage more centrally with plot patterns, tropes and other – broadly speaking – 'literary' characteristics of planning documents and other pragmatic texts as well as with the comparative reading of literary and pragmatic texts.

Here, both the pragmatic functions and affordances of literary texts *and* the 'literary' strategies, patterns and mechanisms of planning texts are of interest.[16] So far, there is a predominance of studies from planning research and planning theory, which frequently use the concept of 'narrative' and other narratological terms and concepts in inflationary and fuzzy ways. There is as yet no substantial narratology of planning documents, though recent work by Lieven Ameel or Bart Keunen and Sofie Verraest and others point in this direction (cf. also Buchenau/Gurr 2016, 2018; Sattler). Such work has been able to highlight how productive analyses of planning texts informed by narratology, the theory of metaphors or rhetoric generally can be: Which *dénouements*, path dependencies, inclusions and exclusions are suggested or even imposed by the plot patterns associated with different genres or by established patterns of narrative sense-making?

Read in this light, planning texts can frequently be shown to function in profoundly 'literary' ways (for a more detailed discussion, cf. Chapters 7 and 8), calling up epic, comic, tragic or melodramatic plot patterns and narrative conventions. In this vein (but without exploring their generic implications), Throgmorton (2003, 142f.) speaks of "at least five broad narratives [that] are commonly told about urban areas in America" and mentions:

1. "the city as a site of opportunity and excitement";
2. "the city as a nightmare";
3. "the city as a site of injustice, oppression, and exclusion (but also hope)";
4. "the environmentalists' interpretation. According to it, the city is a site of activities that are rapidly eroding the ecological base upon which those activities are founded";

5. "the city of ghosts. This offers a narrative of memory, of loss, of small towns drying up and blowing away [...] of neighborhoods being destroyed by urban renewal [or] being eviscerated by deindustrialization".

Though this inventory of narratives is hardly complete, it is clear that each of these patterns suggests different outcomes, inclusions and exclusions.

For this type of analysis, a concept I propose to call "narrative path dependency" may be fruitful: While 'path dependency' is a common concept in planning, it is conceptually surprisingly close to the analysis of plot patterns in literary studies, where the choice of specific plot patterns suggests or even predetermines certain outcomes. In planning, path dependencies are defined as developments in which a situation or decision to a large extent predetermines the future development of a system, so that decisions at one point in time might severely limit the range of options for future decision-makers. In this vein, David Harvey provides the well-known example of the building of a nuclear power station, which creates a legacy not only of dangerous nuclear waste that will need to be safely stored for thousands of years; it also predetermines social processes and power relations: The management of a nuclear power station in critical condition, for reasons of urgency and expertise, obviously cannot be subject to democratic decision-making processes but requires rapid expert intervention (cf. Harvey 229). The decision to build a nuclear power station can thus be said to create multiple – technological, environmental, social and political – path dependencies.

If one assumes that the built environment shapes social processes just as social processes shape the built environment (cf. Harvey), it is clear that planning decisions – especially if they are decisions which either create long-term structures or which generate technological lock-ins – have long-term consequences for the living conditions in cities. Thus – just as decisions for technological standards in markets with a need for a systemic fit of different components create technological lock-ins (think DOS vs. Mac or the printer market) – planning decisions can create path dependencies which impose on future generations the consequences of blind spots or short-sightedness at the time of making the decision. A case in point may be the decision in many post-war European cities as well as in much twentieth-century planning in North American cities, to plan cities around individual automotive mobility at a time when environmental degradation, climate change or geopolitical considerations with regard to fossil fuel dependencies were not an issue. This created path dependencies in terms of functional zoning, the use of space, (dis-) incentives for living in the city or in suburbs, environmental developments, urban public health and many other fields. The million-dollar question for contemporary planning is thus the question of what future generations will recognise as present-day blind spots, limitations or unquestioned preoccupations and which path dependencies they will have led to.

Insights into the limitations of planning in recent decades have further highlighted the need to consider path dependencies in urban planning: this is true both for insights into the role of emergence – spontaneous, unplanned (and unplannable) processes in urban development – as well as for the more general insight into the limits of planning and into the constraints of planning in and for conditions of uncertainty.

More generally, insights into the role of path dependencies for planning and insights into the limits of planning have led to what might be referred to as a 'new modesty in planning' after the perceived failure of many high-flying plans in twentieth-century planning (cf., for instance, much large-scale modernist planning in the wake of Le Corbusier). This more modest type of planning seeks to limit path dependencies by allowing for reversible planning decisions. The city of Portland, Oregon, has often been credited with pioneering such planning principles in the early 2000s (cf. Jain).

In literary studies, where path dependency is not a common concept, the choice of narrative patterns, genres and modes of emplotment can be seen as creating the literary equivalent of path dependencies: Specific modes of emplotment – for instance comedy, tragedy, satire or romance (cf. White "Introduction") – with their generic implications as well as central tropes and references to established patterns of narrative sense-making – can be said to create narrative path dependencies by suggesting or even determining specific outcomes, inclusions and exclusions. Thus, if urban development narratives are formulated in terms of 'growth', 'agency', 'identity formation', 'the finding of a proper voice' or 'attainment of potential', then these are the generic terms of the *Bildungsroman* especially of the late eighteenth and the nineteenth centuries as the narrative of emergent self-confidence, self-realisation and agency. These, however, clash with the more recent generic development of the *Bildungsroman*, which frequently no longer follows such optimistic patterns, but rather stages abortive attempts at rising from poverty or tells stories of racism and glass ceilings preventing the attainment of agency (for the *Bildungsroman* in urban planning, cf. also Ameel 2016).

Another case in point for the need for literary studies analyses of planning documents and urban development discourses is the common – often uncritical – designation of certain groups (often artists, students or members of the LGBTQ community) as 'pioneers of urban change' or, even more incisively, 'pioneers on the frontier of urban revitalisation' (often in gentrification contexts). This can be shown – often unintentionally – to actualise the implications of the frontier trope by raising the question who the 'hostile native Americans' implied in the frontier pattern might be, thus suggesting potentially divisive and agonistic patterns in urban development as well as patterns of inclusion and exclusion (for this, cf. Smith; for the implications of other key metaphors and tropes, cf., e.g., Cresswell; Keunen/Verraest; cf. also my discussion of the conceptual and ideological implications of plot patterns, tropes and metaphors earlier in this chapter). Certain tropes can thus – often unintentionally or even against the 'intended' logic of a planning text – suggest narrative patterns, again with associated outcomes, inclusions and exclusions, and reproduce or reinforce them. This type of research relies on developments in cognitive science and their repercussions in literary and cultural studies, which have foregrounded the power of figurative thought and the way in which cognitive models guiding thought and behaviour rely on figures of speech and thought. In attempts at securing socially integrative planning, attention to the implications of the chosen metaphor or narrative patterns and their suggested path dependencies can thus be vital to detecting and avoiding unintended or counter-intuitive suggestions.

Notes

1 A more detailed discussion of this approach is to be found in Gurr 2013.
2 For a compelling and detailed discussion of narratives in planning, cf. Ameel 2021.
3 While there is a substantial discussion about issues of 'complexity' in planning theory, this is hardly the case with 'ambiguity'. In the few contributions there are, 'ambiguity' generally appears as a problem to be solved (cf. for instance Adhikari/Li). For a more differentiated discussion, in which ambiguity nonetheless clearly seems problematic, cf. Forester 89 *et passim*. For a discussion of ambiguity in the definition of planning problems, cf. the classic account in Rittel/Webber. I am grateful to Patsy Healey for bringing to my attention the fact that 'certainty', 'flexibility' and 'fuzziness' rather than 'ambiguity' are the relevant terms used in different planning debates. In each case, it seems, there are conflicts of interest with regard to the openness as opposed to determinacy of planning policies, regulations and individual plans. While the notion of 'boundary objects' suggests itself here, there appears still to be a tendency to regard ambiguity as ultimately problematic. For a discussion of ambiguity as related to ambivalence and contradiction, cf. Gurr 2017.
4 For the notion of 'boundary objects', cf. the classic account in Star/Griesemer.
5 For the ambivalent effects of ambiguity in strategic planning from a management perspective, cf. Abdallah/Langley.
6 However, literary texts frequently do not attempt to solve a problem by imposing an answer – and even if they do, they are often less interesting for the answer they propose than for having asked the question and raised the problem.
7 The German original reads: "Simulationsräume für ein alternatives Probehandeln mit herabgesetztem Risiko" (Wellershoff 57).
8 In an excellent essay, Lieven Ameel has explored the case of Finnish novelist Hannu Mäkelä, who, in 2009, published a novel expressly commissioned to accompany and foster the development of Helsinki's former port area Jätkäsaari into a gentrification-prone waterfront residential area (cf. Ameel 2016).
9 One specific type of working with scenarios at the intersection between planning studies and literary/cultural studies has recently received more attention, namely research on the potential role of science fiction for planning. In this vein, the German Federal Institute for Building, Urban and Spatial Research (BBSR) in 2015 issued a study entitled *Learning from Science Fiction Cities: Scenarios for Urban Planning* (my translation; cf. BBSR). Moreover, as increasingly frequent collaboration between planning experts and science fiction writers shows, literary texts as models *of* and models *for* urban realities also have a crucial role to play in developing scenarios.
10 For this, cf. also Mandelbrote: "[M]emory and the telling of stories about oneself, allow the expression not only of the human experience of time, and of history, but also of human identity. We are who we are because of the stories which we remember and repeat about ourselves" (339).

11 The French original reads: "Je vois dans les intrigues que nous inventons le moyen privilégié par lequel nous re-configurons notre expérience temporelle confuse, informe et, à la limite, muette" (Ricœur 1983, I, 13).
12 The German original reads: "die Wiederkehr lebensweltlicher Realität im Text" (Iser 21).
13 The German original reads: "literarische Anschlusswelten [...] die unsere Welt in je spezifischer Weise ins Imaginäre fortführen, doch so, dass die Übergänglichkeit selbst erkennbar ist" (Stierle 176).
14 For the classic studies cf. Fauconnier; Fauconnier/Turner; Johnson; Kövecses; Lakoff/Johnson 1980, 1999; Lakoff/Turner; Turner; cf. also Geeraerts/Cuyckens.
15 For a balanced if unorthodox discussion of White and an attempt (based not least on White, Ricœur and cognitive approaches) at exploring the interplay between metaphor, narrative, and emotion, cf. Snævarr.
16 For this, cf. for instance Ameel 2016, 2017, 2019, 2021; Buchenau/Gurr 2016, 2018; Childs; Cohen; Eckstein/Throgmorton; Filep/Thompson-Fawcett/Rae; Healey; Ivory; Kaplan; Keunen/Verraest; Mandelbaum; Sandercock 2003, 2010; Tewdwr-Jones; Throgmorton 1996, 2003; van Hulst.

References

Abdallah, Chahrazad, Ann Langley. "The Double Edge of Ambiguity in Strategic Planning." *Journal of Management Studies* 51.2 (2014): 235–264. doi: 10.1111/joms.12002.

Adhikari, Binay, Jianling Li. "Modelling Ambiguity in Urban Planning." *Annals of GIS* 19.3 (2013): 143–152.

Ameel, Lieven. "A *Bildungsroman* for a Waterfront Development: Literary Genre and the Planning Narratives of Jätkäsaari, Helsinki." *Journal of Urban Cultural Studies* 3.2 (2016): 167–187.

Ameel, Lieven. *The Narrative Turn in Urban Planning: Plotting the Helsinki Waterfront.* New York: Routledge, 2021.

Ameel, Lieven. "The Sixth Borough: Metaphorizations of the Water in New York City's Comprehensive Waterfront Plan Vision 2020 and Foer's 'The Sixth Borough'." *Critique* 60.3 (2019): 251–262. https://doi.org/10.1080/00111619. 2018.1556203.

Ameel, Lieven. "Towards a Narrative Typology of Urban Planning Narratives for, in, and of Planning in Jätkäsaari, Helsinki." *Urban Design International* 22 (2017): 318–330. https://doi.org/10.1057/s41289-016-0030-8.

ARUP. *2050 Scenarios: Four Plausible Futures.* London: ARUP, 2019.

Baßler, Moritz. *Die kulturpoetische Funktion und das Archiv: Eine literaturwissenschaftliche Text-Kontext-Theorie.* Tübingen: Francke, 2005.

BBSR (Bundesinstitut für Bau-, Stadt- und Raumforschung). *Von Science-Fiction-Städten lernen: Szenarien für die Stadtplanung.* Bonn: BBSR, 2015.

Bell, Wendell. *Foundations of Futures Studies: History, Purposes, and Knowledge.* Rev. ed. London: Routledge, 2003.

Berndt, Frauke, Stephan Kammer. "Amphibolie – Ambiguität – Ambivalenz: Die Struktur antagonistisch-gleichzeitiger Zweiwertigkeit." *Amphibolie – Ambiguität – Ambivalenz.* Ed. Berndt, Kammer. Würzburg: Königshausen & Neumann, 2009. 7–30.

Buchenau, Barbara, Jens Martin Gurr. "City Scripts: Urban American Studies and the Conjunction of Textual Strategies and Spatial Processes." *Urban Transformations in the U.S.A.: Spaces, Communities, Representations*. Ed. Julia Sattler. Bielefeld: transcript, 2016. 395–420.

Buchenau, Barbara, Jens Martin Gurr. "On the Textuality of American Cities and their Others: A Disputation." *Projecting American Studies: Essays on Theory, Method and Practice*. Ed. Frank Kelleter, Alexander Starre. Heidelberg: Winter, 2018. 135–152.

Burke, Kenneth. *The Philosophy of Literary Form: Studies in Symbolic Action*. Berkeley: University of California Press, 1974 [reprint; orig. ed.: Baton Rouge: Louisiana State University Press, 1941].

Childs, Mark C. "Storytelling and Urban Design." *Journal of Urbanism* 1.2 (2008): 173–186.

Cohen, Philip. "Stuff Happens: Telling the Story and Doing the Business in the Making of Thames Gateway." *London's Turning: Thames Gateway; Prospects and Legacy*. Ed. Philip Cohen, Michael J. Rustin. Aldershot: Ashgate, 2008. 99–124.

Cresswell, Tim. "Weeds, Plagues, and Bodily Secretions: A Geographical Interpretation of Metaphors of Displacement." *Annals of the Association of American Geographers* 87 (1997): 330–345.

Eckstein, Barbara, James A. Throgmorton, eds. *Story and Sustainability: Planning, Practice, and Possibility for American Cities*. Cambridge, MA: MIT Press, 2003.

Fauconnier, Gilles. *Mapping in Thought and Language*. Cambridge: Cambridge University Press, 1997.

Fauconnier, Gilles, Mark Turner. *The Way We Think: Conceptual Blending and the Mind's Hidden Complexities*. New York: Basic Books, 2002.

Filep, Crystal Victoria, Michelle Thompson-Fawcett, Murray Rae. "Built Narratives." *Journal of Urban Design* 19.3 (2014): 298–316.

Fluck, Winfried. *Das kulturelle Imaginäre: Eine Funktionsgeschichte des amerikanischen Romans, 1790–1900*. Frankfurt/Main: Suhrkamp, 1997.

Forester, John. *Critical Theory, Public Policy, and Planning Practice: Towards a Critical Pragmatism*. Albany: State University of New York Press, 1993.

Geeraerts, Dirk, Hubert Cuyckens, eds. *The Oxford Handbook of Cognitive Linguistics*. Oxford: Oxford University Press, 2010.

Ghamari-Tabrizi, Sharon. *The Worlds of Herman Kahn: The Intuitive Science of Thermonuclear War*. Cambridge, MA: Harvard University Press, 2005.

Glomb, Stefan, Stefan Horlacher, eds. *Beyond Extremes: Repräsentation und Reflexion von Modernisierungsprozessen im zeitgenössischen britischen Roman*. Tübingen: Narr, 2004.

Gurr, Jens Martin. "Views on Violence in Shelley's Post-Peterloo Prose and Poetry: Contradiction, Ambivalence, Ambiguity?" *Romantic Ambiguities: Abodes of the Modern*. Ed. Sebastian Domsch, Christoph Reinfandt, Katharina Rennhak. Trier: WVT, 2017. 83–93.

Gurr, Jens Martin. "'Without contraries is no progression': Emplotted Figures of Thought in Negotiating Oppositions, *Funktionsgeschichte* and Literature as 'Cultural Diagnosis'." *Text or Context: Reflections on Literary and Cultural Criticism*. Ed. Rüdiger Kunow, Stephan Mussil. Würzburg: Königshausen & Neumann, 2013. 59–77.

Gymnich, Marion, Ansgar Nünning, eds. *Funktionen von Literatur: Theoretische Grundlagen und Modellinterpretationen*. Trier: WVT, 2005.

Hallet, Wolfgang. *Fremdsprachenunterricht als Spiel der Texte und Kulturen: Intertextualität als Paradigma einer kulturwissenschaftlichen Didaktik*. Trier: WVT, 2002.

Hallet, Wolfgang. "Methoden kulturwissenschaftlicher Ansätze: Close Reading und Wide Reading." *Methoden der literatur- und kulturwissenschaftlichen Textanalyse: Ansätze – Grundlagen – Modellanalysen*. Ed. Vera Nünning, Ansgar Nünning. Stuttgart, Weimar: Metzler, 2010. 293–315.

Harvey, David. "Contested Cities: Social Process and Spatial Form." *The City Reader*. Ed. Richard T. LeGates, Frederic Stout. London, New York: Routledge, [4]2000. 225–232.

Healey, Patsy. "Planning in Relational Space and Time: Responding to New Urban Realities." *A Companion to the City*. Ed. Gary Bridge, Sophie Watson. Oxford: Blackwell, 2000. 517–530.

Iser, Wolfgang. *Das Fiktive und das Imaginäre: Perspektiven literarischer Anthropologie*. Frankfurt/Main: Suhrkamp, 1993.

Ivory, Chris. "The Role of the Imagined User in Planning and Design Narratives." *Planning Theory* 12.4 (2013): 425–441.

Jain, Arun. "Urban Design Frameworks as a Basis for Development Strategies: A Portland Case Study." 2012. http://mud-sala.sites.olt.ubc.ca/files/2015/08/Arun-Jain-UDFrameworks-as-Basis-for-Development-Strategies.pdf.

Johnson, Mark. *The Body in the Mind: The Bodily Basis of Meaning, Imagination, and Reason*. Chicago: University of Chicago Press, 1987.

Kaplan, Thomas J. "Reading Policy Narratives: Beginnings, Middles, and Ends." *The Argumentative Turn in Policy Analysis and Planning*. Ed. Frank Fischer, John Forester. London: UCL Press, 1993. 167–185.

Keunen, Bart, Sofie Verraest. "Tell-Tale Landscapes and Mythical Chronotopes in Urban Designs for Twenty-First Century Paris." *CLCWeb: Comparative Literature and Culture* 14.3 (2012). https://doi.org/10.7771/1481–4374.2038.

Koschorke, Albrecht. *Wahrheit und Erfindung: Grundzüge einer Allgemeinen Erzähltheorie*. Frankfurt/Main: Fischer, [3]2013.

Kövecses, Zoltan. *Metaphor in Culture: Universality and Variation*. Cambridge: Cambridge University Press, 2005.

Kronenfeld, David B. *Culture as a System: How We Know the Meaning and Significance of What We Do and Say*. New York: Routledge, 2018.

Lakoff, George, Mark Johnson. *Metaphors We Live By*. Chicago: University of Chicago Press, 1980.

Lakoff, George, Mark Johnson. *Philosophy in the Flesh: The Embodied Mind and its Challenge to Western Thought*. New York: Basic Books, 1999.

Lakoff, George, Mark Turner. *More than Cool Reason: A Field Guide to Poetic Metaphor*. Chicago: University of Chicago Press, 1989.

Mandelbaum, Seymour J. "Telling Stories." *Journal of Planning Education and Research* 10.3 (1991): 209–214.

Mandelbrote, Scott. "History, Narrative, Time." *Journal of European Ideas* 22 (1996): 337–350.

Moretti, Franco. *Distant Reading*. London: Verso, 2013.

NEMO (Neue Emscher-Mobilität). Institute of Mobility and City Planning (imobis), University of Duisburg-Essen. www.nemo-ruhr.de.

Quinn, Naomi, Dorothy Holland. "Culture and Cognition." *Cultural Models in Language and Thought*. Ed. Holland, Quinn. Cambridge: Cambridge University Press, 1987. 3–40.

Ricœur, Paul. *Temps et récit*. Vol. 1. Paris: Seuil, 1983.

Ricœur, Paul. *Time and Narrative*. Vol. 1. Trans. Kathleen McLaughlin, David Pellauer. Chicago: University of Chicago Press, 1984.

Rittel, Horst W.J., Melvin M. Webber. "Dilemmas in a General Theory of Planning." *Policy Sciences* 4.2 (1973): 155–169.

Sandercock, Leonie. "From the Campfire to the Computer: An Epistemology of Multiplicity and the Story Turn in Planning." *Multimedia Explorations in Urban Policy and Planning: Beyond the Flatlands*. Ed. Leonie Sandercock, Giovanni Attili. Dordrecht, Heidelberg, New York: Springer, 2010. 17–37.

Sandercock, Leonie. "Out of the Closet: The Importance of Stories and Storytelling in Planning Practice." *Planning Theory & Practice* 4.1 (2003): 11–28.

Sattler, Julia. "Finding Words: American Studies in Dialogue with Urban Planning." *Projecting American Studies: Essays on Theory, Method, and Practice*. Ed. Alexander Starre, Frank Kelleter. Heidelberg: Winter, 2018. 121–134.

Smith, Neil. *The New Urban Frontier: Gentrification and the Revanchist City*. London, New York: Routledge, 1996.

Snævarr, Stefán. *Metaphors, Narratives, Emotions: Their Interplay and Impact*. Amsterdam, New York: Rodopi, 2010.

Star, Susan Leigh, James Griesemer. "Ecology, 'Translations' and Boundary Objects: Amateurs and Professionals in Berkeley's Museum of Vertebrate Zoology, 1907–39." *Social Studies of Science* 19.3 (1989): 387–420.

Stierle, Karlheinz. "Die Fiktion als Vorstellung, als Werk und als Schema – Eine Problemskizze." *Funktionen des Fiktiven*. Ed. Dieter Henrich, Wolfgang Iser. Poetik und Hermeneutik X. Munich: Fink, 1983. 173–182.

Tewdwr-Jones, Mark. *Urban Reflections: Narratives of Place, Planning and Change*. Bristol: Policy Press, 2011.

Throgmorton, James A. "Planning as Persuasive Storytelling in a Global-Scale Web of Relationships." *Planning Theory* 2.2 (2003): 125–135.

Throgmorton, James A. *Planning as Persuasive Storytelling: The Rhetorical Construction of Chicago's Electric Future*. Chicago: University of Chicago Press, 1996.

Turner, Mark. *Reading Minds: The Study of English in the Age of Cognitive Science*. Princeton: Princeton University Press, 1991.

van Hulst, Merlijn. "Storytelling, a Model *of* and a Model *for* Planning." *Planning Theory* 11.3 (2012): 299–318.

Wellershoff, Dieter. *Literatur und Lustprinzip*. Cologne: Kiepenheuer & Witsch, 1973.

White, Hayden. *Metahistory: The Historical Imagination in Nineteenth-Century Europe*. Baltimore: Johns Hopkins University Press, 1973.

Zapf, Hubert, ed. *Kulturökologie und Literatur: Beiträge zu einem transdisziplinären Paradigma der Literaturwissenschaft*. Heidelberg: Winter, 2008.

Zapf, Hubert. "Literature as Cultural Ecology: Notes Towards a Functional Theory of Imaginative Texts with Examples from American Literature." *Literary History/Cultural History: Force-Fields and Tensions*. Ed. Herbert Grabes. Tübingen: Narr, 2001. 85–99.

Zapf, Hubert. *Literatur als kulturelle Ökologie: Zur kulturellen Funktion imaginativer Texte an Beispielen des amerikanischen Romans*. Tübingen: Niemeyer, 2002.

7 'Scripts' in Urban Development

Procedural Knowledge, Self-Description and Persuasive Blueprint for the Future

Barbara Buchenau, Jens Martin Gurr

Cities have been matched with minds, manners and traditions since the heydays of the Chicago School of urban sociology a century ago. Urban infrastructure, then, came alive as a cultural organism developing creative and destructive energies that cannot be contained by its material constraints. Within the past three decades, this turn to culture in the age of American urbanisation transformed into a turn to stories and narrative in the age of global urbanisation.[1] Stories, urban researchers and developers suggest alike, can raise urban structures, with professional and professionalised narrative place-making attracting the majority of the global population to cities and urban agglomerations in the global South and North.[2] With this turn to stories came the rise of urban storytellers – itself a story of professionalisation driven by the 'story turn in planning'.[3] Thus, in 2017, plagued by long-term decline and consistently negative media coverage as a city in ruins, the city of Detroit hired "America's first official 'chief storyteller' " (Helmore n.p.), Aaron Foley. Foley's task was to counter the overwhelmingly discouraging reporting with more positive stories about the city. Other US cities – primarily Denver and Atlanta – have followed suit (cf. Williams). In Sweden, too, a network of cities intent on sustainable and climate-sensitive development, the Viable Cities Network, hired a professional "Chief Storyteller" (Grankvist n.p.). And in Helsinki, a novel was commissioned to promote the development of the city's former port district (cf. Chapter 6; as well as Ameel 2016, 2021).

While city administrations have become increasingly savvy in harnessing the power of stories for urban development, the turn to stories as tools of change has a sharp political edge as well. During the 2016 US elections, in Donald Trump's Inaugural Address, throughout his presidency and again very prominently in response to the 2020 protests against racist violence, storytelling was brought in as an incremental political practice.[4] Donald Trump's heroic and anti-heroic stories integrate punching depictions of urban decline; they reiteratively evoke 'inner cities', thus calling up the long-standing distrust of the city in US culture, while swiftly authenticating and authorising racist and white supremacist rationales.[5] His campaigning until today leverages narratives, medial representations and figural language to endorse, change and exploit anti-urban imaginaries. "Trump thinks-by-narrative", according to Hart, leaving "no gap at all" between "personal experience and public policy"

(101). His happenstance storytelling addresses the convictions and the fears of people who crave to find "narratives designed to heal [their] wounds – both imagined and real" (Hart 98). If "urban structures are built and sustained by layered, conflicting stories and the bodies that live them" (Rhinehart n.p.),[6] then the case of Trump's divisive stories of racially divided inner cities requires us to think twice about "storytelling" as an easy and uncomplicated "model *of* and *for* urban planning" (van Hulst).

This chapter accordingly discusses the ability of fictional accounts, poetic language and audio-visual storytelling to serve as powerful models *of* and *for* urban developments, exploring especially the energetic and potentially disintegrative dynamics unfolding at the intersections of descriptive, re-scriptive and prescriptive uses of texts. We will first discuss the conjunction of textual strategies and spatial processes in urban planning to then introduce the notion of 'scripts' as a new conceptual framework for the study of the art of persuasion in urban development. Scripts are artful combinations of narrative, medial as well as figural acts of framing, inscription, description and prescription.[7] In their combination of stories, tropes and media, scripts serve three contending functions simultaneously: they activate procedural knowledge, they serve as self-description, and they provide blueprints for the future. Thus, scripts establish contingent connective tissues between the past, the present and the future.

We begin our critical inquiry into scripts by asking: Is it possible to relate fundamental strategies of textual representation to key processes of urban development? The turn to stories in the field of urban planning (cf. Sandercock 2003, 2010; Throgmorton 1996, 2003; and others) suggests that this is an easy and effective conjunction. But literary strategies and urban planning do not coincide without conflicts and contradictions. Blends of poetic techniques, social practice and urban form generate imaginative overflows that are potentially productive as well as destructive.[8] Observing the close ties between media, narratives and (urban) spaces, we argue that texts can function as indicative as well as indexical models *for* the city. The conjunction of textual strategies, urban form and urban development opens up multiple spaces of imagination, generating new options for agency as well as narrative control. These dynamics must be acknowledged and thoroughly studied, if the conflictive powers of storytelling in urban development are to be properly understood.

In a previous joint essay (Buchenau/Gurr 2016), we have conceptualised 'condensation', 'inversion' and 'assemblage' as three procedures that conjoin texts, cultures and cities. Condensation, inversion and assemblage are central patterns of urban change. At the same time, they are key strategies of representation in urban cultural production that activate the imaginative drive of literary art. This imaginative drive is built on what Samuel Taylor Coleridge famously called the "willing suspension of disbelief" in 1817 (cf. Coleridge ch. XIV). And it offers catharsis precisely because of its fictional, non-representational stance, as Aristotle understood it.

Cities are sites of 'condensation' – people, infrastructures, medial forms, semiosis and semanticisation meet here; they intersect, clash and collide, multiply and overlap. Needs, desires, hopes and fears are condensed in cities as well. Literary and media strategies of 'condensation' replicate *and* prefigure these urban condensations: figural and "narrative arc[s] through time" fuse past, present and future, establishing "typological bridges between distinct moments in time and space" (Buchenau 2012, 179). Layering, adaptation, plurimedial experiments, multiple references, and textual strategies of convergence and assimilation compress meaning and integrate contradictory affects and arguments. These core techniques of the art of persuasion constrain and thereby focus the imagination of their readers, thus ostensibly strengthening their sense of unity of purpose, place and time. But the reductions and adaptations of 'condensation' also lead to the multiplication of potential applications as well as meanings (cf. Buchenau 2012).

Cities are sites of 'inversion' as well – for instance in de- and reurbanisation and the drastically shifting fate of the inner city, but also in the industrialisation and deindustrialisation of urban fringes. Literary techniques of 'inversion', for instance by irony, metaphor, remediation or by a conjunction of generic conventions as in tragicomedy, conjoin opposites. These inversions allow for contrapuntal games as well as alternate histories, and they celebrate (or lament) the change of fate. But literary and media inversions also draw attention to narrative paths (cf. Rabinowitz 182–185) and path dependencies as well as to contingencies that limit human ambitions of intervention and control (for narrative path dependencies, cf. also Chapter 6).

Finally, cities are sites of combination, juxtaposition, recomposition – and thus of the 'assemblage' of different elements, forms, materialities and functionalities. Textual strategies of 'assemblage' (in the sense of a montage of distinct, seemingly irreconcilable media, genres, conventions, styles or techniques) heighten complexity. They confound *and* liberate readers at the same time, thus enticing readerly engagements and downright reader activism.[9] Literary and media 'assemblage' serves as a signpost for changing uses as well as revolutions of tastes, ideologies and habits.

The textual strategies and techniques of 'condensation', 'inversion' and 'assemblage' have been central to attempts at *rendering* 'cityness'. As literary innovations, they have frequently evolved in response to the challenge of representing urbanity (cf. Chapter 2). More importantly, however, they have been central strategies in *initiating*, blueprinting and thus 'scripting' urban developments. In contemporary urban planning, cities are quite literally 'scripted': the narrative voices of testimonials as well as marketing anecdotes connect seamlessly, but not without friction, with exclusive and occasionally inclusive medial frames and dramatic remediations. As the following example of Essen's campaign for the title of European Green Capital will show, poetic language and literary figuration are rarely missing in strategic urban documents, thus enhancing the degree to which urban planning and development makes deliberate (but not always well-informed) use of the literary and medial arts of persuasion.

Defining 'Scripts'

In 2017, the city of Essen, metonymically standing in for the entire Ruhr region, became the European Green Capital. The first paragraph of the application for the title submitted to the European Commission in 2014 stated:

> The successful 150-year transformation story, from a city of coal and steel to the greenest city in North Rhine-Westphalia, is a role model of structural change for many cities in Europe [...] Green infrastructure is the motor for our sustainable urban development [...] The people's "ability to change" is the key to the success of this process of transformation.
> (Essen 2014, 1)

This paragraph provides, among other things, the diagnosis of an "intrinsic logic ['Eigenlogik']" of a city, as Berking and Löw outline it: Essen is depicted as a city in structural transformation, which today has become remarkably 'green'. But beyond referencing this "intrinsic logic", the introductory sentences of the application text perform a three-step-move of yoking together past, present and future: What is emplotted here is the seamless conjunction of *procedural knowledge* gathered in the history of (post-)industrial transformation; *self-description* capturing the present-day regional and international role of the city; and a *blueprint* for the future envisioning the fully sustainable city. The Green Capital campaign at large underscores this tripartite move through time, using the figure of thought "from green to grey to green" (Essen 2017, 8; our translation) as its motto, an alliterative condensation of a 150-year transformation from pre-industrial via industrial to post-industrial city. The opening sentences first provide the procedural knowledge of the "150-year transformation story" (Essen 2014, 1) recalling the hardships and challenges of more than a century of structural change. Second, the self-description as presently the "greenest city in North Rhine-Westphalia" (Essen 2014, 1) enables a plausible story of an apparently straightforward development from the past of industrial labour into the present of greening, deindustrialising infrastructure. Third, the persuasive blueprint of "the motor for our sustainable urban development" (Essen 2014, 1) elegantly suggests a path into the future of green urbanity.

But this strong and indeed 'transformative' reading of a greening city of coal and steel also singles out from other cities this specific transformation achievement: To be 'green' in locationally privileged cities like Stockholm or Hamburg (the first two European Green Capitals in 2010 and 2011) is easy – for a post-industrial legacy city like Essen to have reached the current state, the passage implies, is the far more impressive achievement.[10] This combination of narrative sense-making, temporal condensation and the suggestive charting of a future-oriented development, enhanced, as we will indicate in what follows, by

Figure 7.1 The kernel script "from green to grey to green" with suggestive illustration in the 2017 European Green Capital image brochure of the City of Essen, Germany (UNESCO World Heritage Site Zollverein, view of the pithead frame of shaft 3/7/10 towards Gelsenkirchen-Rotthausen).

Source: City of Essen, European Green Capital Image Brochure (Essen 2017, 8); photograph by Frank Vinken. Reprinted with permission of the Green Capital Agency, City of Essen.

savvy medial framing and a figurative rendering of structural transformation – the alliteration "green to grey to green" (Essen 2017, 8; our translation) – is an epitome of what we call a 'script'. This particular 'script' also entails the collective personification of a population with a specific "ability to change" (Essen 2014, 1), plotted to appear as a single communal life of 150 years of transformation. This is a 'script' *of* and *for* human and urban change delivered in the combination of just one alliterative headline (the figure), a short paragraph (the narrative) and a photograph (the media; cf. Figure 7.1).

In the text of the 2017 image brochure, the pre-industrial deep past as well as the industrial near past become striking contrasts to today's surprisingly green city:

> The transformation of the city of Essen from a pre-industrial diocese with abbess gardens and imperial parks via a coal-mining and steel metropolis to a green city is impressive. Around 1900, the cityscape of Essen was largely characterized by the Krupp cast steel factory, by tight quarters near the old town, and large Krupp colonies [...] by the chimneys of the coking plants and the framework of blast furnaces, by conveyor towers and slagheaps.[11]
>
> (Essen 2017, 8; translation Phillip Grider)

Epitomised in the figural kernel script "from green to grey to green" (Essen 2017, 8; our translation) of deep past, near past and present, the text is here accompanied by a highly suggestive image of a pithead in the midst of urban greenery (cf. Figure 7.1). The haze looks distinctly 'idyllic', dreamily unreal, *and* it recalls the days of industrial fumes and air pollution – thus again visually, medially yoking together past, present and future.

Scripts such as the one produced by the Green Capital of Europe 2017 combine descriptive, re-scriptive as well as prescriptive elements. They mostly conjoin two to three temporal dimensions and they nearly always communicate figurally, as well as narratively *and* medially. Scripts thus are not stories, they are also not limited to stories. But scripts do incorporate persuasive storytelling into a matter-of-fact world of make-believe. They are assemblages of figural expression (poetic language, tropes, but also numericals and charts), of narrative exposition (story, voice, focalisation, character constellation, emplotment) and of media presentation (frames, schemes, tracks and shots established by images and sound tracks, analogue and digital maps, audiovisual material, diverse forms of writing and printed matter).

'Scripts' across the Disciplines

Of course, the notion of the 'script' is widely used in a range of fields and disciplines outside of the realm of literary studies, such as biblical hermeneutics, critical race theory or artificial intelligence, to name just three fields. The most basic definition of a script is the idea of a "typescript of a cinema or television film; the text of a broadcast announcement, talk, play, or other material" (*OED*, s.v. script), material, that is, that urban developers and planners today continually produce and consume. This standard definition already contains the more descriptive sense of a 'transcript', but also the prescriptive sense of an instruction to be carried out, of a predefined sequence of actions and dialogues to be appropriated and enacted in a specific setting. One particularly intricate application of typescripting in urban development is the case of the Ruhr region's title of the European Capital of Culture in 2010. As Hanna Rodewald explores in her investigation of the RUHR.2010 artistic output and its slogan "Change through Culture – Culture through Change" (our translation), this standard implementation of scripting in urban development transfers and translates to German post-industrial cultural landscapes famous American tropes and plot lines such as the frontier (cf. Rodewald).

The scriptural dedication to norms, rules and laws can be traced back to the context of the systematic interpretation of the Bible, where the notion of 'scripture' applies to all texts that are taken to be "as surely true as Holy Scripture" (*OED*, s.v. scripture 1c). The normative implications of 'Scripture' in the sacred sense – writing that spells out norms and practices of faith in ways that are understood to be sanctified, authoritative, beyond critique – lost its tight grip on the world in the Early Modern period, but lived on in the multiple permutations of, especially, US American civil religion. A much embattled instantiation of a proto-religious scripture of the American Dream is the Statue of Liberty. Its dramatising sculptural commemoration of the abolition of slavery belies the violence and murder of the Jim Crow laws, and the Emma Lazarus sonnet added in 1903 sanctifies immigration and its control. The statue spoke to and impacted the massive growth of metropolitan regions, scripting American standards of social and racial mobility in the urban realm. Chicago's White City, Detroit's Ford River Rouge Complex accompanied by Diego Rivera's artwork or the Zeche Zollverein in the Ruhr region have scripted urban aspirations and dreams in similarly complex ways. They are today iconic and potentially authoritative projects of greening and ostensibly desegregating urban environments, as Juliane Borosch argues in her doctoral project.[12] As examples such as these suggest, writings claiming authority or anything that was perceived as being authoritative served as a kind of 'scripture' broadly conceived. These texts (indeed these are more often text/image/media assemblages) can be understood to control and regulate people's actions and mental spaces (cf. Assmann/Assmann 8).

Before the invention of copy machines, 'scripts' also denoted the originals of a legal document. In this context, the normative implication of the 'true' or 'authoritative' version differentiated it from a merely derivative rescript – an important distinction in all settings in which titles and true scripts were and continue to be needed to claim urban lands, assume ownership or safeguard autonomy and freedom. Think, for instance, of the 'Bracero Program', a post-war initiative attracting four million workers from Mexico under contract in the guest worker programme (cf. Molina ch. 5, "Deportations in the Urban Landscape", 112–138). These workers on contracts were matched by *sin papeles*, workers who lacked the original documents granting them the right to work in agriculture and a wide range of other industries. In common parlance, these undocumented labourers were soon called 'wetbacks' – a term which then became a shorthand or kernel script, "used [...] interchangeably with *Mexican immigrants* in stories on crime, communicable disease, and deporting children" (cf. Molina 114). The non-script of an insufficient legal title here becomes the script of the racialised outsider who can be subjected to deportation. Questions of authority, authorisation and regulation have quite obviously affected uses of the script for the design of urban futures until today. Quite programmatic, if apparently non-political, engineering examples can be found in the difficult international translation of sustainability and green building standards and their explanatory text/charts/media compounds that Katharina Wood investigates in her dissertation.[13]

Another understanding of 'scripts' that is crucial for a better understanding of how stories, figures and media collaboratively shape urban development and especially urban planning comes from the field of social psychology, where 'scripts' are understood as "generic schemata of social events" (Whitney 13522). As schemata, they connect "symbolic and nonverbal elements in an organized and time-bound sequence of conduct through which persons both envision future behaviour and check on the quality of ongoing conduct" (Gagnon 61). Here, the descriptive sense of 'script' as procedural knowledge is inextricably combined with the prescriptive sense of appropriateness and social control. Scripts are so pervasive (and naturally persuasive), because they are immensely adaptable, as Gagnon notes: "their capacity to be assembled or disassembled in creative or adaptive responses to new circumstances is a critical element in our capacity to manage a changing internal and external environment" (62). Literary theorist Paula Moya has brought the notion of the schema that is at the core of this definition of the script to bear on literature proper, noting that schemas are

> structures that have been built up through a person's past behaviour and experiences in specific domains [...] Schemas thus have a temporal dimension characterized by evolution across time – they are anticipatory as well as retrospective, even as they orient a person's behaviour in the present.[14] (15)

Prominent examples beyond the signposts of segregation would be encounters with *stop and frisk* policing. These "symbolic and nonverbal elements" (Gagnon 61) in retrospect and in anticipation manage the expectations and the behaviour of people of colour and of white people. While some are subjected to unwarranted searches when moving in public urban space, the others experience and learn to expect the exposure to a sense of privilege and entitlement in the same spaces.

But scripts are also unconscious life plans developed in response to education and early experiences. They are plans that can be made conscious and can to some extent be re-scripted or at least modified, according to Berne's "transactional analysis" (1958, 1961). Transferred to cities, this suggests that path dependencies can be said to play a significant role, though re-scripting is understood to be possible within reasonable boundaries (cf. Chapter 6). In the Ruhr region, the University of Duisburg-Essen's affirmative action programme for first-generation students *Chance hoch 2* is one example of a structured attempt at reprogramming unconscious life plans; RuhrFutur's educational initiatives and their ambition to craft social change is another, as Chris Katzenberg argues in his doctoral project.[15]

Artificial intelligence (AI) researchers Roger C. Schank and Robert P. Abelson further define a 'script' as "a standard event sequence" (38), as in their well-known example of the "restaurant script" and the internalised familiarity with the sequence of actions from being seated to leaving that a restaurant visit involves. Based on this notion, 'script' here came to be used to refer to cultural models as powerful unconscious or semi-conscious guides of individual and collective human behaviour (for such cultural models, cf. Quinn/Holland as well as Stigler/Hiebert; on frames, cf. Goffman; for a compelling case study on how cultural scripts and models support or impede action, cf. Ungar). Their argument clarifies that scripts are a form of procedural knowledge that effortlessly and without further notice guide people through standard urban situations such as the meal at a restaurant, the use of public transportation or the visit to a tourist attraction, framing and thus guiding people's understanding of the social world. One particularly transformative "standard event sequence" (Schank/Abelson 38) appears to be urban gardening with its twofold promise of recreation and sustenance. Forms of transatlantic 'diversity gardening', under investigation in the dissertation project of Elisabeth Haefs, indicate that the effortless guidance through urban garden patches builds temporary communities dedicated to sustainability, but not necessarily social inclusiveness.[16]

This effortless guidance by scripts is neither harmless nor without discrimination. As Natalia Molina argues, "racial scripts" connect "the lives of racialized groups [...] across time and space [...] thereby affect[ing] one another, even when they do not directly cross paths" (6). These "racial scripts" determine social as well as institutional interactions, they affect everybody individually and all kinds of social and cultural group identification specifically, though they have decisively and dominantly negative effects on racialised groups only. In response to 'racial scripting', "counterscripts" come into action, which "offer alternatives or directly challenge dominant racial scripts" (Molina 7). One particularly powerful example of 'counterscripting' in action is the work of the *Quilomboarte* art collective and the *Tía Chucha's Centro Cultural*, supported and studied by Florian Deckers in his dissertation project on "raising ethnic voices" in New York and Los Angeles.[17] As the scrutiny of street art suggests, the inversion of 'racial scripts' might be possible, but the tipping points that would reverse dynamics of racialised oppression are hard to reach and they are extremely sensitive to reversals and backlashes.

Finally, from the field of architecture and the design of a user's experience of that architecture, Norman M. Klein's notion of "scripted spaces" draws attention to the

> walk-through or click-through environment (a mall, a church, a casino, a theme park, a computer game) [...] designed to *emphasize* the viewer's journey [...] The audience walks *into* the story. What's more, this walk should respond to each viewer's whims, even though each step along the way is prescripted (or should I say preordained?). It is gentle repression posing as free will.
>
> (11 *et passim*; italics original)

Understood in a way that combines all these different definitions and uses, scripts are models *of* and *for* urban development, oscillating between and suggestively – if sometimes problematically – blurring descriptive, re-scriptive and prescriptive components. In the field of urban planning, Christopher Alexander's notion of "patterns" can be seen as a closely related concept: Here, a "pattern" is a modular solution, blueprint or 'recipe' for a specific design challenge, a solution that can be replicated or adapted in comparable contexts to address comparable problems (cf. Alexander/Ishikawa/Silverstein).[18] This notion of a hierarchically ordered system of patterns as a 'language' – with a specific 'vocabulary', 'grammar' and 'syntax' and a formulaic way of outlining them, their contexts and applications – has been widely adopted as a 'travelling concept' (*sensu* Bal) in other disciplines, most prominently in software engineering (cf. for instance Gabriel). Johannes Maria Krickl's doctoral research on waterfront reconquistas in the deindustrialising urban environments of the United States and Germany indicates that the planning, the operation and the re-use of inner harbour spaces is indeed a strong case of a 'pattern language' brought into action, of prescripting and preordaining future developments by forceful imagination.[19]

Flipping Scripts, Exploring the Dynamics Unfolding

Scripts can of course be modified. When Jamie Peck critiqued the "creativity script" popularised by Richard Florida and his many disciples on both sides of the Atlantic, he did not argue for an inversion, or a turn away from a fascination with the so-called 'creative class' of artists, academics and cultural workers (cf. Peck 2005, 2007; for an Emersonian reading of Florida and his functionalist understanding of creativity and the 'creative class', cf. Grünzweig). Instead, he sought to loosen and lessen the tight, normative bonds between the arts, the sciences and capital, wresting academia and the arts, as well as the city, from a notion of creativity that made literature, the arts, scholarship and especially the sciences appear religiously scriptural and therefore unchallenged in their status as canonical authorities who bind together and lead communities of believers (thus replicating the generalised as well as figurative definition of religion, cf. *OED*, s.v. religion, 3a, 4a/b, 5a, 7). Planning scholars such as Courtney Elizabeth Knapp move forward from this critique of the industrial reproduction of creativity, investigating how, when and to what extent divisive and oppressive scripts can be flipped to make sure that the production of knowledge and culture can contribute to transformative social change rather than the normalisation of the status quo. Studying how planners and city officials have sought to change the script behind their cities' development, Knapp points out that since the late 1980s and early 1990s, a generation of urban planners at work in Chattanooga, Tennessee, rewrote the post-industrial script of manufacturing decline by "inspiring a Back to the City movement, and expanding its arts-history-and-culture-based tourist economy" (14). This turn to and celebration of obliterated histories and stories of the city facilitated a "renaissance" of the "Dynamo of Dixie" (Knapp 14), which has brought authoritative exclusions and textually regulated forms of gentrification. A turn to storytelling for the oppressed hence does not guarantee narrative control or even the affordances and allowances of authorship. In response to this intricately de-authorising change, new social movements are currently "working to [again] flip the mainstream script of urban revitalization" (Knapp 16).

One of the rather unproductive generic implications of scripts is that the possible outcomes of a plot are not numberless. If you know the script, you know its narrative trajectory and you might want to try to change it, by flipping genre, voice, imagery or media. But the life of stories, figures and media is never that easy (for narrative path dependencies, cf. also Chapter 6; and Ameel 2016, 2021). An exception to the basic rule of the path dependencies of each individual script is said to be computational script, since it is often understood to promise the invention of real alternatives. At the "Mediated City" Conference in Los Angeles in 2014, for instance, in a presentation entitled "Do We Have to Stick to the Script? Cities, Surveys and Descripting", architect

Eric Haas discussed the "projective" as well as the "prescriptive enterprise" entailed in computational language that turns "land descriptions" into "alternative mediations of the city" (4): "we can import recorded data sets, unleash the potential of computation to produce alternative results, and physicalize the consequences to produce new 'real' cities that participate in a cycle of recreation" (Haas 4f.). In these new mediated and computationally enhanced urban spaces, practices of prioritisation and leisurely trivialisation unfold, which Maria Sulimma explores in her postdoctoral research on "trivial pursuits".[20]

In urban contexts, then, the idea of the 'script' is used to think of regulations that are communally binding and restricting, and that serve to build a consensus – or relay and enhance dissent – on possible styles of interpretation. To speak of scripting is to suggest and even promise a high degree of predictive reliability, even a strong sense of determinism, while at the same time defusing potential reactions by proposing that a script can be adapted or modified. Studying the detailed narrative, figurative and medial processes at the core of each script is a necessary exercise to understand how scribal agency and modes of scripting and deciphering empower legal codes which regulate the underlying obligations and rights of the producers and the users of texts and images: Who is allowed to write/read; who speaks; who is being heard and who is being hurt, to adopt an incisive set of distinctions implemented by a group of scholars gathered by Mahmoud Arghavan, Nicole Hirschfelder, Luvena Kopp and Katharina Motyl;[21] which kind of authority is obtained by the act of writing/reading; who gets to keep the document; which rights are given to the holder of the document; etc. The notion of 'scripts' permits close and detailed observations of the contradictory outcomes of planning practices that operate within the storytelling paradigm, using stories to be persuasive in processes of urban development. Scripts function as powerful cultural tools, suggesting, accompanying, framing or plausibilising specific paths towards the future of cities. In many cases, practitioners are aware of the importance of such scripts – with their specific narratives, media and figures – to their practice, without being experts in *how* they function and *why* they may foster mixed results. This is precisely the key contribution literary and cultural studies can and must make. Despite the strongly normative implications, the power of scripts lies precisely in their threefold nature of being (1) merely a form of happenstance and often unreliable procedural knowledge about the past, (2) a practice of wilful self-description informing the present (and rewriting the past), (3) *and* an ambitiously authoritative, binding and thus strongly prescriptive attempt at blueprinting the future.

As literary and cultural scholars with interests in narratology, media change and figuration, our understanding of how scripts affect urban imaginaries, economies and infrastructures combines three interrelated insights to describe the conflictive condensation at the core of urban scripting processes: (1) the awareness, repeatedly discussed throughout this book, that planning is quintessentially a narrative process, including the ensuing complications arising from the fourfold public use of narrative as an affective access to knowledge, shock, enchantment and awe, to paraphrase Rita Felski (cf. 2008); (2) the debate about the future-oriented, anticipatory, premeditated and performative function of both, the media (cf. Grusin) and of narrative patterns (cf. Koschorke 245); and (3) developments in cognitive science and their repercussions in literary and cultural studies, which indicate how figurative thought and cognitive modelling guide thoughts and behaviour, a procedure only complicated by the ability of figures of speech and thought rather seamlessly to yoke together times present, past and future as well as distinctive places and spaces (cf. Chapter 6; Gurr; Buchenau 2011).

A contentious hermeneutics is at work, then, whenever successful urban transformation seeks to draw on storytelling to bring about the future. The ultimately idle hope of urban developers, municipalities and, for instance, the creative and sustainable industries, is that a script can serve as a neutral tool to tailor urban change. But as Dzudzek and Lindner have noted in their study of the creative economy, a script for the future "is actually the result of an ongoing collective (re)writing and performing endeavour, to which not only 'partners in mind' contribute but also sometimes fierce opponents" (392f.).[22] These scripts are inherently performative: If persuasive enough, they bring about what they often purport merely to describe. This is particularly evident in the case of the 'creative city script' as outlined and promoted by Richard Florida: While in parts allegedly *describing* a pattern of urban development – the accumulation of the 'creative class' in particularly attractive locations offering the 'three T's' of "Talent", "Technology" and "Tolerance" (cf. Florida 2002, 2005) – the ensuing "creativity fix" (Peck 2007; cf. also Dzudzek/Lindner) proposed itself as a blueprint and 'recipe' for cities. The 'creative script' was rolled out in numerous consulting projects by Florida himself and by global consulting firms in his wake. The characteristic oscillation between re-scription, description and prescription inherent to scripts here led to a self-reinforcing global hype of urban development strategies geared towards the attraction of the desirable 'creative class' segment.

In conceptualising the way in which urban agents in their engagement with models combine tradition, everyday practice and innovation, Armin Paul Frank's understanding of "writing strategies" in colonial and new national contexts provides a number of helpful clues (2015, 235; cf. also Frank 2004, 838): "when writers feel moved to assert a new identity in literary terms" (2015, 235), Frank argues, they can – heuristically and with variations and combinations – make use of basic strategies "that fit in with the morphology of the German verb for writing, *schreiben: nachschreiben, weiterschreiben, umschreiben, gegenschreiben*, and *vorbeischreiben*" (2015, 235f.). Thus, original models, in the process of adapting them, can be largely copied ("*nachschreiben*"), continued ("*weiterschreiben*"), changed and adapted ("*umschreiben*"), countered and opposed ("*gegenschreiben*") or circumvented ("*vorbeischreiben*"). Re-scripting (both in the sense of 'scripting again' and of 'changing the script'), scripting further, counter-scripting or circumscripting, it needs to be noted, are not only common writing strategies in literary history (especially in the continuities and discontinuities of (post-)colonial writing), but also common forms of engaging with established self-descriptions, procedural knowledge, as well as blueprints and 'recipes' for urban development.

The detailed analysis of scripts and their use in processes of urban development delineated here requires structured conversations between disciplinary schools: Analyses of the narrative, medial and figural layers of scripts strengthen and occasionally qualify insights from literary studies, since an understanding of the uses, functions and effects of scripts fosters new interdisciplinary perspectives informed by the heated debates with urban planners, urban geographers, urban sociologists, economists and others about the incremental status of narrative, figuration, media and the arts in consequential and often violent as well as destructive urban scenario building.

Applications: Scripting Post-Industrial Urban Futures and the Ubiquity of 'Creative', 'Sustainable' and 'Inclusive' Urban Visions

Good stories, strong images and connective media: these are the ingredients increasingly used by municipalities, urban developers, creative industries as well as NGOs in the fields of culture, society and the environment to embellish – or even develop in the first place – their plans and schemes for urban life after deindustrialisation. Our Graduate Research Group, "Scripts for Postindustrial Urban Futures: American Models, Transatlantic Interventions" (cf. City Scripts), engages in a focused transatlantic comparative analysis that maps and evaluates the range of scripts used to invent a better future for cities in the American Rust Belt and the German Ruhr region. At their best, narratives, figures and media help to imagine viable paths into a better future. At their worst, they unleash anxieties and build scenarios that propel further segregation, conflict and economic disintegration. In an era in which shrinking cities trouble the former Western centres of industrial production, bringing fear especially to the homelands of car and steel manufacturing,[23] the faith in the imaginative forms of procedural knowledge, self-description and blueprint for the future we refer to as 'scripts' is not only unfaltering, but even strengthened. The belief is that scripts with their suggestive combination and deployment of stories, figures and media can bring about urban revitalisation for so-called "legacy cities – older industrial cities that have experienced sustained job and population loss over the past few decades" (Mallach/Brachman, backcover; cf. also Berking/Löw; Florida 2011; Peck 2005, 2007). These scripts for post-industrial urban futures energise real and complicated power dynamics. They work to contribute to a paradigmatic shift that urban planner and geographer Michael Batty has described as "the transition from a world based on energy to one based on information: from an industrial to a postindustrial world" (191).

When scripts give new storylines to cities that lost, or continue to lose, their lifeline industries, they additionally seep into the self-definition of cities that lack an industrial heritage. Cities that are *not* legacy cities in the strict sense of the term use multifaceted imaginative tools – photos, cartoons, drawings, short narratives, film clips – to dress up as post-industrial 'working cities': a consortium of 91 Arizona cities and towns gathering at AZ Cities @ Work. This interactive gateway celebrates old, quaint forms of industrial labour: the 'o' in 'Work' is a stylised cog wheel; simple drawings and illustrations in the style of cartoons and children's literature portray stereotypical working-class scenes and locations; photography and short film clips bring an imagined past into the realm of the present. In contrast to the idealisation of manual and industrial work through this employment of iconic art, the biographical narratives of "the men and women that make AZ cities work" (AZ Cities @ Work) redefine the older idea of work that is connected to big industries and manual labour. This old idea is now refitted so as to suit the young and promising service industry (cf. AZ Cities @ Work). The offspring of this union of old and new labour is the production of a sustainable lifeline for a new type of 'working cities' in this sparsely populated section of the American Sun Belt. Here, municipalities comparatively unaffected by the dissipation of industrial production and the concomitant job losses endorse the concept of hard, often physical work. Yet, the slippage in the meaning of 'work' is deployed to insinuate that cities rather than people must work, i.e. function like a cog wheel at the heart of a productive engine, a rhetorical move placing the advertised location and its communities safely outside the realm of the crisis of deindustrialisation.

What is striking in examples such as this is the persistent use of a fairly limited number of basic scripts used in the projection and prescription of urban futures: Cities in urban development, marketing or urban planning documents are almost invariably imagined as 'creative', 'sustainable' and 'socially inclusive', with two or all three of them frequently conjoined under the heading of the 'smart city' in its various definitions (cf. also Chapter 8). As a globally current example, one might take waterfront redevelopments of former port locations. Waterfront projects in their theming and imagineering activities frequently make use of all three current guiding principles of post-industrial urban development, despite latent or obvious contradictions between them: They are almost invariably marketed as ideal locations for the creative economy and – increasingly important for the frequently up-market clientele – as sites of sustainable living, e.g. by virtue of advanced building technologies used in renovation. Conversely, in order to counter the public image as gentrified elite spaces, they frequently project the image of being family-friendly and socially inclusive, not least by romanticising their harbour past as sites of physical labour, even in places where the harbour as a means for providing jobs and income has ceased to play an important role.

The promotion of one of the most visible of such waterfront development projects and arguably the largest such project in Europe, HafenCity Hamburg, is a picture-book example of the pervasiveness of scripting. Between 2001 and the early 2030s, this project is turning an area of 2.2 square kilometres of former port area just south of the inner city of Hamburg into a mixed-use residential and commercial area, with the Elbphilharmonie as its celebrated icon, a futuristic concert-hall-*cum*-hotel and luxury apartments as well as a publicly accessible plaza with views of the city and the port placed on top of an enormous 1960s red-brick warehouse.[24] Almost any issue of the project's quarterly newsletter, the *HafenCity News*, yields references to all three major scripts. In issue 47, published in July 2017, for instance, a few pages suffice to discuss the

Figure 7.2 Text and visualisation of 'creative', 'sustainable' and 'inclusive' urban development scripts in HafenCity Hamburg.

Source: HafenCity News 47 (7/2017), 4, 9, 10. www.hafencity.com.

building of "Creative Blocks" that will include a residential project "specifically geared towards the needs of [...] the creative economy, architecture, living and media" (9; our translation), while another article entitled "Sustainable and Regional" (4; our translation) references the 'sustainability script'. This article announces the opening of a wholefoods supermarket and a farmer's market offering only organically grown (and largely regional) produce. Finally, under the heading "Apple Juice, Honey and Community Spirit" (10; our translation), this issue promotes local community gardening initiatives including photographs of families happily gardening and a beekeeper on top of a stationary shipping container (cf. Figure 7.2). To be fair, the issue begins with a three-page report on the opening of a memorial to victims of the holocaust deported from a site in what is now the HafenCity, including interviews with historians.

The ease with which these frequently standardising recurrent scripts of the 'creative', 'sustainable' and 'inclusive city' allegedly collaborate rather than collide can also be seen in a text announcing the selection of four Chinese cities as UNESCO Creative Cities in November 2017:

> The United Nations Organization for Education, Science and Culture (UNESCO) has picked four Chinese cities to join its Creative Cities Network (UCCN), the organization said on Tuesday [...] The four Chinese cities, Changsha (media arts), Macao Special Administrative Region

> (gastronomy), Qingdao (Film) and Wuhan (design) are among 64 cities from 44 countries and regions which join the network. The UNESCO said on Tuesday that the four Chinese cities were picked for their efforts to "develop and exchange innovative best practices to promote *creative industries*, strengthen *participation in cultural life* and integrate culture into *sustainable urban development* policies".
>
> (Xinhua; our italics)

Here, too, it seems that notions of the 'creative', the 'sustainable' and the 'inclusive' or 'participatory city' again seamlessly go together. Moreover, the citation of a UNESCO pronouncement on a news portal closely affiliated with the Chinese government appears to document that these scripts are globally circulating and pervasive models for urban development.

The scripts *of* and *for* sustainable, inclusive and/or creative urban development are simple, but not simplistic endeavours to re-scribe the past, describe the present and prescribe the future of cities facing complex problems. These scripts provide a fixed set of generic responses to recurring global challenges of urban environments, of collective action and individual ingenuity. Whether they can be adapted to local conditions and embodied by believers in these scripts, who bring about social changes they deem to be improvements to a given situation, depends on factors such as (a) the credibility and the consistency of concrete forms of storytelling, (b) the effectiveness and understandability of specific figural expressions, and (c) the affiliations enabled by pivotal (re-) mediations among the audiences that translate reduced and condensed arches through time and space, thus developing real-world applications of the stories heard, the visions seen and the mediations decrypted. While this deep and intricate coding of urban development necessarily can profit from literary, cultural and medial analysis, the scripting of urban change also helps the field of literary studies to get a better grip on the contentious battles between a hermeneutics of suspicion and a willingness to be "hooked", as Rita Felski describes it: being caught off-guard, to be dragged out of a readerly habit of distancing oneself from the text and its major leaps of faith. In *Hooked: Art and Attachment*, Felski moves away from an engagement with storytelling that suspects the narrator as much as the characters encountered in literary texts. Her appreciation of the verbal and visual inventions that can take their audiences captive reminds us that it is not an easy game played by city agents who turn to scripts as viable pathways to exit current conflicts. When urban practices and urban narratives collide and coincide, negative energies strengthen their readers' distrust in the future vision portrayed. At the same time, the readers' will to believe and their readiness to suspend disbelief allows for temporary, if shaky, attachments that provide a home for readers in simultaneous pursuit of several conflicting scripts of urban change.

Acknowledgements

This chapter has its intellectual home in our *City Scripts* research group of the University Alliance Ruhr (cf. City Scripts). Generous funding from the VolkswagenFoundation for "Scripts for Postindustrial Urban Futures: American Models, Transatlantic Interventions" (2018–2022) allows the senior and junior members of our group to work closely with urban developers and planners such as the Green Capital Agency Essen, the museum Dortmunder U, the Duisport Group (running Europe's largest inland harbour), a centre for sustainable construction (Öko-Zentrum NRW), RuhrFutur, a collaborative initiative for education in the Ruhr region, the LA community centre *Tía Chucha's Centro Cultural*, the international art collective *Quilomboarte*, the Detroit consulting company Zachary & Associates, as well as the Portland, Oregon, Collaborative for Inclusive Urbanism. We gratefully acknowledge the productive long-standing cooperation with our fellow North American studies researchers that has informed this chapter. Special thanks go to Stephanie Leigh Batiste, UCSB, Courtney Moffett-Bateau, Detroit/Berlin, Kornelia Freitag, Chris Katzenberg, Johannes Maria Krickl, and Michael Wala from the Ruhr-University Bochum, Walter Grünzweig, Randi Gunzenhäuser, Hanna Rodewald, Julia Sattler and Katharina Wood from the Technical University of Dortmund and, at the University of Duisburg-Essen, hub of the *City Scripts* group, Juliane Borosch, Florian Deckers, Elisabeth Haefs, Zohra Hassan-Pieper, Dietmar Meinel, Maria Sulimma and our dear colleague Josef Raab†, whose memory will shape the books to come out of this inter-institutional and transatlantic cooperation.

Notes

1 For the cultural turn, cf. Jameson; for its methodological innovations, cf. Bachmann-Medick. For the narrative turn, cf. Part III, IV and Epilogue in Phelan/Rabinowitz.
2 For the big migration to urban settings, cf. WBGU; for the story turn, cf. Buchenau/Gurr 2016; for the cultural and narrative turn to cities, cf. Buchenau/Gurr 2018.
3 For a discussion of the 'story turn in planning', cf. the Introduction to this book; as well as Sandercock 2003 and 2010; van Hulst. For an account of the societal functions of narrative, cf. Koschorke; for the implications of global urban competition for the self-representation of cities, cf. Reckwitz 382–393; for a critical discussion of the fuzziness brought on by the stellar career of the term 'narrative' in the field of economic and social practice, cf. Griem.
4 As Roderick P. Hart argues with regard to the 2016 US election, "storytelling was one of Trump's go-to weapons. His stories were not Reaganesque, filled with warmth and filigree. They were harsh, soulful, a punch in the face, not a gentle hand on the nation's shoulder. Trump was the protagonist in his stories, almost always their hero [...] Trump is a disciplined storyteller [...] [H]e continually reinforces the same stories" (99).
5 For anti-urban traditions, cf. Conn; White/White. For Trump's attraction to and for small towns and the main street, cf. Eckardt. For samples of Trump's use of the 'inner city trope', cf. Ye Hee Lee.

6 More fully, the passage reads: "[U]rban structures are built and sustained by layered, conflicting stories and the bodies that live them, eternally (re)shaping cities and histories. This 'narrative urbanism' is a patient, organic process revealing every construction site and street corner as a haunted site with stories past and passing by" (Rhinehart n.p.). This nicely illustrates some of our key concerns and might have served as an epigraph.
7 For a detailed discussion of the transhistorical as well as transregional cultural work of 'scripts' and 'scribal agency' in colonial North America, cf. Buchenau 2011.
8 For the Nietzschean double bind between the "destructively creative" as well as "creatively destructive" conjunction of literary strategies of representation, practices of the everyday and urban structures, cf. Bradbury/McFarlane 446.
9 For a popular culture example of literary and medial assemblages that helped to define North American and European immigrant societies, cf. Buchenau 2013.
10 For exemplary investigations of interactions between readers and texts, which highlight how readers establish new contexts for a text and how they defamiliarise established understandings and interpretations, cf. da Costa Fialho; Djikic *et al.* From a philological vantage point, writer response criticism addresses the literary texts produced by transformative readings, cf. Buchenau 2002, 36–51.
11 The German original reads: "Die Wandlung der Stadt Essen von einem vorindustriellen Stift mit Äbtissinengärten und Kaiserparks über eine Kohle- und Stahlmetropole zu einer grünen Stadt ist beeindruckend. Um 1900 war Essens Stadtbild geprägt durch die Kruppsche Gussstahlfabrik, durch enge Quartiere nahe der Altstadt und große Krupp-Kolonien [...] durch Schlote der Kokereien und Gestelle der Hochöfen, durch Fördertürme und Halden" (Essen 2017, 8).
12 For Juliane Borosch's doctoral research on new norms and forms of "jazzing up [...] climate-friendly rehabilitation in Detroit and the Ruhr", cf. www.uni-due.de/cityscripts/projects_jazzing_up_the_climate_friendly_city.
13 For Katharina Wood's exploration of the "ecological standardization and optimization" seeking to produce "green metropoles" and the intricate and occasionally self-defeating effects on conservation regulations, cf. www.uni-due.de/cityscripts/projects_green_metropoles.
14 Moya is building on Markus/Kitayama.
15 For *Chance By 2* (our translation) and its goal of educational justice, cf. Chance hoch 2; for Chris Katzenberg's project on "collective impact" scripts for educational and social reform in post-industrial cities, cf. www.uni-due.de/cityscripts/projects_social_change_for_engaging_cities.
16 For Elisabeth Haefs's work on "diversity gardening" in Essen and Portland, cf. www.uni-due.de/cityscripts/projects_diversity_gardening.
17 For Florian Deckers's investigations of ethnic urban counterscriptings, cf. www.uni-due.de/cityscripts/projects_raising_ethnic_voices.
18 In this vein, the chapter on the 'garden city' idea and its global spread in the early twentieth century in Peter Hall's magnificent *Cities of Tomorrow: An Intellectual History of Urban Planning and Design since 1880* is entitled "The City in the Garden: The Garden-City *Solution*; London, Paris, Berlin, New York, 1900–1940" (90–148; our emphasis). For a reading of the 'garden city' concept as a script, cf. Chapter 8 below.
19 For Johannes Maria Krickl's work on "conflicting scripts for waterfront and port developments", cf. www.uni-due.de/cityscripts/projects_waterfront_reconquista.
20 www.uni-due.de/cityscripts/projects_trivial_pursuits. For an exemplary insight into Maria Sulimma's research on serialised practices of prioritisation and of storytelling, cf. Sulimma, forthcoming.

21 These questions demarcate an almost epic battle about diversity, access, participation and epistemology in the urban as well as the academic realm, a battle wisely condensed into the formula "Liberal Appropriation vs. Critical Intervention" (17) in the ground-breaking volume of essays edited by Mahmoud Arghavan *et al.*

22 It is frequently the competition and interaction between different forms of writing and distinctive styles of mediation that substantially affects urban spaces (cf. Binder; Lindner; Schwanhäußer 2010a, 2010b).

23 For narratives of decline in the infamous American urban crisis of the 1970s and 1980s cf., for instance, Teaford's chapter on "the metropolitan malaise" and the resulting fragmentation of the city (151–156; here 152); Jonnes. On 6 November 1993, *The Economist* 329:7836 followed suit with the caption "Hell is an American City" on its front cover (cf. Punch 13).

24 A similarly iconic office building, the Elbtower, designed by David Chipperfield Architects Berlin, at a projected 233m to be by far the city's tallest conventional building, is to be completed in 2025 as a counterpoint to the Elbphilharmonie.

References

Alexander, Christopher, Sara Ishikawa, Murray Silverstein. *A Pattern Language: Towns, Buildings, Construction.* Oxford: Oxford University Press, 1977.

Ameel, Lieven. "A *Bildungsroman* for a Waterfront Development: Literary Genre and the Planning Narratives of Jätkäsaari, Helsinki." *Journal of Urban Cultural Studies* 3.2 (2016): 167–187.

Ameel, Lieven. *The Narrative Turn in Urban Planning: Plotting the Helsinki Waterfront.* New York: Routledge, 2021.

Arghavan, Mahmoud, Nicole Hirschfelder, Luvena Kopp, Katharina Motyl, eds. *Who can Speak and Who is Heard/Hurt? Facing Problems of Race, Racism and Ethnic Diversity in the Humanities in Germany*. Bielefeld: transcript, 2019.

Assmann, Aleida, Jan Assmann. "Geheimnis und Offenbarung." *Schleier und Schwelle.* Ed. Assmann, Assmann. Munich: Fink, 1998. 7–14.

AZ Cities @ Work. "The Men and Women that Make AZ Cities Work." 2017. http://azcitieswork.com/the-men-and-women-that-make-az-cities-work/.

Bachmann-Medick, Doris. *Cultural Turns: New Orientations in the Study of Culture.* Berlin, Boston: de Gruyter, 2016.

Bal, Mieke. *Travelling Concepts in the Humanities: A Rough Guide.* Toronto: University of Toronto Press, 2002.

Batty, Michael. "The Future Cities Agenda." *Environment and Planning B: Planning and Design* 40.2 (2013): 191–194. doi:10.1068/b4002ed.

Berking, Helmuth, Martina Löw, eds. *Die Eigenlogik der Städte: Neue Wege für die Stadtforschung.* Frankfurt/Main: Campus, 2008.

Berne, Eric. "Transactional Analysis: A New and Effective Method of Group Therapy." *American Journal of Psychotherapy* 12 (1958): 735–743.

Berne, Eric. *Transactional Analysis in Psychotherapy: A Systematic Individual and Social Psychiatry.* New York: Grove Press, 1961.

Binder, Beate. *Streitfall Stadtmitte: Der Berliner Schlossplatz.* Cologne: Böhlau, 2009.

Borosch, Juliane. "Jazzing Up the Climate-Friendly City: Scripts for Sustainable and Climate-Friendly Rehabilitation in Detroit and the Ruhr." www.uni-due.de/cityscripts/projects_jazzing_up_the_climate_friendly_city.

Bradbury, Malcolm, James McFarlane. *Modernism: A Guide to European Literature 1890–1930*. Harmondsworth: Penguin, 1976.

Buchenau, Barbara. "Erdichtetes Wissen über das präkoloniale Amerika. Junge Märkte und Ideen im Bann des *Song of Hiawatha* (1855)." *Von Käfern, Märkten und Menschen: Kolonialismus und Wissen in der Moderne*. Ed. Rebekka Habermas, Alexandra Przyrembel. Göttingen: Vandenhoeck & Ruprecht, 2013. 221–232.

Buchenau, Barbara. *Der frühe amerikanische historische Roman im transatlantischen Vergleich*. Interamericana 2. Frankfurt/Main: Peter Lang, 2002.

Buchenau, Barbara. "Inventing Iroquoia? Migrating Tropes of Similarity and Heritage in Francophone Narratives of Colonial Possession." *FIAR: Forum for Inter-American Research* 4.2 (2011): n.p. http://interamericaonline.org/volume-4-2/buchenau/.

Buchenau, Barbara. "Prefiguring CanAmerica? White Man's Indians and Religious Typology in New England and New France." *Transnational American Studies*. Ed. Udo J. Hebel. Heidelberg: Winter, 2012. 165–182.

Buchenau, Barbara, Jens Martin Gurr. "City Scripts: Urban American Studies and the Conjunction of Textual Strategies and Spatial Processes." *Urban Transformations in the U.S.A.: Spaces, Communities, Representations*. Ed. Julia Sattler. Bielefeld: transcript, 2016. 395–420.

Buchenau, Barbara, Jens Martin Gurr. "On the Textuality of American Cities and their Others: A Disputation." *Projecting American Studies: Essays on Theory, Method and Practice*. Ed. Frank Kelleter, Alexander Starre. Heidelberg: Winter, 2018. 135–152.

Chance hoch 2. www.uni-due.de/chancehoch2/.

City Scripts. Graduate Research Group "Scripts for Postindustrial Urban Futures: American Models, Transatlantic Interventions." www.cityscripts.de.

Coleridge, Samuel Taylor. *Biographia Litteraria* [1817]. Princeton: Princeton University Press, 1985.

Conn, Steven. *Americans Against the City: Anti-Urbanism in the Twentieth Century*. Oxford: Oxford University Press, 2014.

da Costa Fialho, Olívia. "Foregrounding and Refamiliarization: Understanding Readers' Response to Literary Texts." *Language and Literature* 16.2 (2007): 105–123.

Deckers, Florian. "Raising Ethnic Voices: Counter-Discourses in the Contemporary Cultural Scenes of New York City and Los Angeles." www.uni-due.de/cityscripts/projects_raising_ethnic_voices.

Djikic, Maja, Keith Oatley, Sara Zoeterman, Jordan B. Peterson. "On Being Moved by Art: How Reading Fiction Transforms the Self." *Creativity Research Journal* 21.1 (2009): 24–29.

Dzudzek, Iris, Peter Lindner. "Performing the Creative-Economy Script: Contradicting Urban Rationalities at Work." *Regional Studies* 49.3 (2015): 388–403.

Eckardt, Frank. "Trump on Main Street." *Dérive: Zeitschrift für Stadtforschung* 68.3 (2017): 4–8.

Essen. "European Green Capital Image Brochure." 2017. https://media.essen.de/media/egc2017media/egc2017_dokumente/ghe_imagebroschuere.de.pdf.

Essen. "Grüne Hauptstadt Europas: Bewerbung." 2014. https://media.essen.de/media/wwwessende/aemter/59/gruene_hauptstadt_europas_1/00_GHE_Einleitung_web.pdf.

Felski, Rita. *Hooked: Art and Attachment*. Chicago: University of Chicago Press, 2020.

Felski, Rita. *Uses of Literature*. Oxford: Blackwell, 2008.

Florida, Richard. *Cities and the Creative Class*. New York: Routledge, 2005.

Florida, Richard. *The Rise of the Creative Class: And How It's Transforming Work, Leisure and Everyday Life*. New York: Basic Books, 2002.

Florida, Richard. *The Rise of the Creative Class, Revisited.* New York: Basic Books, 2011.

Frank, Armin Paul. "A Rationale for a Comprehensive Study of the History of United States Literary Culture." *The International Turn in American Studies.* Ed. Marietta Messmer, Armin Paul Frank. Frankfurt/Main: Peter Lang, 2015. 231–270.

Frank, Armin Paul. "Translation Research from a Literary and Cultural Perspective: Objectives, Concepts, Scope." *Übersetzung, Translation, Traduction: Ein Internationales Handbuch zur Übersetzungsforschung.* Ed. Armin Paul Frank, Harald Kittel, Norbert Greiner, Theo Hermans, Werner Koller, Jose Lambert, Fritz Paul, in association with Juliane House, Brigitte Schultze. Berlin: de Gruyter, 2004. Vol. 1, 790–851.

Gabriel, Richard P. *Patterns of Software: Tales from the Software Community.* Oxford: Oxford University Press, 1996.

Gagnon, John H. "Scripts and the Coordination of Sexual Behaviour" [1974]. *The Interpretation of Desire: Essays in the Study of Sexuality.* Ed. Gagnon. Chicago: Chicago University Press, 2004. 59–87.

Goffman, Erving. *Frame Analysis: An Essay on the Organization of Experience.* London: Harper & Row, 1974.

Grankvist, Per. "Explaining and Exploring Our Common Future." Viable Cities Network 2019, 13 October 2019. https://medium.com/viable-cities/explaining-the-future-44d5ba787a82.

Griem, Julika. "Vom Nutzen und Nachteil des Narrativs für die Analyse des Hochschulsystems." Excerpt from a presentation at the conference *Differenzierung im Hochschulsystem zwischen Bildungsauftrag und Selbstentwurf.* Vienna, May 2017.

Grünzweig, Walter. "Parasitic Simulacrum. Ralph Waldo Emerson, Richard Florida, and the Urban 'Creative Class'." *Urban Transformations in the U.S.A.: Spaces, Communities, Representations.* Ed. Julia Sattler. Bielefeld: transcript, 2016. 81–97.

Grusin, Richard. *Premediation: Affect and Mediality after 9/11.* New York: Palgrave, 2010.

Gurr, Jens Martin. "'Without contraries is no progression': Emplotted Figures of Thought in Negotiating Oppositions, *Funktionsgeschichte* and Literature as 'Cultural Diagnosis'." *Text or Context: Reflections on Literary and Cultural Criticism.* Ed. Rüdiger Kunow, Stephan Mussil. Würzburg: Königshausen & Neumann, 2013. 59–77.

Haas, Eric. "Do We Have to Stick to the Script? Cities, Surveys and Descripting." *The Mediated City Conference.* Architecture_MPS, Los Angeles, 1–4 October 2014. http://architecturemps.com/wp-content/uploads/2013/09/HAAS-ERIC_DO-WE-HAVE-TO-STICK-TO-THE-SCRIPT.pdf.

Haefs, Elisabeth. "Diversity Gardening: Validating the 'Script of Green Strategies for Inclusive Urbanism'." www.uni-due.de/cityscripts/projects_diversity_gardening.

HafenCity Hamburg GmbH. *HafenCity News* 47 (2017) [quarterly publication, print and online]. www.hafencity.com/upload/files/files/170630_HC_News_47_FINAL_kl_kl.pdf.

Hall, Peter. *Cities of Tomorrow: An Intellectual History of Urban Planning and Design since 1880.* Chichester: John Wiley & Sons, [4]2014.

Hart, Roderick P. *Trump and Us: What He Says and Why People Listen.* Cambridge: Cambridge University Press, 2020.

Helmore, Edward. "Detroit Redefined: City Hires America's First Official 'Chief Storyteller'." *Guardian*, 5 September 2017.

Jameson, Frederick. *The Cultural Turn: Selected Writings on the Postmodern, 1983–1998*. London: Verso, 1998.

Jonnes, Jill. *South Bronx Rising: The Rise, Fall, and Resurrection of an American City*. New York: Fordham University Press, 1988.

Katzenberg, Chris. "Social Change for Engaging Cities – Translating Urban 'Collective Impact' Initiatives between the Rust Belt and the Ruhr." www.uni-due.de/cityscripts/projects_social_change_for_engaging_cities.

Klein, Norman M. *The Vatican to Vegas: A History of Special Effects*. New York: The New Press, 2004.

Knapp, Courtney Elizabeth. "Flipping the Script: Toward a Transformative Urban Redevelopment Agenda in Chattanooga, Tennessee." *Progressive Planning* 195 (Spring 2013): 14–17.

Koschorke, Albrecht. *Wahrheit und Erfindung: Grundzüge einer Allgemeinen Erzähltheorie*. Frankfurt/Main: Fischer, [3]2013.

Krickl, Johannes Maria. "Waterfront Reconquista: Conflicting Scripts for Waterfront and Port Developments in Inland Harbor Cities." www.uni-due.de/cityscripts/projects_waterfront_reconquista.

Lindner, Rolf. "Textur, '*imaginaire*', Habitus. Schlüsselbegriffe der kulturanalytischen Stadtforschung." *Die Eigenlogik der Städte: Neue Wege für die Stadtforschung*. Ed. Helmuth Berking, Martina Löw. Frankfurt/Main: Campus, 2008. 83–94.

Mallach, Alan, Lavea Brachman. *Regenerating America's Legacy Cities*. Cambridge: Lincoln Institute of Land Policy, 2013.

Markus, Hazel Rose, Shinobu Kitayama. "Culture and the Self: Implications for Cognition, Emotion, Motivation." *Psychological Review* 98.2 (1991): 224–253.

Molina, Natalia. *How Race is Made in America: Immigration, Citizenship, and the Historical Power of Racial Scripts*. Berkeley: University of California Press, 2014.

Moya, Paula M.L. *The Social Imperative: Race, Close Reading, and Contemporary Literary Criticism*. Stanford: Stanford University Press, 2016.

Oxford English Dictionary. "Religion, n." Oxford: Oxford University Press, 2014.

Oxford English Dictionary. "Script, n." Oxford: Oxford University Press, 2014.

Oxford English Dictionary. "Scripture, n." Oxford: Oxford University Press, 2014.

Peck, Jamie. "The Creativity Fix." *Fronesis* 24 (2007): 1–19.

Peck, Jamie. "Struggling with the Creative Class." *International Journal of Urban and Regional Research* 29.4 (2005): 740–770.

Phelan, James E., Peter J. Rabinowitz, ed. *A Companion to Narrative Theory*. Malden, MA: Blackwell, 2005.

Punch, Maurice. *Zero Tolerance Policing*. Bristol: Policy Press, 2007.

Quinn, Naomi, Dorothy Holland. "Culture and Cognition." *Cultural Models in Language and Thought*. Ed. Holland, Quinn. Cambridge: Cambridge University Press, 1987. 3–40.

Rabinowitz, Peter J. "They Shoot Tigers, Don't They? Path and Counterpoint in *The Long Goodbye*." *A Companion to Narrative Theory*. Ed. James E. Phelan, Peter J. Rabinowitz. Malden, MA: Blackwell, 2005. 181–191.

Reckwitz, Andreas. *Die Gesellschaft der Singularitäten*. Berlin: Suhrkamp, 2017.

Rhinehart, Zoë-Eve. "MONU [Magazine on Urbanism] #29/*Narrative Urbanism*." *Medium*, 30 December 2018. https://medium.com/@zoeeve/review-of-monu-29-narrative-urbanism-e8b2eedd8b8c.

Rodewald, Hanna. "Artsy Rust Belts: Narratives of the Creative Class in Post-Industrial Cities from a Transatlantic Perspective." www.uni-due.de/cityscripts/projects_artsy_rust_belts.php.

Sandercock, Leonie. "From the Campfire to the Computer: An Epistemology of Multiplicity and the Story Turn in Planning." *Multimedia Explorations in Urban Policy and Planning: Beyond the Flatlands*. Ed. Leonie Sandercock, Giovanni Attili. Dordrecht, Heidelberg, New York: Springer, 2010. 17–37.

Sandercock, Leonie. "Out of the Closet: The Importance of Stories and Storytelling in Planning Practice." *Planning Theory & Practice* 4.1 (2003): 11–28.

Schank, Roger C., Robert P. Abelson. *Scripts, Plans, Goals and Understanding: An Inquiry into Human Knowledge Structures*. Hillsdale: Lawrence Erlbaum, 1977.

Schwanhäußer, Anja. *Kosmonauten des Underground: Ethnografie einer Berliner Szene*. Frankfurt/Main: Campus, 2010a.

Schwanhäußer, Anja. "Stadtethnologie: Einblicke in aktuelle Forschungen." *Dérive: Zeitschrift für Stadtforschung* 40 (2010b): 106–113.

Stigler, James W., James Hiebert. *The Learning Gap: Best Ideas from the World's Teachers for Improving Education in the Classroom*. New York: Free Press, 1999.

Sulimma, Maria. "Surviving the City: *Zombies, Run!* and the Horrors of Urban Exercise." *Video Games and Spatiality in Amercian Studies: Playing the Field II*. Ed. Dietmar Meinel. Berlin: de Gruyter (forthcoming).

Sulimma, Maria. "Trivial Pursuits: The Practices and Politics of Prioritization in Postindustrial Urban Spaces." www.uni-due.de/cityscripts/projects_trivial_pursuits.

Teaford, Jon C. *The Twentieth-Century American City: Problem, Promise, and Reality*. Baltimore: Johns Hopkins University Press, 1986.

Throgmorton, James A. "Planning as Persuasive Storytelling in a Global-Scale Web of Relationships." *Planning Theory* 2.2 (2003): 125–135.

Throgmorton, James A. *Planning as Persuasive Storytelling: The Rhetorical Construction of Chicago's Electric Future*. Chicago: University of Chicago Press, 1996.

Ungar, Sheldon. "Knowledge, Ignorance and the Popular Culture: Climate Change versus the Ozone Hole." *Public Understanding of Science* 9 (2000): 297–312.

van Hulst, Merlijn. "Storytelling, a Model *of* and a Model *for* Planning." *Planning Theory* 11.3 (2012): 299–318.

WBGU [German Advisory Council on Global Change]. *Humanity on the Move: Unlocking the Transformative Power of Cities*. Berlin: WBGU, 2016.

White, Morton Gabriel, Lucia White. *The Intellectual Versus the City: From Thomas Jefferson to Frank Lloyd Wright*. Cambridge, MA: Harvard University Press and MIT Press, 1962.

Whitney, Paul. "Schemas, Frames, and Scripts in Cognitive Psychology." *International Encyclopedia of the Social & Behavioral Sciences*. Ed. Neil J. Smelser, Paul Baltes. Oxford: Elsevier, 2001. 13522–13526.

Williams, Joseph P. "'Chief Storytellers': The Newest City Trend?" US News.com, 14 May 2019. www.usnews.com/news/cities/articles/2019-05-14/denver-atlanta-and-detroit-hire-chief-storytellers-to-shape-city-narratives.

Wood, Katharina. "Green Metropoles: Conserving Whose World? Sustainability Standards in the U.S. and Germany." www.uni-due.de/cityscripts/projects_green_metropoles.

Xinhua. "Four Chinese Cities Picked as UNESCO Creative Cities." China.org.cn, 1 November 2017. www.china.org.cn/travel/2017-11/01/content_41828399.htm.

Ye Hee Lee, Michelle. "President Trump's claim that he has done 'far more than anyone' for 'inner cities'." *The Washington Post*, 17 August 2017. www.washingtonpost.com/news/fact-checker/wp/2017/08/17/president-trumps-claim-he-has-done-far-more-than-anyone-for-inner-cities/.

8 From the 'Garden City' to the 'Smart City'

Literary Urban Studies, Policy Mobility Research and Travelling Urban Models

Introduction

'Smart City', 'Sustainable City' – a.k.a. 'Eco-City', or 'Green City' – 'Inclusive City': The global diffusion of blueprints for the future of cities is a major factor in global policy development, and numerous attempts, frequently with an urban focus, have been made to identify key actors, mechanisms and contextual factors crucial to its understanding. However, the ways in which policies concretely travel still remains understudied – and even where contributions do analyse specific documents, this analysis is generally limited to a content analysis with little regard for rhetoric, imagery, tropes or other strategies of generating persuasiveness. In this chapter, I argue that a literary and cultural studies approach that proceeds by means of a close reading of the material and pays attention, for instance, to rhetoric, iconography or intertextuality can profitably supplement existing approaches to the study of policy mobility and diffusion. What will be central to this endeavour is the notion of 'scripts' as developed in Chapter 7. Thus, in a conception which deliberately combines descriptive as well as prescriptive definitions of the term from a range of fields and disciplines (including literary studies, social psychology, law, biblical scholarship and artificial intelligence research), I regard 'scripts' as combining procedural knowledge, self-description and blueprints for the future.

This type of research situates itself at the intersection between urban literary and cultural studies, policy mobility research in political science, economics, and in human geography, as well as planning research on 'global urbanism'. While seeking to contribute to all of them, it is firmly rooted in literary urban studies in terms of method and corpus, but goes further than most previous approaches to literary urban studies in more consistently shifting attention to non-literary texts. This chapter thus seeks to develop an approach to policy mobility that is informed by guiding questions and methods from literary and cultural studies in order to elucidate a blind spot in existing policy mobility research. In doing so, I draw on numerous concepts developed in the previous chapters (texts as qualitative models of and for the city, texts and scenario building, the scripted nature of urban development, narrativity of planning documents and planning processes). Hence, the chapter ties together virtually all strands of the book.

As a case study, I analyse the 'garden city' concept and its virtually global spread in the early twentieth century as a 'script'. I therefore discuss later manifestations of the 'garden city script' side by side with its founding text, Ebenezer Howard's *Garden Cities of To-Morrow* (1902). In his magisterial *Cities of Tomorrow: An Intellectual History of Urban Planning and Design since 1880*, Peter Hall writes about this travelling model: "What was astonishing about the garden-city movement was how easily it was exported from its homeland, but also how strangely it became transformed in the process" (132). A reading especially of Howard's text will point out both its suggestive combination of English and American strands of anti-urbanism *and* its deployment of figurative, narrative and medial strategies of persuasion to promote utopian promises of an alternative to life in crowded industrialised cities. The discussion of its global adaption, in turn, will illustrate key mechanisms in such processes of policy diffusion and translation.

In sum, taking my cue from the notion of 'script' as developed with Barbara Buchenau in Chapter 7, I argue that the frequently scripted nature of blueprints for urban development relies on narrative acts, generic formula, medial forms and structures, figural thought, and cognitive models, and thus on processes of narrativisation, mediation and figuration (both in the sense of personification and condensation into figures of thought). A literary studies approach to policy diffusion might therefore profitably complement existing approaches.

On a Central Gap in Policy Mobility Research

Recent decades have seen an unprecedented global diffusion of ideas, recipes and blueprints for urban development, many of which, it can be noted, can be subsumed under a fairly limited number of labels such as 'smart', 'sustainable', 'creative' and 'socially inclusive' urban development: Sustainable or climate-sensitive urban development, water-sensitive planning, creative cities policies, post-industrial waterfront development, ideas for inclusive urbanism and other concepts have – wholesale or piecemeal – quickly spread across the globe. Thus, much of the research in policy mobility generally has focused on cities – both in the sense that 'urban policies' have been a key focus and in the sense that cities are the key nodes in networks of policy diffusion where conferences, fact-finding visits, etc. take place (cf. Prince 319). This type of "transnational urbanism" (Smith), however, is only part of a much more general tendency: the global diffusion of "institutions, policies, programmes, procedures, ideologies, justifications, attitudes and ideas" generally (de Jong/Mamadouh 20). Under the headings of 'policy mobility', 'policy diffusion' or 'institutional transplant/transfer', this phenomenon has attracted an enormous amount of scholarly attention in various disciplines ranging from comparative law (cf. Teubner) and political science (cf. for instance Castles; Dobbin/Simmons/Garrett; Dolowitz/Marsh; Hudson/Kim; Stone), sociology and comparative education (cf. Strang/Meyer; Sun; Tan), economics and business administration (cf. Herrmann-Pillath/Zweynert; Taube), (critical) urban geography (cf. Fricke; McCann/Ward; Peck/Theodore) to comparative urban studies, planning studies and architectural research (cf. Abram; Healey; Healey/Upton; Hein 2014, 2016; McNeill, Sanyal 2005, 2016; Schmitt; Smith; Zimmermann). Broadly speaking, emphasis in this research has shifted from largely non-contextual, positivist-rationalist 'policy transfer' or 'transplant' to a more context-oriented, constructivist 'policy mobilities' paradigm.[1] Despite different guiding questions and preoccupations, these various traditions share an interest in identifying factors that may enable or impede 'successful' transfers (cf. especially de Jong; de Jong/Mamadouh/Lalenis 2002a, 2002b; Delpeuch/Vassileva; Inkpen/Pien).

Thus, policy mobility has come to be recognised as a major factor in global policy developments and there has been a consistent interest in systematising and understanding key actors, mechanisms and contextual factors. In the wake especially of Dolowitz and Marsh's influential account, there has been highly differentiated research on the types of agents involved (e.g. elected officials, political parties, think-tanks, supranational organisations, consultants, corporations, academics, philanthropic foundations, etc.) (cf. Dolowitz/Marsh; Stone).[2] As for the different mechanisms in the global exchange and diffusion of policies, Dobbin, Simmons and Garrett, for instance, distinguish between "coercion" by powerful states or organisations, "competition" (which may enforce the adoption of certain policies to remain competitive), "policy learning", i.e. the rational takeover of ideas; and "emulation", designating an opportunistic or strategic adoption of a policy if this is perceived as being politically advantageous (cf. also Liu/Leisering 110). Finally, research on contextual factors has long assumed that similar political or legal systems, common linguistic and cultural traditions and conventions, or other – broadly speaking – 'cultural similarities'[3] might make successful policy transfers more likely (for an account of this approach, cf. Lalenis/de Jong/Mamadouh).[4] However, there is strong empirical evidence against such assumptions (cf. de Jong/Mamadouh/Lalenis 2002a, 288; Inkpen/Pien; Liu/Leisering).

Arguing that scholars have been "focusing little on the specific processes and practices" (108) by means of which policies travel, McCann proposes a research agenda of studying more closely the "global circulation of urban policies" (109). He states the need to avoid both the view of policy mobility as the purely rational activity of globally informed best practice seekers on the one hand and the view of urban policies as freely transferable 'plug and play' modules, as it were (cf. McCann 109). Thus, McCann seems more aware than most that "[s]omething happens to policy knowledge along the way, *in the telling*" (117; my emphasis) and argues the need "to explore *how* urban policy gets done in global context – through the prosaic routines, practices, technologies, interpersonal connections, and travels of key actors" (110). McCann speaks of the "products of the work of experts [...] – stories, articles, reports, PowerPoint presentations, maps [...] conferences, meetings, fact-finding-visits" – which "reflect, travel through, and produce circuits of policy knowledge" (116, 120).[5] Moreover, he argues that "two crucial elements of policy mobilities are site visits and conference attendance; that face-to-face interactions in these globalizing microspaces play a central role in shaping policies and policy learning" (McCann 123). However, as argued earlier, the ways in which policies concretely travel still remains understudied: The overwhelming majority of studies on policy mobility across disciplines – whether they take an institutional, actor-centric approach, a 'cultural fit' approach studying the compatibility of belief systems, or a global convergence approach – appears to have a blind spot in the analysis of *how*, i.e. in what material form, such ideas actually travel. Is it expert presentations, photographs, investor brochures, plans and visualisations, policy papers or scholarly studies? Moreover, even where contributions do mention 'document analysis' as a research method (cf. for instance Liu/Leisering 108; Liu/Sun; McCann 113; Romano 38; Sun 375), there is generally little to no engagement with the materiality, mediality and narrativity of the actual documents, speeches, etc. involved (cf. also Honeck 133 for a similar diagnosis). Such an analysis, I believe, might significantly strengthen discussions of how to account for 'successful' or 'unsuccessful' transplants.[6]

Without for a moment seeking to invalidate the various existing research traditions and their findings, I nonetheless suggest that closer attention to the concrete material that actually travels, that is, a literary and cultural studies approach that proceeds by means of a close reading of the material and pays attention, for instance, to rhetoric, iconography and intertextuality, might profitably supplement existing approaches to the study of policy mobility and diffusion. More specifically, I argue that the notion of 'scripts' will prove a powerful supplement to existing approaches.

Case Study: The 'Garden City Script' and its Diffusion in the Early Twentieth Century

In 1898, the untrained (though remarkably well-read) English social reformer-turned-planner Ebenezer Howard published *To-Morrow: A Peaceful Path to Real Reform* and thus initiated the concept of the 'garden city', "one of the most powerful ideas that urbanism came up with in the early 20th century" (Monclús/Díez Medina 13). In a section of hardly more than 15 pages, he here outlined how to solve the then prevalent problem of mass migration from the depopulating countryside to crowded and unhealthy industrial cities by means of a system of 'garden cities'. Persuasively illustrating them in his famous "three magnets" diagram (cf. Figure 8.1), Howard sought to combine the benefits of the town with those of the country: "beauty of nature" *and* "social opportunity", "low rents" *and* "high wages", "pure air and water [...] no smoke, no slums" *and* "flow of capital [...] plenty to do [...] freedom" would, he argued, draw people to the "Town-Country", as manifested in his 'garden cities' (Howard 1898, 8).

These were meant to be made up of a central city of some 50,000 inhabitants surrounded by further settlements with a population of around 30,000. Each of these 'garden cities' enclosed by a community-owned greenbelt that was to contain farms and allotments as well as institutions like an "agricultural college" and "convalescent homes" (Howard 1898, 12), together forming a

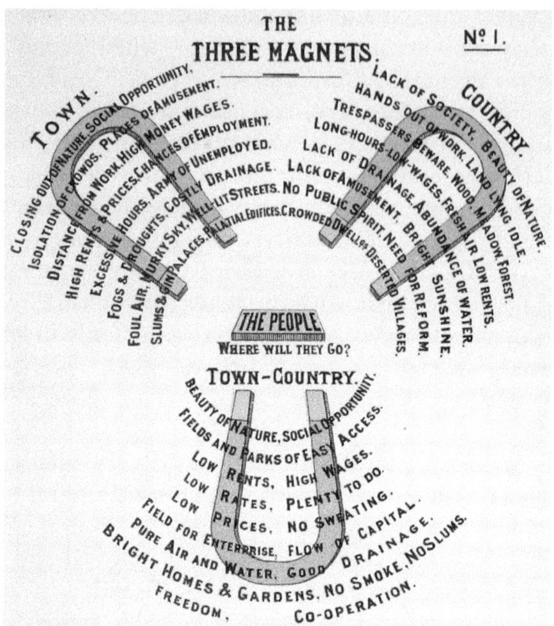

Figure 8.1 "The Three Magnets", illustrating the ills and benefits of country and city and the combined advantages of the "Town-Country" or "Garden City"; diagram from Ebenezer Howard's 1898 *To-morrow: A Peaceful Path to Real Reform.*

Source: Howard (1898, 8).

city of some 250,000 inhabitants. Land would be owned and managed by the community, making this a case of radical self-government bordering on anarchism.

By far the major part of Howard's book (1898, 20–167) is then largely dedicated to financing schemes and revenue calculations, administrative questions and, not least, to pre-emptively answering likely objections:

> Its entire revenue is derived from rents; and one of the purposes of this work is to show that the rents which may very reasonably be expected from the various tenants on the estate will be amply sufficient, if paid into the coffers of Garden City, (a) to pay the interest on the money with which the estate is purchased, (b) to provide a sinking fund for the purpose of paying off the principal, (c) to construct and maintain all such works as are usually constructed and maintained by municipal and other local authorities out of rates compulsorily levied, and (d) (after redemption of debentures) to provide a large surplus for other purposes, such as old-age pensions or insurance against accident and sickness.
>
> (1898, 20f.)

What gained traction, however, was largely only the physical planning essence of Howard's concept, the permeation of human-scale settlements with extensive green spaces. Thus, with the Garden City Association, founded in 1899, the 'garden city' idea – or significant variations of it – successively spread globally, within less than two decades reaching places, for instance, in Britain, Germany, the United States, Australia and New Zealand (cf. Monclús/Díez Medina; as well as Hall 101–148). It is already telling for this process of diffusion that Howard's book is now universally known by the title of the revised second edition of 1902: In contrast to the original title *To-Morrow: A Peaceful Path to Real Reform*, the new title *Garden Cities of To-Morrow* significantly replaced the reference to Howard's radically reformist *end* with the physical *means* he proposed for its realisation. Indeed, so successful was the spatial planning essence of the 'garden city' – with the reformist agenda at its core virtually eviscerated – that Hall rightly regards Howard as having been widely misunderstood. The gravest of all misreadings, Hall argues, is to "see him as a physical planner, ignoring the fact that his garden cities were merely the vehicles for a progressive reconstruction of capitalist society into an infinity of cooperative commonwealths" (91). How, it is to be asked, did a radically reformist programme based on decentralised, virtually anarchist self-government, for which the 'garden city' scheme was merely a means to an end, come to be globally diffused as a spatially based planning blueprint for green and healthy urban development?

A brief discussion of the intellectual origins of Howard's concept might contribute to an explanation. In what remains the most detailed study of Howard's intellectual outlook, Beevers points to the English dissenting tradition as the source of virtually all of Howard's key ideas (cf. 24). While this refers primarily to Howard's social and political ideas, the connection between ruralism and socio-political reformism also, of course, has a long (and partly identical) tradition. This lineage, which George McKay in *Radical Gardening: Politics, Idealism & Rebellion in the Garden* (2011) pithily termed "horti-countercultural politics", extends from Winstanley's seventeenth-century manifestos for the agrarian proto-communist community of "Diggers" via Owen's radically utopian Topolobampo community in Mexico in the 1880s (cf. also Howard 99) to contemporary guerrilla gardening (for the tradition of "alternative communities", cf. also Monclús/Díez Medina 15). Moreover, the vernacular English tradition of romanticising the countryside in the wake, not least, of Wordsworth, also appears to be a strong presence. Thus, Wordsworth's familiar complaint about "the encreasing accumulation of men in cities" in his 1802 "Preface to *Lyrical Ballads*" (597),[7] seems to resonate in Howard's constant references to "over-crowded cities" (119 *et passim*). Wagner largely credits the distrust in metropolitan centres and large agglomerations in Howard and the early garden city movement to early social medicine's miasma theory of disease and to early (European) sociology's criticism of the city (cf. 46). It is important to note, however, that Howard spent six formative years in his 20s (1871–1876) in the United States, briefly as a failing farmer in Nebraska and then in Chicago from 1872 to 1876, when the city was still known as the 'garden city', surely the origin of Howard's 'garden city' designation (cf. Hall 93). As a farmer on the frontier in Nebraska, Howard had first-hand experience with the 1862 Homestead Act and its promises (cf. Hall 92). Hall does refer to Howard's ideas of self-reliant small communities as "a peculiarly American vision, the homesteading spirit, brought back home to industrial England" (99). However, he largely appears to underestimate the impact of American intellectual traditions. Wagner, too, in his otherwise compelling account almost entirely disregards the influence of Howard's six years in the United States on the development of his ideas (cf. 40f.). Thus, while "the first stirrings" of Howard's interest in the connection between urban form and "the social question" have been traced to his time in the United States (Beevers 1), the impact of a specifically American type of anti-urbanism, which Howard can be shown to have read and internalised, has almost entirely been overlooked (for this tradition, cf. Conn; White/White). One of the classic early American instances of associating urban density with moral and political degradation is of course Jefferson's 1787 letter to James Madison, significantly written from Paris:

> I think our governments will remain virtuous for many centuries; as long as they are chiefly agricultural; and this will be as long as there shall be vacant lands in any part of America. When they get piled upon one another in large cities, as in Europe, they will become corrupt as in Europe.
>
> (Jefferson 422)

It can be argued that this American tradition of Jeffersonian pastoralism, though never quite explicit, is nonetheless a clear presence in Howard's text – and was repeatedly to make itself felt in the history of the garden city movement. Moreover, Howard's reading during his time in the United States has been disregarded, although it can be shown to have left its mark on his outlook. Thus, Howard there read and met Whitman, Emerson and Lowell, and read Hawthorne (cf. Beevers 6), the latter two being cited prominently in *Garden Cities of To-Morrow*.[8] Further, as a motto to the entire book, Howard cites the final stanza of J.R. Lowell's 1845 poem "The Present Crisis", an abolitionist classic later frequently quoted by Martin Luther King Jr. References to the "Pilgrims" and the "Mayflower" implicitly cast the struggle for garden city reform as the dissenting pioneers' arduous quest for a better future on new shores:

> New occasions teach new duties;
> Time makes ancient good uncouth;
> They must upward still, and onward,
> Who would keep abreast of Truth.
> Lo, before us, gleam her camp-fires!
> We ourselves must Pilgrims be,
> Launch our 'Mayflower,' and steer boldly

Through the desperate winter sea,
Nor attempt the Future's portal
With the Past's blood-rusted key.[9]
(Howard 1898, unpaginated imprint page)

Thus, several intellectual traditions come together in Howard's conception: First, a vernacular English ruralist tradition of distrust in 'crowded cities' is coupled with a dissenting tradition of "horti-countercultural" alternative communities (*sensu* McKay). These are joined by a specifically American system of beliefs, myths and symbols combining the "Pilgrims'" religious quest for a better community, missionary zeal, and Jeffersonian ruralism and distrust of big cities – acquired, imaginatively amalgamated and supplemented by means of wide reading in quintessentially canonical *and* countercultural American literature (*sensu* Bercovitch).

The convergence of these literary and cultural traditions already becomes manifest in one of the illustrations, "Group of Slumless, Smokeless Cities"[10] (cf. Figure 8.2). Here, the names of the outer cities surrounding the central city – "Gladstone", "Justitia", "Rurisville", "Philadelphia", "Concord" and "Garden City" – point to English liberalism and ruralism as well as to specifically American republican intellectual traditions (cf. below for a more detailed discussion of the narrative, medial and figural patterns of the 'garden city script').[11]

How did the 'garden city' concept travel so quickly – and what was it that actually travelled? People for site visits and conferences, scholarly papers, or design manuals and advertising materials? Or is the spread of 'garden city' ideas merely an unsurprising case of comparable solutions inspired by comparable challenges (green space advocacy to bring fresh air and opportunities for exercise into rapidly growing, unhealthy industrial cities)? In the rapid diffusion of 'garden city' ideas, all of these mechanisms can be shown to play a role.

This can be exemplified by studying side by side Howard's founding text, its early English realisations – the first garden city of Letchworth (1903) and the garden suburb of Hampstead (1905–1907) – as well as the early German reception and selected later exponents. After Letchworth, Hampstead as the second manifestation of Howard's idea was already conceived as a mere garden suburb. What is more, Hampstead – like the other garden cities and suburbs – very much against Howard's original ideas, "became a small-scale elitist suburb" (Monclús/Díez Medina 16). Arguably the most important German manifestation of the garden suburb idea – its "outstanding expression" (Hall 123) – is Essen's Margarethenhöhe neighbourhood (since 1906) and the work of its key planner, Robert Schmidt. In this development, Howard's politically, socially and economically radical ideas were quickly watered down and in parts virtually written out of the 'garden city script'. The garden city movement thus really only gained national and international traction in its reduced form as a blueprint for the physical planning of 'garden suburbs' (cf.

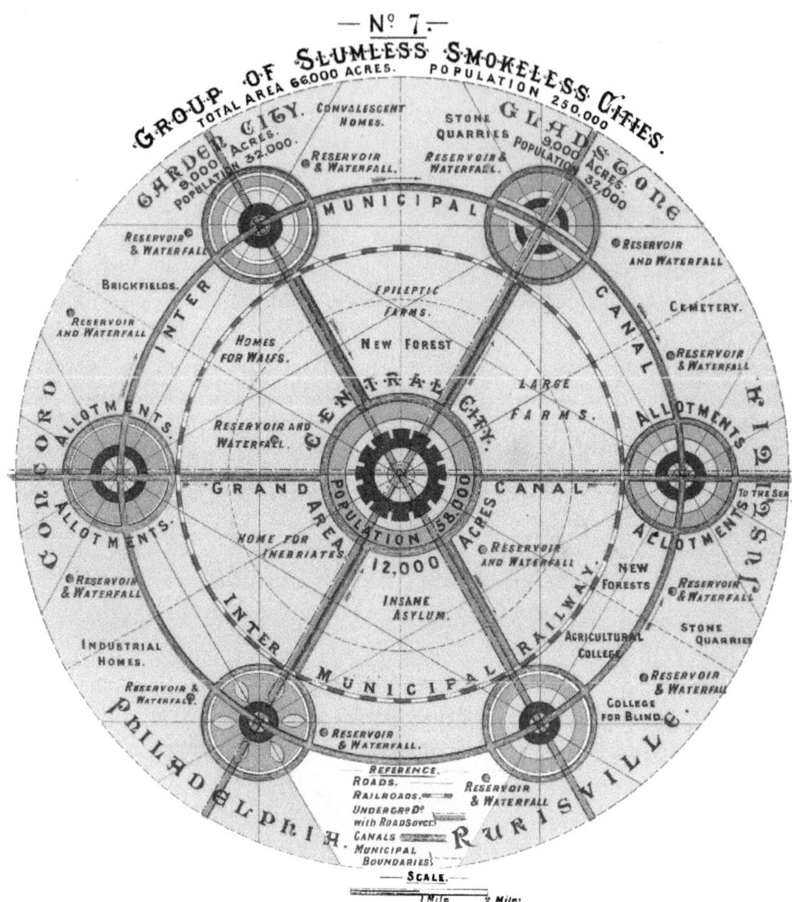

Figure 8.2 Visualisation of central city and outlying 'garden cities' with telling place names from Ebenezer Howard's 1898 *To-morrow: A Peaceful Path to Real Reform.*

Source: Howard (1898, 12).

Hall 101–148). This development was largely owed to Howard's key British associates, architects Raymond Unwin and Barry Parker, who quickly came to spearhead the movement and who were responsible for the early designs.

As for the German reception and implementation of Howard's ideas, the "*Deutsche Gartenstadtgesellschaft*" was already founded in 1902, inspired by a translation of Howard's book into German and with a similarly reformist agenda (cf. Hall 121f.). Essen Margarethenhöhe, a garden suburb of what was then a centre of the coal and steel industries, was, though instituted top-down by the Krupps, the "outstanding expression" of garden city (really garden suburb) design in Germany (cf. Hall 123). With its curving streets, a market square, an entrance gateway and – closely inspired by Unwin and Parker's designs – decidedly anti-modern, retro-architecture, it closely echoed medieval small towns (at least in external appearance – the housing construction is surprisingly standardised and grid-based). Margarethenhöhe, designed by architect Georg Metzendorf in close cooperation with Robert Schmidt, is hailed as "a milestone in the national and international history of urban planning" (von Petz 58) with a significant amount of scholarly material devoted to it.

We here largely need to consider the work of Robert Schmidt (1869–1934), chief planner of the city of Essen (1901–1920) and later the first director of the regional planning association in the Ruhr region (1920–1932). His 1912 discussion of foundations for a general settlement plan for the industrial Ruhr region in his *Denkschrift*[12] is a landmark in the early history of integrated regional planning and remarkably far-sighted in recognising the importance of green spaces for urban health promotion.[13] Schmidt was apparently a liberal social democrat (for Schmidt's leftist politics, cf. von Petz 32 *et passim*), who clearly had strong sympathies for Howard's political and social reformism and was profoundly influenced by the resulting planning ideas. Schmidt appears to have undertaken several study trips to England[14] to observe 'garden city' developments first-hand and already met Unwin and other protagonists of the garden city movement as early as 1903 (cf. von Petz 27).[15]

The successful diffusion of central 'garden city' concepts, I argue, is not least the result of their packaging in the form of a 'script'. In other words, the specific combination of narrative presentation, persuasive appeal to various literary and cultural traditions, and suggestive images, may to a large extent account for its unique appeal. In this vein, Howard's original 1898 book, and especially the revised 1902 edition *Garden Cities of To-Morrow*, despite its allegedly expository nature, is a profoundly *literary* text full of narrative strategies, literary references and suggestive illustrations. Literary references include, for instance, quotations (largely as chapter epigraphs) from the biblical Book of Job (76), Goethe's *Maximen und Reflexionen* (114), Dickens's *Our Mutual Friend* (70), Scott's *The Heart of Midlothian* (134), Hawthorne's *The Scarlet Letter* (126) or Lowell's "The Present Crisis" (cf. my discussion earlier in this chapter). Howard's proposal, then, taps into and amalgamates several literary traditions, each with their specific – and frequently topical – associations. Thus, as one epigraph to the chapter on "The Town-Country Magnet", which describes the allure of the 'garden city', Howard cites William Blake's hymn "Jerusalem", widely known as England's unofficial anthem, with its topical juxtaposition of "these dark Satanic mills" (generally read as a reference to the ills of industrialisation) and "England's green and pleasant land":

> I will not cease from mental strife,
> Nor shall my sword sleep in my hand,
> Till we have built Jerusalem
> In England's green and pleasant land.
> – *Blake* (qtd. in Howard 1898, 12)

After the exhortation from Lowell's "The Present Crisis" in the epigraph to the entire book – "We ourselves must Pilgrims be,/Launch our 'Mayflower,' and steer boldly/Through the desperate winter sea" – this is again the expression of a willingness to struggle for the 'new Jerusalem', the model city upon which the eyes of all the world will be set – here formulated in the highly topical and suggestive terms of a city in "green and pleasant land". The second epigraph to Howard's first chapter in the second edition,[16] from John Ruskin's "Sesame and Lilies", presents, as it were, the outcome of the struggle and virtually functions as an epitome of the 'garden city' concept with its description of a "clean and busy street within and the open country without, with a belt of beautiful garden and orchard round the walls, so that from any part of the city perfectly fresh air and grass and sight of far horizon might be reachable in a few minutes walk" (qtd. in Howard 1902, 20).

Howard's language is frequently highly metaphorical, virtually poetic in places in its suggestive exhortation of the beauties of nature and its benefits for human health and happiness:

> Yes, the key to the problem how to restore the people to the land – that beautiful land of ours, with its canopy of sky, the air that blows upon it, the sun that warms it, the rain and dew that moisten it – the very embodiment of Divine love for man – is indeed a *Master-Key*, for it is the key to a portal through which, even when scarce ajar, will be seen to pour a flood of light on the problems of intemperance, of excessive toil, of restless anxiety, of grinding poverty – the true limits of Governmental interference, ay, and even the relations of man to the Supreme Power [...] [This will lead to the] spontaneous [i.e. unforced, voluntary] movement of the people from our crowded cities to the bosom of our kindly mother earth, at once the source of life, of happiness, of wealth, and of power.
>
> (1898, 5, 7)

Throughout, the text relies on suggestive contrasts between the ills of life in industrial cities and the beauty of nature: In the city, "the sunlight is being more and more shut out, while the air is so vitiated that the fine public buildings, like the sparrows, rapidly become covered with soot" (Howard 1898, 8), while the country provides "beautiful vistas, lordly parks, violet-scented woods, fresh air, sounds of rippling water" (Howard 1898, 8). These benefits of nature, Howard maintains, can be retained in city life "by so laying out a Garden City that, as it grows, the free gifts of Nature – fresh air, sunlight, breathing room and playing room – shall be still retained in all needed abundance" (1898, 114).

Like many of the writings indebted to Howard, Schmidt's *Denkschrift*, too, highlights the centrality of nature to urban health – from the micro-scale of the individual building that is to provide sun and fresh air to the individual all the way to the provision of intercommunal greenbelts, the planning of which takes up more than 16 out of 102 pages (65–75, 90–96). Thus, the *Denkschrift* contains a "[s]chematic illustration of how green spaces are to permeate a city plan",[17] in which the town is surrounded by a greenbelt, from which green spaces extend into the town centre, thus providing all residential areas with access to extensive green spaces. Moreover, individual residential areas are each to contain smaller, separate parks and green spaces. Though clearly distinct from Howard, the description of their function in organicist metaphors – "regenerators of air in the urban organism" (Schmidt 66; my translation)[18] – is remarkably similar. Furthermore, despite the otherwise sober expository tone and academic *look and feel* of the *Denkschrift*, which also manifests itself in 25 large fold-out maps and illustrations as well as 45 tables with impressively detailed statistics on demographic development, population and building densities, building types and heights, etc., Schmidt occasionally waxes lyrical[19] with stark (and suggestively gendered) contrasts between industry's "smoking funnels, rattling conveyor belts, dusty slag heaps, toxic blast furnace gases, noisy steam hammers and rams" (68; my translation)[20] on the one hand and the "beauty of the scenery [...] rich and waving, curved silhouettes of landscape, groves and meadows, hollows and hills" (68; my translation).[21] In many places, his text works by means of personification, anthropomorphisation and suggestive contrasts between the beauty of pristine nature and industrial waste lands with rivers as open sewers:

> The term "walking trail" is as relative as that of the avenue or the murmuring brook, which can be a silvery trout stream or the Emscher [a river then used as an open sewer], indicative of the mass accumulation of people, on whose green-yellow-brownish surface melancholy willow trees dream of the definitive success of the Emscher Association [the regional water management body].[22]
>
> (Schmidt 77; my translation)

Besides, the *Denkschrift* also relies on personification: Thus, the threats of unhealthy dwellings and the significantly increased mortality rates of their occupants are here drastically personified by means of the "child, deprived of sun, light, and air, an innocent sentenced to death in the rear building" (Schmidt 41; my translation).[23]

But the 'scripted' nature of the 'garden city' concept goes beyond figurative and often poetic language generally: Given the opposition of 'nature' and 'city' in the 'industrial present' and their fortunate combination in the happy 'garden city to be', the 'garden city script' lends itself to being expressed in figures of thought and speech that suggest a reconciliation of opposites (for an inventory of figures of thought in dealing with binary oppositions, cf. Gurr 2013). Thus, Howard frequently invokes the contrast between "crowded, unhealthy cities" on the one hand and "the keen and pure delights of the country" on the other hand (1902, 15) and argues that "[t]own and country *must be married*, and out of this joyous union will spring a new hope, a new life, a new civilisation" (1902, 18; italics original). Similarly, Letchworth Garden City was advertised as a union of opposites with the slogan "Health of the Country, Comforts of the Town" (Monclús/Díez Medina 16).

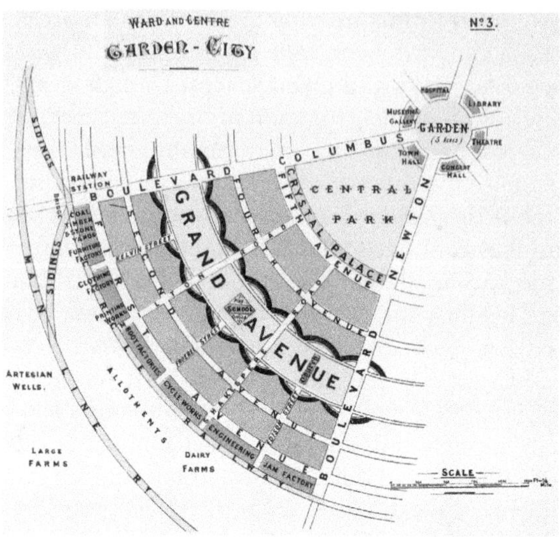

Figure 8.3 Illustration of one ward of a 'garden city' with telling street names and spatial configurations from Ebenezer Howard's 1898 *To-morrow: A Peaceful Path to Real Reform.*

Source: Howard (1898, 14).

The 'garden city script' also, however, evinces the suggestive use of illustrations arguably inherent to scripts. Thus, in the conceptual illustration of the layout of one of the city's wards (cf. Figure 8.3), we find a highly telling combination of street names and intriguing connections established by some of the streets.

Together with the place names in Figure 8.2 – "Gladstone", "Justitia", "Rurisville", "Philadelphia", "Concord" – the place names here – "Columbus Boulevard", "Newton Boulevard", "Froebel Street" (leading to the school), "Kelvin Street", "Edison Street" (leading from the engineering facilities to the church), "Shakespeare Road", "Milton Road", as well as "First Avenue", "Second Avenue" and "Central Park" – each evoke specific European or American cultural icons. Together, these place names suggest a felicitous conjunction of reason, discovery, science and progress on the one hand and of literary and cultural sophistication on the other hand, virtually, one might say, a happy reconciliation of "the two cultures" (*sensu* Snow).[24] While it is important to note that Howard's idealised illustration is explicitly referred to as "a diagram only – plan must depend on site selected" (14), this as well as the other illustrations from Howard's book have frequently been reprinted and adapted, and their conceptual suggestiveness, cultural allusiveness and appealing combination of geometrical precision and harmonious ornamentality surely contributed to their virtually global appeal.

Finally, in the outline of the nature of scripts (cf. Chapter 7), the argument was that – even where they manifest themselves in allegedly sober, discursive texts or visual materials – scripts for their persuasiveness frequently rely on narrative patterns. In this vein, it is interesting to note that Howard's description of the garden city, too, is not presented discursively, but in the form of a narrative of walking through the city with a local "friend" familiar with the city and its principles:

> *Passing out of the Crystal Palace on our way to the outer ring of the town, we cross Fifth Avenue* – lined, as are all the roads of the town, with trees – fronting which, and looking on to the Crystal Palace, *we find* a ring of very excellently-built houses, each standing in its own ample grounds; and, *as we continue our walk, we observe* that the houses are for the most part built either in concentric rings, facing the various avenues [...] or fronting the boulevards and roads, which all converge to the centre of the town. *Asking the friend who accompanies us on our journey* what the population of this little city may be, *we are told* about 30,000 in the city itself [...] *Noticing the very varied architecture* and design which the houses and groups of houses display [...] *we learn* that general observance of street line or harmonious departure from it are the chief points as to house-building over which the municipal authorities exercise control, for, though proper sanitary arrangements are strictly enforced, the fullest measure of individual taste and preference is encouraged.
>
> *Walking still toward the outskirts of the town, we come upon "Grand Avenue".*
>
> (1898, 15f.; my emphasis)

Moreover, even the sense of a trajectory from past through present to glorious future inherent in the notion of scripts – while already evoked in Howard's title *Garden Cities of To-Morrow* – is present in the garden city movement (cf. Figure 8.4).

This 1920s advertising poster for Welwyn Garden City traces a path from "Yesterday: Living and Working in the Smoke" via "Today: Living in the Suburbs – Working in the Smoke" to "To-morrow: Living & Working in the Sun at Welwyn Garden City". It thus explicity frames a blueprint for urban development as a path from a dark past into a bright future, a future occasionally celebrated, as we have seen, with religious zeal and virtually clothed in an exceptionalist "city upon a hill" rhetoric and iconography. The latter is evident, for instance, in Louis de Soissons's plans for Welwyn Garden City (cf. Figure 8.5), founded by Howard himself in 1920.[25]

Given these findings about the appeal of the 'garden city' concept, one might wonder about its reception in very different cultural contexts. Here, the early Japanese reception of the garden city in a 1907 adaptation of Howard's study by the Japanese Ministry of Internal Affairs offers an interesting test case (cf. Figure 8.6). This text, for instance, closely reproduces Howard's illustrations with Japanese captions and translated toponyms (for an initial discussion of the Japanese reception of the 'garden city', cf. Oshima).

Figure 8.4 1920s advertisement for Welwyn Garden City.
Source: Monclús/Díez Medina 19.

Here, the central task, it seems, is to explain the appeal of Howard's concept to Japanese planners. Rather than by means of references to British and American literary and cultural traditions, the adoption of Howard's concept in Japan must have worked differently. Here, it would be tempting to think that adoption was eased by the visual and conceptual appeal of Howard's designs: Conceptually in their systematic integration of green spaces into the urban fabric and visually in their combination of ornamentality and geometrical clarity, these may seem compatible with Japanese traditions of landscape gardening and iconic visual representations of urban landscapes, such as Hiroshige's celebrated *One Hundred Famous Views of Edo* (1856–1858). It seems, however, that Japanese and European garden traditions were regarded as so distinct – apparent even in different terminology for European and Japanese gardens and parks – that, at a time of significant interest in Western architectural and landscaping traditions

Figure 8.5 "City upon a Hill" iconography in the original 1920 de Soissons plan for Welwyn Garden City.

Source: Reproduced by permission of Louis de Soissons Limited, London.

(one might recall the hiring of European architects and planners such as Josiah Conder to train Japanese architects at the time), it was precisely the appeal and prestige of a very *different* tradition that eased the adoption of the concept in Japan.[26]

Given this enormous variability of implementations, Hall's diagnosis of the ultimate fate of the garden city movement is fairly devastating: "Howard would fail to see much resemblance to his vision" in virtually any place that claims his legacy – "that vision is nowhere to be found: the shell is there, but not the substance. These are not anarchist self-governing commonwealths of free artisans" (148). Thus, if wholesale adoption is the criterion of success, the garden suburbs to be seen the world over are indeed sorry remnants of Howard's far-reaching ideas and ideals (for a problematisation of 'successful' diffusion, cf.

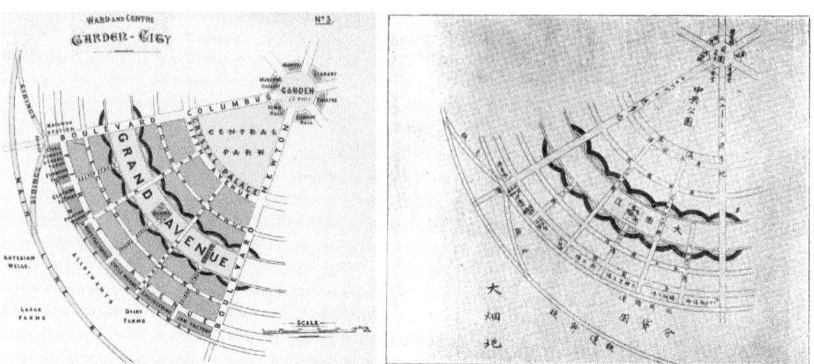

Figure 8.6 Juxtaposition of an illustration from Howard's 1898 *To-morrow: A Peaceful Path to Real Reform* with its adaptation in an official 1907 Japanese publication.

Source: Howard (1898, 14) (8.6a); Japanese Ministry of Internal Affairs (1907) (8.6b).

de Jong; Romano). However, if we assume that the effective kernel of the script is the strategy of greening neighbourhoods to ensure healthier urban living, Howard's concept has been remarkably successful. After all, the numerous explicit or implicit references to Howard in a lot of these developments make clear that this has been more than simply a case of similar challenges (unhealthy neigbourhoods with too little light and fresh air) being addressed by means of a similar – 'obvious' or close-at-hand – solution (providing more green spaces). Thus, the case of the garden city movement supports the notion of scripts as both normative *and* flexible: They are strongly normative at the core but surprisingly adaptive – garden city designs have appealed both to utopian socialists and to proto-Nazi ideologues of blood and soil (for a right-wing interpretation of the garden city in Germany, cf. Schubert; as well as Hall 121). A narratological perspective is helpful here: Narratives which leave room for interpretation and negotiation are *more* rather than *less* socially binding than precise narratives, and thus *more* likely to appeal to a broad audience (cf. Koschorke 349–352 *et passim*; programmes of political parties are a classic case in point).[27] Thus, it is precisely the adaptability and, where necessary, the de-ideologised deployment of a 'script' that supports its success. The change of title from *To-Morrow: A Peaceful Path to Real Reform* (1898) to *Garden Cities of To-Morrow* (1902), which, as I have noted, replaced the reference to Howard's reformist end with the physical means for its realisation, is precisely such a de-ideologising move and makes a pragmatic approach possible.

In sum, what has generally been regarded as the global diffusion of a quintessentially 'English' script – the establishment of greener, less crowded cities (in effect mostly really suburbs) as a response to the living conditions in industrial cities under free-market capitalism – on closer inspection turns out to have been based on a far more complex transatlantic (and later global) exchange of ideological preconceptions, interpretive patterns, narratives, imaginaries and iconographies. With these insights, we might want to reconsider Peter Hall's assessment quoted earlier: "What was astonishing about the garden-city movement was how easily it was exported from its homeland, but also how strangely it became transformed in the process" (132). While "astonishing" from a planning perspective, the fate of the garden city movement – both its rapid global spread and its significant variability – is far less so if studied from a literary and cultural studies perspective on policy diffusion which reads the 'garden city' concept as a script.

'Green', 'Sustainable', 'Inclusive', 'Competitive', 'Smart Cities': Further Applications

I further argue that even more recent globally pervasive strategies of harnessing 'green' urban development measures to foster social inclusiveness might ultimately be traced to Howard's central principle of deploying 'green' for social purposes (for the influence of Howard's 'garden city' ideas on recent 'eco-city' developments, cf. Caprotti 2019; Hassenpflug 2019).[28] Here, too, there is a remarkably limited set of strategies and models, such as the establishment of water-sensitive public spaces (e.g. playgrounds, parks), community gardens, collective clean-up-the-city initiatives, public subsidies for greening neighbourhoods, etc. However, such initiatives designed to promote social inclusiveness through 'green' measures frequently do not succeed if the impact of local political regulations and governance structures as well as culturally divergent practices and patterns of civic engagement are not sufficiently observed. Thus, Glover, Shinew and Parry, while emphasising the fostering of sociability, democratic commitment and community values, also use their demographic data of a sample of community gardeners in St. Louis, Missouri, to show that the majority of them are, in fact, white and fairly affluent (cf. 84).[29] Moreover, success – here understood as a policy or initiative that actually supports social inclusiveness – is frequently fairly limited, if conflicts between 'sustainable' and 'inclusive' urban development are not addressed (for instance if advanced – and expensive – low-energy building technologies and the greening of former industrial waterfronts induce gentrification-like processes). New York City's High Line Park and its impact on the local real estate market and on neighbourhood demographics is an illustrative and much-discussed example (cf. Betsky; Lang/Rothenberg). Here, 'ecologically sustainable' in practice often means 'socially exclusive'. In this vein, Wachsmuth, Cohen and Angelo succinctly outline what has come to be known as 'environmental gentrification':

> As districts become greener, they become more desirable and expensive. The premiums placed on neighbourhood amenities – such as walkability, public transport and the proximity of parks, farmers' markets and "greenways" such as hiking trails and bike paths – by residents who can afford to pursue them raise the cost of living.
>
> (392)

Especially high-profile projects such as High Line Park or the Atlanta Beltline (for a critical discussion, cf. Immergluck/Balan) would lend themselves to discussions of the overlaps and conflicts between the different narratives deployed in their promotion. In this vein, Lang and Rothenberg, however without any detailed analysis of narrative strategies and visualisation, have pointed to the "strong graphic identity" (1751) and the "discourse of win-win" (1752) in the promotion of the High Line project.

Similar analyses might be conducted, I suggest, for other globally pertinent patterns of urban development and the underlying 'scripts': For instance, waterfront redevelopment, i.e. the transformation of former port areas into frequently up-market residential or mixed-use districts – with iconic early examples in New York City's waterfronts or the London Docklands – has long clearly been a globally circulating blueprint. Arguably, this has to some extent simply been a case of similar (obvious) solutions to the identical challenge of finding new uses for abandoned former port areas in potentially attractive locations on the water. This understanding, however, would significantly underestimate the impact of powerful narrative and visual strategies of promoting such developments, which have led to remarkably similar iconographies of successful development, frequently with virtually interchangable architecture in very different locations. Apart from some few truly iconic buildings – Gehry's Guggenheim in Bilbao, Herzog & de Meuron's Elbphilharmonie in Hamburg, or Kengo Kuma's V & A in Dundee, Scotland, and a handful of further examples – who would be able to tell entire waterfronts in Hamburg HafenCity from developments in Düsseldorf's MedienHafen, or from, say, San Francisco, Baltimore, London, Amsterdam or Tokyo – attractively green and sustainable or creative-friendly (if often hardly socially inclusive) as they might be? (for the role of narratives in the planning and promotion of waterfront developments in Helsinki, cf. Lieven Ameel's *The Narrative Turn in Urban Planning: Plotting the Helsinki Waterfront*).[30]

Arguably the most pervasive recent travelling model is the ubiqitous 'smart city'. Promoted largely by global tech companies such as IBM, Cisco or Google, such developments – whether in Korea, China, the United States, Canada or different European countries – are frequently marketed with utopian promises of residential comfort, liveability, safety and sustainability, often intersecting with 'eco-city' concepts (for the intersections, cf. Bibri). However, Rob Kitchin has argued that even critical scholarship on the 'smart city' discourse, although "vital in countering the supposedly pragmatic, non-ideological, commonsensical visions of the smart city" (132), has been dominated by "one-size fits all narratives and canonical examples" (134). Moreover, he has diagnosed a "lack of in-depth empirical case studies of a range of smart city developments and comparative research of similar initiatives in different locales" (Kitchin 134). Despite initial analyses of the narratives deployed in these developments (cf., for instance, Söderström/Paasche/Klauser; Wiig), there is as yet little or no systematic literary and cultural studies research.[31] Robert Cowley's 2016 paper on "Science Fiction and the Smart Eco-City" points out a direction such research might take by perceptively commenting on the "science fictional aesthetic evident in the promotion of many 'eco-city' initiatives, and particularly in their more recent hi-tech and 'smart' incarnations" (1). Against more critical assessments of such cultural references, he has argued that "'story-telling' is one of the few remaining legitimate ways for urban policy-makers to relate to the future" (Cowley 1). However, the origins and global spread of the 'smart city' idea and its limited set of scripts, despite a wealth of 'smart city' research in urban geography, planning studies, political science and other disciplines, would merit a literary studies monograph of its own.[32]

All in all, we can observe a fairly limited set of globally prevalent urban development models, the vast majority of which fall under the headings of the 'green' or 'sustainable city', the 'smart city', the 'competitive/prosperous/growing city' and, more recently, and with less corporate backing, the 'inclusive city'.[33] Blueprints such as the 'creative city' concept can largely be identified as varieties of the 'competitive city' (for these models as 'scripts', cf. Chapter 7).

Many documents central to urban policy mobility – whether in the fields of 'sustainable', 'smart', 'inclusive' or 'competitive' urban development – through their titles already point to the fact that these are recipes, blueprints, how-to manuals, toolkits or roll-out instructions: Thus, the Gehl Institute's 2012 *Inclusive Healthy Places – A Guide to Inclusion & Health in Public Space: Learning Globally to Transform Locally* already indicates it is meant to foster and support the global diffusion of a set of recipes. The 'how-to' formula similarly announcing transferability is used in a 2019 report by the Brookings Global Cities Initiative entitled *Metro-to-Metro Economic Partnerships: How to Network Global Assets to Fuel Regional Growth* (Gootman/Barker/Bouchet). As a further variation, both Rivero Moreno and Rivas's *Placebranding Toolkit: Cultural Heritage as a Driver for Branding the Contemporary City*[34] and Charles Landry's influential *The Creative City: A Toolkit for Urban Innovators*, by being referred to as "toolkits" similarly announce their suitability for virtually global implementation. Such packages, however, are rarely 'plug and play', but, like corporate software packages, need to be customised and adapted in consulting projects, for which freely available brochures, rankings, survey papers, etc. merely function as appetisers. For instance, consultancy firm Copenhagenize Design Co. publishes a freely accessible index of bicycle-friendly cities and then sells manuals and consulting projects on how to 'Copenhagenize' a city, i.e. how to become as bicycle-friendly as the long-term number one city in such rankings, Copenhagen.

A marketing-driven segue from analysis to prescription is almost invariably part and parcel of such survey papers and policy documents. This is apparent, for instance, in consultancy empirica's report on "*Schwarmstädte*", literally "flock cities" (because young people allegedly 'flock' to them). This 2015 report outlines how a number of German cities experience above-average growth in the segment of the population under 35 ("cumulative cohort growth rate"). This is descriptively outlined in a report, which tentatively and vaguely lists features that might make these cities attractive; more concrete recommendations of what cities need to do to become or remain a 'flock city', however, are then only available in paid consulting projects (cf. GdW 2015).

The performative logic of such scripts observed with Richard Florida (cf. Chapter 7) is at work here, too: By persuasively describing a development, the 'flock city script' generates a need to create similar conditions, thus partly bringing about or at least reinforcing developments the report allegedly only describes and analyses.

One might not quite want to go as far as urban thinker and consultant Arun Jain, who has argued that "reliance on well-known development models and the literal copying of best practices is pure intellectual laziness. While knowing what's out there is helpful, the blind copying of formulas disregards what is crucial to urban development: local context". However, a more critical look at travelling urban models and policies that does not de-contextualise and over-rationalise the causes for their success or failure clearly seems in order. It would be in keeping with the more recent constructivist approaches to policy diffusion and translation – and it would benefit from the kind of 'literary studies'-informed analysis proposed here.

Notes

1 For discussions of this paradigm shift and critical accounts of the history and the various traditions in research on policy mobilities, cf. especially Peck; Peck/Theodore. For discussions of the implications of the various metaphors that have been used, cf. Teubner, who comments on the implications of the medical metaphor of the 'transplant'; as well as Prince; and Levi-Faur/Jordana 192. In an illuminating essay on key metaphors in the study of global networks that helped spread the notion of 'creativity' as crucial to post-industrial urban development, Prince also persuasively engages with Actor-Network-Theory (ANT) and its adoption in policy mobility studies in the wake, for instance, of Mol/Law. Despite significant benefits, he critiques ANT because, given its focus on structures and networks, in analyses informed by it, "not only are people marginalized, but so are the power relations they are embedded in" (Prince 328).

2 For the helpful distinction between a supply side (global consultants, architects, planners) and a demand side (municipal governments, interest groups, investors), cf. McCann 109.

3 With reference to Castles, groups of nations with – allegedly – similar patterns are frequently referred to as "families of nations". For a discussion and problematisation of transfers between such "families of nations", cf. Lalenis/de Jong/Mamadouh.

4 A related notion – and one that has not, to my knowledge, been employed in policy mobility research – is that of culturally specific systems of collective symbols ("*Kollektivsymbolsysteme*", Parr). Parr notes that "the synchronic systems of collective symbols differ significantly between different cultures" (30; my translation), which he illustrates by contrastively outlining the systems of collective symbols prevalent in contemporary Germany (as well as the significantly different one formerly prevalent in the GDR) and in the United States, but also in Luxembourg. These differences in the systems of collective symbols – leading to different "culturally constructed spatial models" (Parr 30; my translation), different cultural frames, interpretive patterns and thus to different plausibilities of the same 'script' – might go some way towards explaining the comparative ease (or lack thereof) of policy mobilities between different communities. For an illustration, cf. Hassenpflug's discussion of Chinese cultural patterns as evident in the urban fabric of Chinese

cities and especially his discussion of the non-acceptance of selected Western-style neigbourhoods built by Western architects in China (2010, 113–124); cf. also Tan 197. While it is obvious that the field of education is particularly sensitive in terms of the 'cultural fit' of imported concepts, this is surely no less the case with fields such as dwellings or neighbourhood development, which are also highly charged with cultural preferences, culturally sensitive symbolic meanings and specific interpretive patterns.

5 Cf. also Liu/Leisering, who account for policy diffusion by "a variety of mechanisms like development cooperation, exchange of elites and study abroad, migration, global campaigns, international conferences and covenants, policy tourism [i.e. delegation visits of experts and practitioners for the purpose of studying policies and practices in a model region], social movements or mere observation of the experience of others" (109). Following a common distinction, they note the difference between "'vertical' diffusion by international organizations [...] and 'horizontal' diffusion between countries" (Liu/Leisering 108).

6 Who, moreover, defines 'success' or 'failure'? Might not a partial transfer that is deemed a 'failure' by the policy donor be perceived as a resounding success in the host context – and might not a complete transfer that appears a 'success' to the donor fail to meet the objectives of key agents in the recipient context? For a problematisation, cf. de Jong; Romano.

7 For the complex relationship of British romanticism to the city, cf. Chandler/ Gilmartin; Gurr 2017; Gurr/Michel; and Peer.

8 Later, Howard also repeatedly cited American writer Edward Bellamy's 1888 utopian novel *Looking Backward: 2000–1887* as a key influence (cf. Hall 95).

9 The poem is here reproduced the way it is printed in Howard's book, i.e. with each of Lowell's octameter lines broken up into two tetrameters, thus somewhat obscuring the rhyming couplets and triplets.

10 This illustration from the 1898 edition does not appear in full in the 1902 edition, which here only has the detailed illustration of one segment of the ensemble (cf. Howard 128). The combination of English and American distrust of big cities – Wordsworthian ideas of "the increasing accumulation of men in cities" (597), and Jeffersonian ideas of pastoral moral integrity (cf. also the "three magnets" diagram in Figure 8.1) are also to be found in numerous passages such as this: "It is well-nigh universally agreed by men of all parties, not only in England, but all over Europe and America and our colonies, that it is deeply to be deplored that the people should continue to stream into the already over-crowded cities" (Howard 1902, 11); cf. also the moralising overtones and the suggestion of moral and political integrity in references to "the keen and *pure* delights of the country" (Howard 1902, 15; my emphasis).

11 While – especially together with "Justitia" – "Concord" superficially refers merely to the classic political virtue of unity, it also – especially if considered in sequence next to "Philadephia" – resonates with more specifically 'American' associations, mainly recalling Concord, Massachusetts, as the place associated, most prominently, with Emerson, Thoreau and Hawthorne and, beyond that, with the American War of Independence and its beginning in the battles of Lexington and Concord.

12 The German title is *Denkschrift betreffend Grundsätze zur Aufstellung eines General-Siedelungsplanes für den Regierungsbezirk Düsseldorf (rechtsrheinisch)*. This is the area containing the Western part of the industrial Ruhr region, here encompassing Landkreis Dinslaken, Duisburg, Mülheim an der Ruhr and Essen, but also Düsseldorf, Landkreis Mettmann and the Wupper cities of Elberfeld and

Barmen (merged with Cronenberg, Ronsdorf and Vohwinkel to form Wuppertal in 1929).

13 The 100 pages of Schmidt's *Denkschrift* do not contain any references. Since his library and correspondence were lost in the Second World War, there is no external evidence of his reading (von Petz 38). A number of influences are unmistakable, however.

14 His early years in Essen are poorly documented and there are no records of such a study tour, though both Schmidt and Unwin later recalled a first meeting in 1903 and Schmidt's designs from this period show clear debts to Unwin and Parker's designs (cf. von Petz 52f., 151). For the connections between the English 'garden city' practitioners and other German advocates, cf. Monclús/Díez Medina 21. In addition to English medieval traditions, Unwin and Parker's designs closely echo German medieval designs such as those in Rothenburg o.d. Tauber (cf. Hall 99, 112 *et passim*). Hall even refers to their style as "quasi-Teutonic" (134). Margarethenhöhe is thus an interesting re-import, as it were, of older German forms by means of a detour through their recent English adaptations.

15 In 1922, Schmidt became an honorary member of the British Town Planning Institute and during the 1920s met Howard at several conferences of the International Federation for Town and Country Planning and Garden Cities, which Howard had founded in 1913 and chaired as President until his death in 1928 (for these connections, cf. von Petz 147–152; Wagner 347 *et passim*). The Federation was renamed several times in the 1920s and was later to become the International Federation of Housing and Planning (IFHP).

16 There are a few changes in the choice of epigraphs between the two editions, but these are hardly relevant to the argument I make in this chapter.

17 The German original reads: "Schematische Darstellung der Durchdringung einer Stadtanlage mit Grünflächen".

18 The German original reads: "Luftregeneratoren im Stadtorganismus" (Schmidt 66).

19 Schmidt's considerable artistic and literary sensibilities are apparent in a life-long attachment to the violin (cf. von Petz 24) and already in a letter to his parents about his experiences during the early days of his studies in Hannover (qtd. in von Petz 209–212), a letter in the mock-epic form of dactylic hexameters reminiscent, not least, of Goethe's *Hermann und Dorothea.*

20 The German original reads: "qualmenden Schornsteinen, klappernden Förderbändern, staubenden Schlackenhalden, giftigen Hochofengasen, lärmenden Dampfhämmern und Schlagwerken" (Schmidt 68).

21 The German original reads: "landschaftliche Schönheit [...] reich und wellig gestalteten, geschwungenen Landschaftssilhouetten [...] Baumgruppen und Wiesenflächen, Talmulden und Hügel" (Schmidt 68).

22 The German original reads: "[D]er Begriff Wanderweg ist ebenso relativ aufzufassen, wie der Begriff der Allee oder des murmelnden Baches, der ein silberner Forellenbach und eine das Massenauftreten des Menschen dokumentierende Emscher sein kann, auf deren grüngelbbraunem Spiegel melancholische Weidenbäume von dem endgültigen Erfolge der Emschergenossenschaft träumen" (Schmidt 77).

23 The German original reads: "[D]as von Sonne, Licht und Luft entwöhnte Kind [wird] im Hinterhause unschuldig zum Tode verurteilt" (Schmidt 41).

24 Though only diagnosed in these terms by C.P. Snow in 1959, the debate between "the two cultures" had repeatedly flared up throughout the nineteenth century with the controversies between Peacock and Shelley in the early 1820s and between T.H. Huxley and Matthew Arnold in the early 1880s as only the most prominent ones.

25 A specifically American re-appropriation, as it were, of the community ideals within the 'garden city script' is apparent in C.A. Perry's 1929 *The Neighborhood Unit: A Scheme of Arrangement for the Family-Life Community* and in Perry's *Housing for the Machine Age* (1939): "The square [at the centre of a 'garden city' neighbourhood] itself will be an appropriate location for a flagpole, a memorial monument, or an ornamental fountain. In the common life of the neigborhood it will function as the place of local celebrations. Here, on Independence Day, the Flag will be raised, the Declaration of Independence will be recited, and the citizenry urged to patriotic deeds by eloquent orators" (Perry 1939, 65; qtd. in Hall 135). For the transatlantic exchange of 'garden city' designs in the first half of the twentieth century, cf. Hall 133–144 ("Garden Cities for America").

26 I am most grateful to Christian Tagsold, one of the foremost experts on Japanese garden culture, for a discussion of these points and for preventing me from the error of looking for Japanese traditions here. For an account of "Japanese Gardens and the West", cf. Tagsold's book. As for the role of Western architects in Japan, I am grateful to Beate Löffler for many productive discussions on her work in the field of architectural knowledge exchange between Japan and the West since the Meiji period.

27 For an excellent review of discussions on the benefits and pitfalls of ambiguity in strategic planning from a management perspective, cf. Abdallah/Langley.

28 For a critical account of what they in their title tellingly refer to as "the 'ubiquitous eco-city'" and "the internationalisation of eco-city policy and practice", cf. Joss/Cowley/Tomozeiu, who also point out the often one-sidedly technology-driven understanding of 'eco-cities'.

29 For the intersections of and the tensions between 'green' and 'socially inclusive' scripts, cf. also Braswell; Caprotti 2014; Gerhard/Marquardt; Gurr/Butler; Haase *et al.*; Hall/Ward; Jonas; Martinez; Miller; Rosol/Béal/Mössner; Wachsmuth/Cohen/Angelo; as well as several contributions in Wilson; Wirth *et al.*

30 A literary studies approach to research on policy mobility and travelling blueprints for urban development would also be applicable to globally prevalent phenomena such as the conversion and restoration of industrially used urban rivers and waterbodies (e.g. the Emscher conversion project in Germany's Ruhr region, False Creek in Vancouver, the Klang River in Malaysia and many others). In a related vein, brownfields conversion and re-use of industrial sites and disused traffic infrastructures also frequently come with fairly generic scripts and recurring strategies of visualisation; cf., for instance, the case of Lake Phoenix [Phoenixsee] in Dortmund, where the site of a former steel mill was turned into a lake. Here, too, the familiar conflicts between environmental, economic and social goals were to be observed, prompting discussions of gentrification-like processes.

31 For an illuminating technology-driven, distant-reading exercise in identifying key collocations and discursive trends in a corpus of texts on 27 'smart cities' in Europe, North America, Asia and Australia, cf. Joss *et al.*

32 For recent discussions of the 'smart city', cf. for instance Albino/Berardi/Dangelico; BBSR; Bibri; Caprotti/Cowley; Cugurullo; Gonella; Joss *et al.*; Kitchin; Libbe; Söderström/Paasche/Klauser; Wiig.

33 As merely one example, the Asian Development Bank in 2012 announced "Green Cities", "Inclusive Cities" and "Competitive Cities" as the "three major themes of [its work] in the urban sector over the coming years" (viii).

34 The complete title is *ROCK Placebranding Toolkit: Cultural Heritage as a Driver for Branding the Contemporary City*, with ROCK signifying "Regeneration and Optimization of Cultural Heritage in Creative and Knowledge Cities". The project was funded by the European Commission.

References

Abdallah, Chahrazad, Ann Langley. "The Double Edge of Ambiguity in Strategic Planning." *Journal of Management Studies* 51.2 (2014): 235–264. doi: 10.1111/joms.12002.

Abram, Simone. "Culture? And Planning?" *Planning Theory and Practice* 17.4 (2016): 654–657.

Albino, Vito, Umberto Berardi, Rosa Maria Dangelico. "Smart Cities: Definitions, Dimensions, Performance, and Initiatives." *Journal of Urban Technology* 22.1 (2015): 3–21.

Ameel, Lieven. *The Narrative Turn in Urban Planning: Plotting the Helsinki Waterfront*. New York: Routledge, 2021.

Asian Development Bank. *Green Cities*. Ed. Michael Lindfield, Florian Steinberg. Urban Development Series. Mandaluyong City, Philippines: Asian Development Bank, 2012.

BBSR (Bundesinstitut für Bau-, Stadt- und Raumforschung). *Smart City Charter: Making Digital Transformation at the Local Level Sustainable*. Troisdorf: Rautenberg Verlag, 2017. www.bmi.bund.de/SharedDocs/downloads/DE/veroeffentlichungen/themen/bauen/wohnen/smart-city-charta-kurzfassung-de-und-en.pdf?__blob=publicationFile&v=4.

Beevers, Robert. *The Garden City Utopia: A Critical Biography of Ebenezer Howard*. London: Macmillan, 1988.

Bercovitch, Sacvan. "The Problem of Ideology in American Literary History." *Critical Inquiry* 12 (1986): 631–653.

Betsky, Aaron. "The High Line Effect: Are Our New Parks Trojan Horses of Gentrification?" *Metropolis*, 13 December 2016. www.metropolismag.com/architecture/ landscape/high-line-effect-new-parks-trojan-horses-gentrification.

Bibri, Simon Elias. *Advances in the Leading Paradigms of Urbanism and their Amalgamation: Compact Cities, Eco-Cities, and Data-Driven Smart Cities*. Cham: Springer, 2020.

Braswell, Taylor Harris. "Fresh Food, New Faces: Community Gardening as Ecological Gentrification in St. Louis, Missouri." *Agriculture and Human Values* 35.4 (2018): 809–822.

Caprotti, Federico. "Eco-Urbanism and the Eco-City, or, Denying the Right to the City?" *Antipode* 46.5 (2014): 1285–1303.

Caprotti, Federico. "From Shannon to Shenzhen and Back: Sustainable Urbanism and Inter-city Partnerships in China and Europe." *Remaking Sustainable Urbanism: Space, Scale and Governance in the New Urban Era*. Ed. Xiaoling Zhang. Singapore: Palgrave Macmillan, 2019. 101–119.

Caprotti, Federico, Robert Cowley. "Varieties of Smart Urbanism in the UK: Discursive Logics, the State and Local Urban Context." *Transactions of the Institute of British Geographers* 44.3 (2019): 587–601. https://doi.org/10.1111/tran.12284.

Castles, Francis G., ed. *Families of Nations: Patterns of Public Policies in Western Democracies*. Aldershot: Dartmouth Publishing, 1993.

Chandler, James, Kevin Gilmartin, eds. *Romantic Metropolis: The Urban Scene of British Culture, 1780–1840*. Cambridge: Cambridge University Press, 2005.

Conn, Steven. *Americans Against the City: Anti-Urbanism in the Twentieth Century*. Oxford: Oxford University Press, 2014.

Copenhagenize Design Co. "The 20 Most Bike-Friendly Cities on the Planet, Ranked." 2019. https://copenhagenizeindex.eu.

Cowley, Robert. "Science Fiction and the Smart Eco-City." University of Westminster, 2016. www.westminster.ac.uk/sites/default/files/science-fiction-and-the-smart-eco-city-cowley.pdf.

Cugurullo, Federico. "The Origin of the Smart City Imaginary: From the Dawn of Modernity to the Eclipse of Reason." *The Routledge Companion to Urban Imaginaries*. Ed. Christoph Lindner, Miriam Meissner. New York: Routledge, 2019. n.p. www.taylorfrancis.com/books/e/9781315163956.

de Jong, Martin. "China's Art of Institutional Bricolage: Selectiveness and Gradualism in the Policy Transfer Style of a Nation." *Policy and Society* 32.2 (2013): 89–101.

de Jong, Martin, Virginie Mamadouh. "Two Contrasting Perspectives on Institutional Transplantation." *The Theory and Practice of Institutional Transplantation: Experiences with the Transfer of Policy Institutions*. Ed. Martin de Jong, Virginie Mamadouh, Konstantinos Lalenis. Dordrecht: Kluwer Academic Publishers, 2002. 19–32.

de Jong, Martin, Virginie Mamadouh, Konstantinos Lalenis. "Drawing Lessons about Lesson Drawing: What the Case Reports Tell us about Institutional Transplantation." *The Theory and Practice of Institutional Transplantation: Experiences with the Transfer of Policy Institutions*. Ed. de Jong, Mamadouh, Lalenis. Dordrecht: Kluwer Academic Publishers, 2002a. 283–300.

de Jong, Martin, Virginie Mamadouh, Konstantinos Lalenis, eds. *The Theory and Practice of Institutional Transplantation. Experiences with the Transfer of Policy Institutions*. Dordrecht: Kluwer Academic Publishers, 2002b.

Delpeuch, Thierry, Margarita Vassileva. "Des transferts aux apprentissages: réflexions à partir des nouveaux modes de gestion du développement économique local en Bulgarie." *Critique internationale* 48 (2010): 25–52.

Dobbin, Frank, Beth A. Simmons, Geoffrey Garrett. "The Global Diffusion of Public Policies: Social Construction, Coercion, Competition, or Learning?" *Annual Review of Sociology* 33.1 (2007): 449–472.

Dolowitz, David P., David Marsh. "Learning from Abroad: The Role of Policy Transfer in Contemporary Policymaking." *Governance* 13.1 (2000): 5–23.

Fricke, Carola. "Implications of Metropolitan Policy Mobility: Tracing the Relevance of Travelling Ideas for Metropolitan Regions." *Metropolitan Regions, Planning and Governance*. Ed Karsten Zimmermann, Daniel Galland, John Harrison. Cham: Springer, 2020. 117–132.

GdW Bundesverband deutscher Wohnungs- und Immobilienunternehmen e.V. *Schwarmstädte in Deutschland: Ursachen und Nachhaltigkeit der neuen Wanderungsmuster*. Berlin, 2015.

Gehl Institute. *Inclusive Healthy Places – A Guide to Inclusion & Health in Public Space: Learning Globally to Transform Locally*. New York: Gehl Institute, 2012.

Gerhard, Ulrike, Edith Marquardt. "The Greener, the Happier? Urban Sustainability in the Knowledge City: Policies, Programs and the Practices in the German Context." *The Politics of the Urban Sustainability Concept*. Ed. David Wilson. Champaign: Common Ground Publishing, 2015. 65–86.

Glover, Troy D., Kimberly J. Shinew, Diana C. Parry. "Association, Sociability, and Civic Culture: The Democratic Effect of Community Gardening." *Leisure Sciences* 27 (2005): 75–92.

Gonella, Francesco. "The Smart Narrative of a Smart City." *Frontiers in Sustainable Cities* 1.9 (2019): n.p. https://doi.org/10.3389/frsc.2019.00009.

Gootman, Marek, Rachel Barker, Max Bouchet. *Metro-to-Metro Economic Partnerships: How to Network Global Assets to Fuel Regional Growth*. Brookings Global Cities Initiative, 31 July 2019. www.brookings.edu/research/metro-to-metro-economic-partnerships/.

Gurr, Jens Martin. "Urban Romanticism." *Handbook of British Romanticism*. Ed. Ralf Haekel. Berlin, Boston: de Gruyter, 2017. 88–103.

Gurr, Jens Martin. "'Without contraries is no progression': Emplotted Figures of Thought in Negotiating Oppositions, *Funktionsgeschichte* and Literature as 'Cultural Diagnosis'." *Text or Context: Reflections on Literary and Cultural Criticism*. Ed. Rüdiger Kunow, Stephan Mussil. Würzburg: Königshausen & Neumann, 2013. 59–77.

Gurr, Jens Martin, Martin Butler. "On the 'Cultural Dimension of Sustainability' in Urban Systems: Urban Cultures as Ecological 'Force-Fields' in Processes of Sustainable Development." *Healthy and Liveable Cities/Gesunde und lebenswerte Städte*. Ed. Stefanie Caeners, Michael Eisinger, Jens Martin Gurr, J. Alexander Schmidt. Stuttgart: avedition, 2013. 138–151.

Gurr, Jens Martin, Berit Michel, eds. *Romantic Cityscapes: Selected Papers from the Essen Conference of the German Society for English Romanticism*. Trier: WVT, 2013.

Haase, Dagmar, Sigrun Kabisch, Annegret Haase, Erik Andersson, Ellen Banzhaf, Francesc Baró, Miriam Brenck, Leonie K. Fischer, Niki Frantzeskaki, Nadja Kabisch, Kerstin Krellenberg, Peleg Kremer, Jakub Kronenberg, Neele Larondelle, Juliane Mathey, Stephan Pauleit, Irene Ring, Dieter Rink, Nina Schwarz, Manuel Wolff. "Greening Cities – To be Socially Inclusive? About the Alleged Paradox of Society and Ecology in Cities." *Habitat International* 64 (2017): 41–48.

Hall, Peter. *Cities of Tomorrow: An Intellectual History of Urban Planning and Design since 1880*. Chichester: John Wiley & Sons, [4]2014.

Hall, Peter, Colin Ward. *Sociable Cities: The 21st-Century Reinvention of the Garden City*. London: Routledge, [2]2014.

Hassenpflug, Dieter. "Chinesische Neustädte V – Lingang New Town." *Baumeister: Das Architekturmagazin*. Blog entry, 25 June 2019. www.baumeister.de/chinesische-neustaedte-v-lingang-new-town/.

Hassenpflug, Dieter. *The Urban Code of China*. Basel: Birkhäuser, 2010.

Healey, Patsy. "Circuits of Knowledge and Techniques: The Transnational Flow of Planning Ideas and Practices." *International Journal of Urban and Regional Research* 37.5 (2013): 1510–1526. https://doi.org/10.1111/1468-2427.12044.

Healey, Patsy, Robert Upton, eds. *Crossing Borders: International Exchange and Planning Practices*. London, New York: Routledge, 2010.

Hein, Carola. "The Exchange of Planning Ideas from Europe to the USA after the Second World War: Introductory Thoughts and a Call for Further Research." *Planning Perspectives* 29.2 (2014): 143–151.

Hein, Carola. "Japanese Cities in Global Context." *Journal of Urban History* 42.3 (2016): 463–476.

Herrmann-Pillath, Carsten, Joachim Zweynert. "Institutionentransfer durch kulturelles Unternehmertum." *Transfer von Institutionen*. Ed. Thomas Apolte. Berlin: Duncker & Humblot, 2014. 85–111.

Hiroshige. *One Hundred Famous Views of Edo*. Ed. and with commentary by Melanie Trede, Lorenz Bichler. Cologne: Taschen, 2010.

Honeck, Thomas. "A Touch of Post-Truth: The Roles of Narratives in Urban Policy Mobilities." *Geographica Helvetica* 73 (2018): 133–145.

Howard, Ebenezer. *Garden Cities of To-Morrow*. London: Swan Sonnenschein, 1902 [rev. 2nd ed. of Howard. *To-Morrow: A Peaceful Path to Real Reform*. London: Sonnenschein, 1898].

Howard, Ebenezer. *To-Morrow: A Peaceful Path to Real Reform*. London: Swan Sonnenschein, 1898.

Hudson, John, Bo-Yung Kim. "Policy Transfer Using the 'Gold Standard': Exploring Policy Tourism in Practice." *Policy & Politics* 42.4 (2014): 495–511.

Immergluck, Dan, Tharunya Balan. "Sustainable for Whom? Green Urban Development, Environmental Gentrification, and the Atlanta Beltline." *Urban Geography* 39.4 (2018): 546–562. https://doi.org/10.1080/02723638.2017.1360041.

Inkpen, Andrew C., Wang Pien. "An Examination of Collaboration and Knowledge Transfer: China-Singapore Suzhou Industrial Park." *Journal of Management Studies* 43.4 (2006): 779–811.

Jain, Arun. Personal conversation with the author, 28 June 2018.

Jefferson, Thomas. "Letter to James Madison, December 20, 1787." *The Papers of Thomas Jefferson*. Ed. Julian P. Boyd. Princeton: Princeton University Press, 1955. Vol. XII, 422.

Jonas, Andrew E. G. "Beyond the Urban 'Sustainability Fix': Looking for New Spaces and Discourses of Sustainability in the City." *The Politics of the Urban Sustainability Concept*. Ed. David Wilson. Champaign: Common Ground Publishing, 2015. 117–135.

Joss, Simon, Robert Cowley, Daniel Tomozeiu. "Towards the 'Ubiquitous Eco-City': An Analysis of the Internationalisation of Eco-City Policy and Practice." *Urban Research & Practice* 6.1 (2013): 54–74.

Joss, Simon, Frans Sengers, Daan Schraven, Federico Caprotti, Youri Dayot. "The Smart City as Global Discourse: Storylines and Critical Junctures across 27 Cities." *Journal of Urban Technology* 26.1 (2019): 3–34.

Kitchin, Rob. "Making Sense of Smart Cities: Addressing Present Shortcomings." *Cambridge Journal of Regions, Economy and Society* 8.1 (2015): 131–136.

Koschorke, Albrecht. *Wahrheit und Erfindung: Grundzüge einer Allgemeinen Erzähltheorie*. Frankfurt/Main: Fischer, [3]2013.

Lalenis, Konstantinos, Martin de Jong, Virginie Mamadouh. "Families of Nations and Institutional Transplantation." *The Theory and Practice of Institutional Transplantation: Experiences with the Transfer of Policy Institutions*. Ed. de Jong, Mamadouh, Lalenis. Dordrecht: Kluwer Academic Publishers, 2002. 33–52.

Landry, Charles. *The Creative City: A Toolkit for Urban Innovators* [2000]. London: Earthscan, [2]2008.

Lang, Steven, Julia Rothenberg. "Neoliberal Urbanism, Public Space, and the Greening of the Growth Machine: New York City's High Line Park." *Environment and Planning A* 49.8 (2017): 1743–1761. https://doi.org/10.1177/0308518X16677969.

Levi-Faur, David, Jacint Jordana. "Regulatory Capitalism: Policy Irritants and Convergent Divergence." *Annals of the American Academy of Political and Social Science* 598.1 (2005): 191–197.

Libbe, Jens. "Smart City." *Handbuch Stadtkonzepte: Analysen, Diagnosen, Kritiken und Visionen*. Ed. Dieter Rink, Annegret Haase. Stuttgart: Barbara Budrich, 2018. 429–449.

Liu, Tao, Lutz Leisering. "Protecting Injured Workers: How Global Ideas of Industrial Accident Insurance Travelled to China." *Journal of Chinese Governance* 2.1 (2017): 106–123.

Liu, Tao, Li Sun. "Urban Social Assistance in China: Transnational Diffusion and National Interpretation." *Journal of Current Chinese Affairs* 45.2 (2016): 29–51.

Martinez, Miranda J. *Power at the Roots: Gentrification, Community Gardens, and the Puerto Ricans of the Lower East Side*. Plymouth: Lexington Books, 2010.

McCann, Eugene. "Urban Policy Mobilities and Global Circuits of Knowledge: Toward a Research Agenda." *Annals of the Association of American Geographers* 101.1 (2001): 107–130.

McCann, Eugene, Kevin Ward, eds. *Mobile Urbanism: Cities and Policymaking in the Global Age*. Minneapolis: University of Minnesota Press, 2011.

McKay, George. *Radical Gardening: Politics, Idealism & Rebellion in the Garden*. London: Frances Lincoln, 2011.

McNeill, Donald. *The Global Architect: Firms, Fame and Urban Form*. New York: Routledge, 2009.

Miller, Byron. "Sustainability for Whom? Sustainability How?" *The Politics of the Urban Sustainability Concept*. Ed. David Wilson. Champaign: Common Ground Publishing, 2015. 107–116.

Mol, Annemarie, John Law. "Regions, Networks and Fluids: Anaemia and Social Topology." *Social Studies of Science* 24.4 (1994): 641–671.

Monclús, Javier, Carmen Díez Medina. "Garden Cities and Garden Suburbs (1898–1930)." *Urban Visions: From Planning Culture to Landscape Urbanism*. Ed. Díez Medina, Monclús. Cham: Springer, 2018. 13–22.

Oshima, Ken Tadashi. "Denenchōfu: Building the Garden City in Japan." *Journal of the Society of Architectural Historians* 55.2 (1996): 140–151.

Parr, Rolf. "Räume, Symbole und kulturelle Konfrontationen: Kollektivsymbolsysteme als 'mental maps'." *Räumliche Darstellung kultureller Begegnungen*. Ed. Nicole Colin, Carla Dauven-van Knippenberg, Christian Moser, Rolf Parr, Anna Seidl. Heidelberg: Synchron, 2015. 15–35.

Peck, Jamie. "Geographies of Policy: From Transfer-Diffusion to Mobility-Mutation." *Progress in Human Geography* 35.6 (2011): 773–797.

Peck, Jamie, Nik Theodore. *Fast Policy: Experimental Statecraft at the Thresholds of Neoliberalism*. Minneapolis: University of Minnesota Press, 2015.

Peer, Larry H., ed. *Romanticism and the City*. New York: Palgrave Macmillan, 2011.

Perry, Clarence A. *Housing for the Machine Age*. New York: Russell Sage Foundation, 1939.

Perry, Clarence A. *The Neighborhood Unit: A Scheme of Arrangement for the Family-Life Community*. New York: Arno Press, 1974 [rpt. of the 1929 original].

Prince, Russel. "Metaphors of Policy Mobility: Fluid Spaces of 'Creativity' Policy." *Geografiska Annaler. Series B, Human Geography* 94.4 (2012): 317–331.

Rivero Moreno, Luis D., Miguel Rivas. *ROCK Placebranding Toolkit: Cultural Heritage as a Driver for Branding the Contemporary City*. ROCK project report, European Commission, 2019. http://branding-toolkit.rockproject.eu.

Romano, Giulia C. "Organisational Learning Analysis and Transfers of 'Eco-City' Concepts to China: The Example of Yangzhou." *China Perspectives* 1 (2017): 37–43.

Rosol, Marit, Vincent Béal, Samuel Mössner. "Greenest Cities? The (Post-)Politics of New Urban Environmental Regimes." *Environment and Planning A* 49.8 (2017): 1710–1718.

Sanyal, Bish. *Comparative Planning Cultures*. New York: Routledge, 2005.

Sanyal, Bish. "Revisiting Comparative Planning Cultures: Is Culture a Reactionary Rhetoric?" *Journal of Planning Theory and Practice* 17.4 (2016): 658–662.

Schmidt, Robert. *Denkschrift betreffend Grundsätze zur Aufstellung eines General-Siedelungsplanes für den Regierungsbezirk Düsseldorf (rechtsrheinisch)*. Essen: Klartext, 2009 [rpt. of the 1912 original].

Schmitt, Peter. "Learning from Elsewhere? A Critical Account of the Mobilisation of Metropolitan Policies." *Metropolitan Regions, Planning and Governance*. Ed. Karsten Zimmermann, Daniel Galland, John Harrison. Cham: Springer, 2020. 79–95.

Schubert, Dirk. "Theodor Fritsch and the German (völkische) Version of the Garden City: The Garden City Invented Two Years before Ebenezer Howard." *Planning Perspectives* 19 (2004): 3–35.

Smith, Michael Peter. *Transnational Urbanism: Locating Globalisation*. Malden, MA: Blackwell, 2001.

Snow, C.P. *The Two Cultures* [1959]. Ed. Stefan Collini. Cambridge: Cambridge University Press, 1998.

Söderström, Ola, Till Paasche, Francisco Klauser. "Smart Cities as Corporate Storytelling." *City* 18.3 (2014): 307–320.

Stone, Diane. "Transfer and Translation of Policy." *Policy Studies* 33.6 (2012): 483–499.

Strang, David, John W. Meyer. "Institutional Conditions for Diffusion." *Theory and Society* 22 (1993): 487–511.

Sun, Kim. "Culture Matters in Educational Policy Transfers: The Case of Curricular Reforms in the Two Koreas during the Soviet and US Military Occupation." *Journal of Education Policy* 32.3 (2016): 372–385.

Tagsold, Christian. *Spaces in Translation: Japanese Gardens and the West*. Philadelphia: University of Pennsylvania Press, 2017.

Tagsold, Christian. Telephone conversation with the author, 26 June 2020.

Tan, Charlene. "Education Policy Borrowing and Cultural Scripts for Teaching in China." *Comparative Education* 51 (2015): 196–211.

Taube, Markus. "Zur Bedeutung transnationaler Institutionentransfers für den Aufbau einer marktwirtschaftlichen Ordnung in der VR China." *Transfer von Institutionen*. Ed. Thomas Apolte. Berlin: Duncker & Humblot, 2014. 123–168.

Teubner, Gunther. "Legal Irritants: Good Faith in British Law or How Unifying Law Ends up in New Divergences." *The Modern Law Review* 61.1 (1998): 11–32.

von Petz, Ursula. *Robert Schmidt, 1869–1934: Stadtbaumeister in Essen und Landesplaner im Ruhrgebiet*. Tübingen: Wasmuth, 2016.

Wachsmuth, David, Daniel Aldana Cohen, Hillary Angelo. "Expand the Frontiers of Urban Sustainability." *Nature* 536 (25 August 2016): 391–393.

Wagner, Phillip. *Stadtplanung für die Welt? Internationales Expertenwissen 1900–1960*. Göttingen: Vandenhoeck & Ruprecht, 2016.

White, Morton Gabriel, Lucia White. *The Intellectual Versus the City: From Thomas Jefferson to Frank Lloyd Wright*. Cambridge, MA: Harvard University Press and MIT Press, 1962.

Wiig, Alan. "IBM's Smart City as Techno-utopian Policy Mobility." *City* 19.2–3 (2015): 258–273.

Wilson, David, ed. *The Politics of the Urban Sustainability Concept*. Champaign: Common Ground Publishing, 2015.

Wirth, Peter, Jiang Chang, Ralf-Uwe Syrbe, Wolfgang Wende, Tinghao Hu. "Green Infrastructure: A Planning Concept for the Urban Transformation of Former Coal-Mining Cities." *International Journal of Coal Science and Technology* 5.1 (2018): 78–91.

Wordsworth, William. "Preface to *Lyrical Ballads* (1802)." *Major Works*. Ed. Stephen Gill. Oxford: Oxford University Press, 2008. 595–615.

Zimmermann, Karsten. "From Here to There: Mapping the Metropolitan Politics of Policy Mobilities." *Metropolitan Regions, Planning and Governance*. Ed Karsten Zimmermann, Daniel Galland, John Harrison. Cham: Springer, 2020. 97–115.

Conclusion

The aim of this book has been to chart the field of literary urban studies. To this end, I have taken as a starting point and heuristic tool an approach to modelling theory that understands texts as qualitative urban models and looks at them both as descriptive models *of* cities (i.e. the 'established' study of literary representations of cities and the urban condition) and as prescriptive blueprints *for* cities (i.e. the more recent discussion of texts and their role in blueprinting and scenario building for cities) (Introduction). In suggesting a contribution of literary urban studies to the broadly interdisciplinary field of urban research, I have – with reference to the primarily *descriptive*, representational function of literary texts – argued that, given their focus on specificity, individuality and patterns of sense-making, they can function as complements to generalising quantitative models currently dominant in urban studies (Chapter 1). I have here argued that simultaneity – as a key component of urban complexity – poses the main representational challenge to texts seeking to simulate the urban experience (Chapter 2). Moreover, in detailed discussions of "The Waste Land" as arguably the quintessential 'city poem' and of Norman Klein's database narrative *Bleeding Through: Layers of Los Angeles 1920–1986*, I have discussed a number of structural and functional analogies between cities and texts that allow texts to function as persuasive qualitative urban models (Chapter 3).

In arguing for a reversal of perspective from the analysis of literary texts as descriptive representations of cities to the complementary analysis of literary and pragmatic texts and their functions in scenario building and blueprinting for urban futures, I have sought to combine the 'story turn in planning' as advanced by James Throgmorton, Barbara Eckstein, Leonie Sandercock, Merlijn van Hulst and others with literary studies insights into the narratology of planning as pursued especially by Lieven Ameel, Bart Keunen, or Sofie Verraest. Walter Benjamin's notion of "superposition" rather than the more established 'palimpsest' has here been conceptualised as an analytical tool to understand layers of urban memory in physical and textual cities (Chapter 4). Furthermore, I have used several types of urban activist writing to point out the transition from the critical representation of urban conditions to the blueprinting of different – more economically viable, sustainable, just and socially inclusive – urban futures (Chapter 5). Attempting to develop a theoretical framework for the comparative analysis of the real-world functions of literary texts and of the – broadly speaking – literary strategies deployed in pragmatic texts such as planning documents, I have built on recent narratological research on planning texts in literary urban studies (especially the work of Lieven Ameel) to propose the notion of what I call "narrative path dependencies" in planning texts (Chapter 6).

Here, the notion of 'scripts' as developed jointly with Barbara Buchenau provides an analytical tool to help understand how narrative templates, various forms of figuration as well as strategies of visualisation and other forms of medial representation can explain the persuasiveness of a limited set of 'recipes' for urban development (Chapter 7). Finally, I have drawn on planning theory and various notions of global urbanism as well as on a core 'literary studies' set of analytical tools in the study of narratives, plots, tropes, rhetoric, cultural concepts and collective symbols to propose a literary studies contribution to policy mobility research, which can help to make sense of travelling urban models and policies past and present (Chapter 8).

Thus to conceptualise literary urban studies by heuristically understanding texts as models *of* and models *for* the city and to alternate between and combine conceptual theoretical work and more extended case studies yields several central results: First, it questions the assumption that any model is equally a 'model of' and a 'model for' something. Second, it provides an insight into the achievements and limitations of both quantitative and qualitative models *of* the city and thereby, third, contributes to an understanding of *those* aspects of urban complexity which cannot be measured, quantified or captured in terms of information theory. This approach, fourth, offers a complementary understanding of how literary texts function as, to an extent, prescriptive models for urban developments – for instance in the development of scenarios – and, on the other hand, of the literary and affective strategies, functions and effects of pragmatic, allegedly purely expository planning texts. Thus, in charting the field of literary urban studies along the lines of the heuristic *distinction* between models *of* and models *for*, I also hope to have shown the productivity of adapting a general theory of models to literary studies and more specifically to literary urban studies.

If, in keeping with this understanding of the aims, objects and methods of literary urban studies and with important work by fellow practitioners such as Lieven Ameel, Jason Finch, Julia Sattler, Sherry Lee Linkon, Bart Keunen, Sofie Verraest and others, the field continues more systematically to take into account pragmatic texts and to read, for instance, planning texts and policy documents side by side with literary texts, I see significant benefits for the field of literary studies:

1. New materials not traditionally studied by literary scholars as well as the need and potential to develop new methods for research.
2. Options for closer cooperation with economics, sociology, urban geography, urban and regional planning, architecture, or public health, but with interdisciplinarity not understood as an end in itself but rather as a

way to do justice to the complexity of cities and to the intricacies of central urban challenges, which can no longer be adequately addressed in siloed disciplinary and sectoral fashion.

3. Improved urban development strategies through heightened awareness of different cultures of planning, participation, civic engagement and a better understanding of the persuasive (and potentially manipulative) use of narrative packaging, visualisation and references to familiar cultural concepts and collective symbols.
4. Urban Development as an innovative field of employment for graduates in literary and cultural studies.

In an interdisciplinary MA programme entitled "Urban Culture, Society and Space", which I have been directing for some ten years at the University of Duisburg-Essen and in which the subjects, methods and forms of cooperation envisaged here have been piloted, we have indeed found that fields of employment not previously open to graduates in literary studies have become an option for them. In taking their skills to the market, I tell my students, they have two options: They can capitalise on what they know, for instance, about the functioning and power of narratives to help developers sell real estate or to help consulting firms promote urban development strategies; or they can act – the colloquialism may be forgiven as appropriate – as 'bullshit detectors', helping municipalities see through some of the narratives promulgated by advocates of, say, purely technology-driven 'smart cities', and can thereby help craft better scripts for more sustainable, resilient as well as socially and ethnically inclusive futures of their cities.

Finally, as for the politics of promoting our discipline in debates about the 'public humanities', while I insist we also continue to teach literary history and any author, text, period or genre we individually see fit, the field of literary urban studies and an engagement in the future of cities will, I believe, help us abdicate our dual role as academia's 'unloved children kept under the stairs' but also as the 'cry-babies of the university', as I would facetiously (if largely, I think, adequately) describe a common (self-)perception. Confidently and realistically claiming a role in shaping the future of cities will make it very much easier to carve out a more significant and rewarding role for literary and cultural studies within the university of the twenty-first century.

Postscript (20 June 2020): COVID-19, the Future of Cities and Literary Urban Studies

As I am completing this book, the world is going through the COVID-19 pandemic, in which cities worldwide have been and continue to be hot spots. And although reports of the 'death of cities as we know them' to me seem premature or grossly exaggerated, the pandemic is already having drastic and foreseeably long-term consequences for cities – and the concomitant narratives are already taking shape. Three months after the beginning of the 'COVID-19 shutdown' (in most regions of Germany, in mid-March 2020), it seems clear that density, precisely the factor that has made cities hot spots of economic activity and cultural buzz, is now making them hot spots of infection: Public transport, for which density is essential to economic viability, looks set to face a major crisis that is unlikely to go away quickly, while cycling infrastructure appears to benefit. The crisis of the retail and hospitality sector is already leading to bankruptcies and to concentration, raising questions as to how to revitalise inner cities. Remote work and conferencing tools clearly appear to make inner-city office space less attractive and sought-after. Moreover, the pandemic is also leading to seismic shifts in what had previously seemed a booming share economy (think Airbnb or car-sharing). Finally, it seems unlikely city tourism will be back anywhere near pre-COVID-19 revenues in the near future.

However, there are also a number of key open questions: How will the pandemic affect efforts to mitigate climate change? How sustainable is the reduction of traffic and industrial emissions during the shutdown – and can the crisis help promote a green post-growth economy? Will, for instance, the reduction of global air travel offset the increased CO_2 emissions due to the decline in the use of public transport and the return to motorised individual mobility? Will the significant impact of scientists on policy-making during the pandemic help give science a stronger voice once the climate crisis regains attention? Will the pandemic lead policy-makers finally to confront the glaring inequalities in cities the crisis has highlighted so dramatically? Then, while the pandemic has drastically made it clear that public health, resilience and even the economy of cities and communities cannot be left to 'the market' and has reaffirmed the role of state institutions, it is unclear whether increased solidarity and social cohesion or growing inequality will, in retrospect, be seen as the prevalent outcome.

As for academia and the funding of research, it seems likely that, given the billions that are rightly and necessarily being spent to fight the social and economic consequences of the COVID-19 crisis, funding for the humanities may become more precarious – surely more drastically so in more market-driven academic systems such as the United States and Britain than, say, in Germany. Hence, the need to justify the relevance of the humanities generally and of literary studies specifically may further increase. Here, too, it may help if we can show to have a real-world commitment and to have an impact on the future of cities. Unfortunately, even some literary scholars, oblivious to our privileged position and to the very unequally distributed options for avoiding risk, have in the COVID-19 crisis been ignorant enough to recommend for everyone the 'literary studies lifestyle' of staying at home and reading a book.

Whichever way the pandemic will affect cities in the long run, one may anticipate a limited set of revitalisation strategies for inner cities in the wake of the COVID-19-induced crises in the urban retail, hospitality, entertainment and culture sectors. Moreover, as firms will surely seek to benefit from increasing remote work by consolidating inner-city office space, the competing scripts in response to this trend are also already emerging: Just as 9/11 prompted predictions about the end of building skyscrapers as high-risk targets, COVID-19, too, according to one variant of the 'urban decline script', is set to lead to the decline of inner cities as sites of economic activity and urbanity, while others predict the conversion of office space into student accommodation and a younger, more diverse, more artistic residential population in inner cities (one can see familiar revitalisation recipes reappear here). Finally, one can foresee urban consultants rolling out strategies for more sustainable post-COVID-19 'quality tourism' that, in common parlance, 'leverages the assets of cities' without overburdening the local population in former hot spots of city-hopping tourism such as Amsterdam, Barcelona or Paris, currently still largely deserted by tourists. More generally, social inclusiveness, environmental justice, efforts at improved and increasing urban public health, sustainability and resilience will be crucial to cities, and – against the familiar 'gloom and doom script' for cities – the competing scripts for how to achieve them, suggestively emplotted and persuasively visualised, are already emerging and will shape the future of our cities. In critically reviewing these scripts as well as in the crafting of more sustainable and more inclusive scripts, there is work for us to do.

Index

Note: Page numbers in *italic* refer to Figures